Oriental
Philosophies

Oriental
Philosophies

by JOHN M. KOLLER   RENSSELAER POLYTECHNIC INSTITUTE

CHARLES SCRIBNER'S SONS · NEW YORK

Library of Congress Catalog Card Number 70–99010

FOR CHRISTY

Preface

This book has been written with two basic aims in mind. First, it is intended to make possible an understanding and appreciation of Oriental thought and life. Second, it is intended to introduce the reader to certain fundamental and characteristic problems in philosophy as they are considered in the Oriental traditions. This is done in an attempt to make it possible for the reader to understand some of the answers given to the basic questions in life. The author is of the opinion that the traditions of Oriental philosophy are no less valuable and important than the traditions of Western philosophy. The assumption that a person can be introduced to philosophy only by considering the major thinkers and problems in the Western tradition is so obviously parochial that it is amazing that it continues almost completely unchallenged.

In the West philosophy is usually thought of in terms of the classical philosophers of the Western world. But in terms of understanding the nature of philosophy and philosophical problems there is no special advantage to studying philosophers who happen to have lived in the Western Hemisphere; geography is irrelevant here. Of course, there is an advantage in studying Western philosophers if the aim is not merely an understanding of the nature of philosophical activity and familiarity with certain philosophical positions, but also that of using the philosophical traditions as a means of understanding those ideas which have shaped the present condition of man in the Western Hemisphere. But by the same token, there is an advantage in studying the Oriental philosophers, for in addition to acquainting one with the nature of philosophy, one also gains understanding of the present condition of man in the Orient.

The reader who is accustomed to reading only Western philosophy will find it tempting to pigeonhole some of the material in this book as religion, or psychology, or even etiquette. He may dismiss certain areas of discussion (and the rest along with it) as "unphilosophical." But why should we force Western definitions of philosophy on the Orient? So far as I know, no one has ever demonstrated the superiority of Western concepts of philosophy over Oriental. And until this is done (if, indeed, it were possible!) Eastern thought should be studied within its own terms.

The important questions of life are no different for the Orient than for the West. Questions like, What is man? What is the nature of the universe in which man lives? In what does the good life consist? and, How can we know if the claims we make about the nature of man, the universe, and the good life are true? are basic philosophical questions, common to human beings the world over because they arise whenever and wherever man reflects upon his experience. Of course, these questions arise in different contexts and assume different forms for people living at different times and in different places, and the answers given may differ considerably. But these are the questions of man as man, arising out of the curiosity attending man's self-conscious nature and the innate urge to improve the conditions of his existence, and no human being can live without considering them. The question is not whether to answer or not answer these questions, but whether the answers will be explicit, thought-out, and well-argued, or whether they will be merely assumed, hidden, and implicit in the actions that constitute the history of a person.

On the easy assumption that an understanding of these questions as posed by philosophers and an analysis of the answers they have given will enable a person to understand and evaluate better the answers he or she gives to these questions, it seems obvious that it is important to know the forms and contexts of basic philosophical questions and answers, not just as they have appeared in the Western tradition, but as they have appeared in the whole philosophical tradition of man. This knowledge is needed to provide the imagination with the insights into man's experience which are required to provide an interpretation of experience that is worthy of the human animal. Ignoring the philosophical traditions of a majority of mankind and thereby depriving oneself of insights and knowledge needed for constructing a satisfactory philosophy of life is surely rash and unjustified.

The individual's need to construct for himself a philosophy of life is, I believe, imperative in our time. Therefore I have endeavored to make available to the lay reader some of the insights of the Oriental philosophers. To understand these ideas does not require any previous acquaintance with technical philosophy. Philosophical concepts and theories universally have their origin in, and depend for their justification and meaning upon, ordinary human experiences with which everyone is familiar. So it is possible, by tracing the relevant reflections on various aspects of experience, to show how a particular concept or theory developed, what it means, and how it can be justified. The present work not only does not assume prior acquaintance with philosophy, but should itself serve as an introduction.

These are among the reflections that have led to this attempt to provide an introduction to philosophy emphasizing the Oriental philosophical traditions. There is no doubt that in our own age we put our very existence in jeopardy by allowing ourselves to remain ignorant of at least half of the world. Never has the need been greater to come to an understanding of all the peoples of the world. Consequently, upon the assumption that to understand what a people have done and what they are likely to do it is necessary to understand their basic attitudes about life as reflected in their views of the nature of man, the good life, the nature of the universe, and the ways in which we can know reality, it is imperative that the philosophies of the Orient be studied and understood. Thus, the two functions which this book is intended to serve—to introduce the reader to an understanding of the Asian mind and to indicate the different ways in which fundamental philosophical questions have been considered in the Orient—grow out of the same basic concern, the concern to maintain and improve human existence.

Contents

xi

INTRODUCTION

THE story of philosophy is the story of man's reflections on life. The problems of life are the source and touchstone of philosophy. If man's practical needs were provided for and his curiosity satisfied it is unlikely that there would be any philosophical activity in the world, for the two principal sources of philosophy are man's curiosity about himself and his surroundings and a desire to overcome all kinds of suffering. Man's practical needs and his theoretical curiosity lead to philosophical activity because it is his nature to be self-reflective. He not only has needs and is curious, but he is aware of himself having these needs and this curiosity. Seeing himself in the context of his surroundings as a being struggling to overcome pain and suffering and trying to uncover the mysteries of existence, man comes to examine the kind of being he is, the kind of world he lives in, and the sources of value and knowledge that are so characteristic of his existence. It is this self-reflective activity of man that constitutes philosophy, for philosophy is not to be identified with the problems of man, but with man's critical reflections on his problems.

To persons accustomed to hearing about the "deepness" and abstractness of philosophy it may appear difficult to see how any enterprise with its roots in the problems of human existence can be isolated from life. And perhaps true philosophy cannot be isolated from life. But the problems of getting food, shelter, and water are not philosophical problems. They are problems to be solved by technology, not by self-understanding and wisdom. And often the problems of the spirit, especially the problems connected with the meaning and value of life and the problem of death, are not recognized as the most basic and urgent of life's problems. It is when life is held over against death that the question "What is life?" arises. And if death and life are not understood, then what assurance is there that all of the rest of man's activities rest upon the right foundation? For all the other activities of man are aimed at preserving and making valuable life itself.

Theories about the meaning of life and death are caught up with speculation concerning how things come into existence and pass out of existence. As man reflects upon his speculations earlier theories come to be questioned. Alternative theories are proposed; these are questioned in turn and new ones proposed. Reflective persons consider the theories of others and reflect on their own experience as they attempt to find a philosophy that in its explanations accounts for all of man's experiences and assures him of the value and meaning of life.

In the process of working out satisfactory explanations, each formulation of the question and each aspect of the proposed solution must be examined from every side. Eventually the questions are raised, "Are things really the way we think they are? Is what we call *knowledge* really knowledge?" The philosopher, reflecting on what we know about our knowledge, may seem very far removed from the ordinary problems of life, though in reality he is not. It is not enough that he ask a question or propose a solution; he must also attempt to justify the proposed solution as a satisfactory answer to the original question. If he discovers that what he took to be knowledge was, in fact, opinion, perhaps mistaken opinion, his whole theory which seemed to explain the meaning and value of life may have to change. And when it does, the philosopher's orientation toward the good life—and his idea of the best means of achieving it—may also change. Could anything be more practical or closer to everyday life than that, even if it be abstract and subtle?

The charge is sometimes made that the philosophers dwell in ivory towers, that they concentrate on logical subtleties and minutiae, while ignoring the major concerns of life. They seem to hide in their abstractions. There is, of course, the possibility that the speculations of the philosophers may cease to be connected with the philosophy of the ordinary people. When this happens philosophy loses much of its relevance; it no longer serves the ordinary person in reflecting upon his own existence in the world, and fails to provide him with the materials needed for the construction of a personal philosophy of life. In the West we are accustomed, in large part, to thinking of philosophy as something apart from life.

In the East the gap between the philosophers and the ordinary people is not nearly as great. Oriental philosophers keep closely in touch with life, returning to the touchstone of human experience to test their theories. The ordinary people stretch beyond their day-to-day concerns and struggle to see their existence in perspective, to understand it in philosophical terms.

This difference between East and West, which is, to be sure, a matter of degree, is due in part to the Oriental insistence on the wholeness of life and knowledge. Unlike Westerners, Easterners dislike cutting up and compartmentalizing life and knowledge. The result is that they do not separate the various fields of philosophy, such as theory of knowledge, theory of being, theory of art, theory of action, theory of political organization, etc. There is no clear-cut distinction between Eastern philosophy and Eastern religion, between philosophy and psychology, or philosophy and science. One consequence of this is the Easterner's tendency to take philosophy seriously. Philosophy in the Orient is not an abstract academic matter with little or no relevance to daily life—it is regarded as life's most basic and most important enterprise.

In China, after Confucianism became the state philosophy, it was impossible to get a government job without knowing the works of Confucius. Chinese history tells of many kings, artists, and scholars who were philosophers. The Chinese regard thought and practice as inseparable from each other, as aspects of the same activity. The central problems of Chinese philosophy are reflected in the questions "How can man achieve a harmony with his fellow men?" and "How can man achieve a harmony with nature?" These two questions turn out to be closely related, because as philosophy developed in China, there was an increasing tendency to identify nature with human nature. To the extent that this identification took place, the problem of achieving harmony with nature was the problem of man being in harmony with himself. In turn, being in harmony with himself was regarded as the necessary basis for achieving a harmony with other men. Being in harmony with himself and in harmony with the rest of humanity is "the highest good" in Chinese philosophy. Because the basic nature of man is seen as essentially moral, the dominant concern of much Chinese philosophy has been with morality. The questions "How can I be good?" and "What is the basis of goodness?" are basic questions throughout the history of Chinese philosophy.

India is famous for the high regard it accords the seeker of wisdom and for its reverence and respect for wise persons. The accumulated practical wisdom of India takes the form of self-discipline (*yoga*) aimed at the total integration of life. In order that this discipline be available to all persons, it is channeled through the activities of worship and devotion, the activities of work, and the activities of knowledge and concentration. These paths of self-discipline are simply the philosophic wisdom of the ages being put into practice by the people. The source of this wisdom of self-discipline is to be found in that combination of deep, intense personal experience and highly abstract rational explanation which is so characteristic of the Indian mind.

Long before Jesus of Nazareth, the sages of India were pondering what man is in his deepest being, and what nature is in its ultimate reality. Pursuing these two questions the philosophers of the Upanishads came to the wonderful realization that man in his deepest being is one with the ultimate nature of reality. The immediate practical problem arising from this discovery was how to realize this inner Self and thereby identify with the very essence of the universe. The search for an answer prompted a variety of developments in *yoga* and religion as well as the construction of moral and social philosophies. The theoretical problems raised by this discovery centered around the difficulty of relating the multiplicity and diversity of experienced reality with the Upanishadic insight into the unity of all existence. Furthermore it was difficult to ascertain how knowledge of such an ultimate reality could be achieved. These problems—which can be formulated in terms of questions about the basis of morality, the nature and function of society, the means of valid knowledge, the principles of logic, and the relation between appearance and reality—all have a common basis in the practical question "How can man achieve the spirituality that is his true nature?"

In Buddhist Asia millions have embraced the teachings of the wisdom-seeking Guatama Siddhartha as the solution to all of life's sufferings. The central problem of Buddhism is that of overcoming suffering. The essential teachings of the Buddha revolve around the questions, What is suffering? How does it arise? How can suffering be eliminated? and, How should man live so as to achieve a suffering-less existence? These questions, however, cannot be answered without inquiring into the nature of the self that suffers and the nature of the world that constitutes a source of suffering for the self. The question, How is suffering caused? leads to a general theory of causation which shapes the theories of man and reality which constitute Buddhist metaphysics. The problems of justifying the claims made about the nature of the self and the nature of reality lead to a general theory of logic and knowledge. Thus, the eminently practical problem of overcoming suffering provokes the reflections that constitute the theoretical principles of Buddhist philosophy.

Despite the many differences between the philosophies of India, China, and Buddhist Asia, they share a common concern with living and being as well as with learning and knowing. Consequently, philosophy and the philosophers have primary importance in all Oriental cultures. In order to understand the life and the attitudes of the Oriental peoples, it is necessary to understand their philosophies. In order to understand their philosophies, it is necessary to look to the traditions wherein these philosophies were born and lived.

PART ONE

The Hindu Systems

Dancing Shiva. *The Metropolitan Museum of Art, Harris Brisbane Dick Fund, 1964*

DOMINANT FEATURES
OF INDIAN PHILOSOPHY

THE story of Indian philosophy is long and exciting. From its beginnings in the speculations of the Vedic seers about six thousand
years ago to its present condition, Indian philosophical thought presents
a richness, subtlety, and variety which constitute an almost awesome
testimony to the human spirit. There is practically no insight or shade
of speculation known to man that is not found in Indian thought. This
richness and complexity makes it impossible to sum up Indian philosophy in clichés, slogans, or easy generalizations. Nevertheless, one
can point out certain dominant features provided one keeps in mind that
there are exceptions to every generalization. The following remarks
must, therefore, be understood as an attempt to select those features
of Indian thought which could be called dominant because of their
endurance, their popularity with a considerable number of philosophers,
or their widespread use in the lives of a majority of the people in India.
In some cases, all three of these criteria apply.

Next to its richness and comprehensiveness, the most striking feature
of Indian philosophical thought is its practical character. From the
very beginning, the speculations of India's sages were aimed at solving
life's basic problems. Their philosophy grew out of their attempts to
improve life. Confronted with physical, mental, and spiritual suffering,
India's early sages sought to understand the reasons and causes for this

suffering. They attempted to improve their understanding of man and the universe because they wanted to uproot the causes of suffering and to achieve the best possible life. The solutions achieved—and the reasons for the conclusions underlying the solutions—constitute the philosophies of these early sages.

India's philosophies, then, responded to both practical and speculative incentives. Practically, there was the acquaintance with ordinary forms of pain and suffering—disease, poverty, starvation, and the knowledge that ultimately death would overtake the sufferer. Speculatively, there was the innate human curiosity to order and to understand human experience. Practical considerations led men to seek ways to overcome the various forms of suffering. Speculative considerations led them to construct explanatory accounts of the nature of reality and of human existence. These considerations were not undertaken separately. The understanding and knowledge derived from speculative curiosity was utilized in the attempt to overcome suffering.

The primacy of the practical considerations involved in Indian phi-losophies gives them substance, while the necessity of the speculative considerations determines their structure. Consequently, though the practical problems involved in determining the nature of the good life—including the social life—are always in the fore, the theoretical explanations—concerning the nature of self, reality, and knowledge—used to justify proposed solutions to the practical problems have great importance in Indian philosophies.

In all philosophy there are two fundamentally different approaches to the problem of suffering which are based upon and characterized by two different attitudes. Both approaches recognize that suffering is the result of a gap between what one is and has, and what one wants to be and wants to have. A man is poor; wanting the wealth he lacks, he suffers. A man desires deathlessness though he knows death is inevitable; fearing this inevitability, he suffers. If there were no difference between what one is and has, and what one wants to be and to have, there would be no suffering. When there is a difference, suffering is inevitable. This being the case, the solution to the problem is obvious: what is and what is desired must be made identical.

But how can this identity be achieved? One approach to the solution lies in adjusting what one is and has to what is desired. If a man is poor but desires wealth, he should endeavor to accumulate wealth. The other approach consists in adjusting one's desires to what one has. If one is poor and desires wealth, he can overcome the resulting problem by removing the desire.

It should be noted here that many shades of compromise between the two approaches are possible. If, theoretically, a pure form of each approach is possible, in practice there is always a compromise: the analyst can only observe how the emphasis falls upon one or the other. Basically it is the second approach that Indian philosophy has taken. India chose to emphasize control of desires. As a result, the philosophies of India tend to insist on self-discipline and self-control as prerequisite to happiness and the good life. Self-control rather than the satiation of desires is the basic way to eliminate suffering.

This need to regulate and control desires threw extraordinary emphasis on knowledge of the self: knowing and controlling the self could do far more than the sciences of nature to alleviate suffering. Consequently, the practice of Indian philosophy became, at best, the art of living in complete control of oneself.

The practical character of Indian philosophy is manifested in a variety of ways. The very word which is usually translated "philosophy" points to this. *Darshana* literally means vision. It is what is seen. In its technical sense it means what is seen when the ultimate is investigated. Thus the ancient seers of India, seeking the solution to life's sufferings, investigated the conditions of suffering and looked to the nature of man and the nature of the external universe to find the causes of suffering and the means for its cessation. What they found constituted their *darshana*, their vision or philosophy.

Of course it is possible to be mistaken in one's vision; one may not see things as they really are. Consequently, the philosopher must justify his vision by providing evidence of its truth. Historically, two methods of justifying philosophical visions are encountered. According to the first method, logical analysis is used to determine whether or not a particular view is justified. If the concepts and statements expressing the vision are inconsistent with each other the vision may be discarded as self-contradictory. For example, if according to the vision in question it is claimed that all things that are born must die, and if it is also held that man is born but will not die, then the vision contains two views which are incompatible with each other. Obviously, the vision cannot be accepted without somehow overcoming this internal inconsistency, for one cannot at the same time accept as true both the claim "all born things die," and the claim "not all born things die," for these claims are contradictory. Any vision which attempts to embrace both of these claims is self-contradictory and cannot be accepted.

But suppose that several visions, each consistent within itself, are mutually incompatible. For example, one vision consistently maintains that all born things die, and the other vision consistently maintains that nothing that is born dies. What reasons are there for preferring one over another? Logic alone is not enough to determine this, for the question is not primarily one of consistency.

The second method, in recognition of the insufficiency of logic alone, is pragmatic, finding the justification of views or theories in the quality of resulting practice.

Indian philosophers have always insisted that practice is the ultimate test of truth. Philosophical visions must be put into practice and life lived according to the ideals of the vision. The quality of the life lived according to those ideals is the ultimate test of any vision. The better life becomes, the closer the vision approaches complete truth.

The criteria for determining the quality of life are, in turn, derived from the basic impetus for philosophy: the drive to eliminate suffering. The vision that makes possible a life devoid of suffering is properly called a true philosophy. Degrees of philosophic truth are determined according to the degree of alleviation of suffering. Put in a positive way, views are true according to the extent they improve the quality of life.

Placing the positive emphasis for justification of a philosophy on experience rather than logic (though logic is not excluded) requires putting philosophy into practice. In India, this has meant the working-out of a way to the realization of the good life wherein suffering is eliminated. The path is part of the vision, and if the way to the realization of the goals of the vision cannot be followed the vision is itself regarded as inadequate. "Good in theory, but not in practice," is a remark that makes no sense when applied to Indian philosophies. Good in theory necessarily means good in practice. If a theory cannot be put into practice there is something wrong with it.

The identification of the way to the good life with the vision of the good life itself is the integrating factor between religion and philosophy in India. When philosophy is regarded as being concerned only with the *theory* of the good life, concern with the practical means of attaining the good life is not considered philosophical. The means of life may then be regarded as falling within the religious or economic spheres, but not the philosophical. When the good life is thought to be "at a higher level" than this ordinary life, the means of achieving it are usually thought of as religious. When a materialistic view of the good life prevails, the means of achieving it are often thought to be economic. In neither case does the matter lie within the philosopher's domain—if religion and economics are practical matters and philosophy is theoretical, the consequent differences of scope, goal, and approach will sharply delineate one approach from another. But in India a philosopher's theory of the good life had to be tested by practice, and the philosopher had to devise a means for achieving the good life in order to be a philosopher. No sharp distinction existed between theory and practice; philosophy and religion were not considered to be two separate activities.

The Indian insistence upon practice as a test of philosophical truth had another effect—it emphasized the introspective approach. To avoid suffering, the philosopher had to look into himself, into his life, and note what was happening. To see the changes taking place and to evaluate these changes it is necessary for the individual to continue his self-examination, to observe what he is and what he is becoming. This necessitates a constant subjectivity.

The subjective is emphasized in two senses in Indian thought. In one sense the subjective is considered as the opposite of objective; the criteria of truth are qualitative rather than quantitative. According to the other sense, subjective refers to the subject as opposed to the object. An object is anything that can be entertained or witnessed by a subject. The subject, however, is always witness or entertainer; never the witnessed or entertained.

Indian philosophy is concerned with the suffering of human beings, and the human subject is of greater importance than the objects that come within the experience of the subject. The self that suffers is always the subject. To treat it otherwise is to regard it as a thing, which places the consideration outside the immediate bounds of philosophy. The ultimate self of man is described in the philosophical literature as pure subject, or subject which can never become object—"The one without a second." It is the subjective or qualitative experience of the subject that is of primary concern.

The emphasis on the subjective, in both senses of that expression, tends to promote a synthetic attitude. The relevant philosophical criteria are not quantitative and public. They belong to subject as subject. Therefore it is impossible for one person to subscribe to one philosophy as alone being true and to regard the others as completely false. Truth in philosophy depends upon the human subject, and another's experience can be known only as an object. There is no knowing—according to ordinary ways of knowing, at least—the other as subject. Consequently, there is no rejecting the other's experience as inadequate or unsatisfactory. Recognition of this has led to a tolerant synthetic attitude which is commonly expressed by saying that while it may be that no vision, by itself, is absolutely true and complete, nevertheless, each vision contains some glimpse of the truth, and by assuming the viewpoints and experiences assumed by the various visions one comes closer to the absolute truth and the complete vision. Philosophical progress is not made by proceeding from falsehood to truth, but by proceeding from partial to more complete truth.

In addition to these features of Indian philosophy which stem from its practical orientation, there is a widespread tendency in Indian thought to presuppose universal moral justice. The world is seen as a great moral stage directed by justice. Everything, good, bad, and indifferent is earned and deserved. The impact of this attitude is to place the responsibility for man's condition squarely upon man himself. An individual is responsible for what he is and what he becomes. He himself has determined his past and will determine his future. In the sacred writings, the Vedas, the concept of *rita* (moral law) denoted justice as the ruler of the universe. As the duties of man in response to justice came to be emphasized, the concept of *dharma* as determined by the moral structure of the universe became dominant. The concept of *karma* came to refer to the relation between what one did and what he was, pointing, as it did, to the causal efficacy of human actions, standing for the self-determination of man.

There is also rather widespread agreement in Indian philosophical thought concerning non-attachment. Suffering results from attaching oneself to what one does not have or even to what one cannot have. These attached objects then become the causes of suffering insofar as they are not attained or are lost. Therefore, if a spirit of non-attachment to the objects of suffering could be cultivated the suffering itself could be eliminated. Thus, non-attachment is recognized as an essential means to the realization of the good life.

Because of the above features of Indian thought, the people of India have usually accorded the highest respect to the philosopher, and philosophy has been regarded as the highest knowledge and wisdom.

CHAPTER 2

HISTORICAL SURVEY
OF INDIAN PHILOSOPHY

INDIAN philosophy began before recorded history. The first bits of speculation which could be called philosophical date back over five thousand years, to about 4000 B.C. Since those beginnings, now dimmed and obscured by time, India has acquired a vast wealth of philosophical vision, speculation, and argument. It is difficult to approach Indian philosophy chronologically, however, as a history in terms of names, dates, and places is a most unsure thing. In India so much emphasis has been put on the content of the thought and so little on person, place, and time that in a majority of cases it is not known who is responsible for the particular philosophy in question. And when the author is unknown, the time and the place can be reckoned only indirectly. Because of this, time is usually reckoned in terms of centuries rather than years or decades, and authorship is attributed to schools rather than to individual persons. Nevertheless, it is possible to see changes in philosophical thinking occurring in a certain sequence. That is, it is possible to see the antecedents and successors of various philosophical problems and solutions.

The historical approach is facilitated by adopting a more or less arbitrary classification of periods in the development of the philosophical traditions in India. The Vedic period stretches from about 4000 B.C. to 700 B.C. The Epic period occurred between 1000 B.C. and 200 A.D. The

Sutra period lasted from about 400 B.C. to 500 A.D. The Commentary
period commenced about 600 A.D. and continued until about 1700 A.D.
The Renaissance period, which is still in progress, began around 1800 A.D.

THE VEDIC PERIOD: It was during the Vedic period that the Aryan
peoples moved from Central Asia into the Indus Valley. The cultural
traditions they brought with them mingled with the traditions and
customs of the people they met, and what can properly be called Indian
culture began to take shape, a growth nourished by the climates and
conditions of two earlier cultures.

The philosophical fruit of this early period is contained in the collection of writings called the Upanishads, which represent the culmination
of philosophical speculation of this first period, and in the earlier literature of the Vedic *Samhitas, Brahmanas,* and *Aranyakas,* which are, for
the most part, religious. Finding themselves in a new land, in many
ways cut off from their familiar routines of life, these early peoples
formulated questions about the world around them and their place in
it. What made the wind blow? What was responsible for the monsoon?
And the sun, giver of warmth and light—who put it in the sky? And
how is it that broad-bosomed earth brings forth these myriad life-forms?
These are typical of the questions entertained in the early portions of
the Vedic period—questions which at first received answers attributing
all these things, both wonderful and terrible, to the gods.

Questions of how and why are the roots of philosophical speculation.
At first men tried to answer these questions in terms of the human person, and they attributed events in nature to superhuman persons, or
gods. This tended to encourage religious activity rather than specifically
philosophical speculation. Inquiring minds, however, continued to
probe into the why's of nature and man, so in addition to developing the
Vedic ritual and worship found in the *Sama* and the *Yajur Vedas,* they
also developed the cognitive inquiry which is the spirit of philosophy.
This is attested to by the literature of the Aranyakas and the Upanishads.
In this later literature a universal law of cause and effect called *rita* is
important. So by the time of the Upanishads that most wonderful of all
discoveries already had been made—the discovery that the ultimate
source and power of all existence is identical with one's ultimate self.

The literature of this period (all of it termed *Veda*) can be divided into
the following categories: *Rig-Veda, Sama Veda, Yajur Veda,* and *Atharva
Veda.* Each of the first three Vedas contain hymns to the gods as well as
various questions (the *Samhita* portion), arrangements of the *Samhita*

portion for use in sacrifices (the *Brahmana* portion), interpretations of the rituals (*Aranyaka* portion), and speculations on the basic questions underlying religious practices (the *Upanishads*). Though all of this literature was composed prior to 700 B.C. it has exerted a very great influence on the people of India right up to our own times.

THE EPIC PERIOD: The wisdom of the Vedic literature was part of a sacred and jealously guarded tradition, often unavailable to many members of the society, or where available, beyond understanding. To compensate for this there grew up a folklore recited in stories and poems which managed to transmit many of the ideals of the sacred tradition to the majority of the people. The two most notable collections of materials constituting this literature are the *Mahabharata* and the *Ramayana*.

The *Mahabharata* is an epic of considerable length (the English translation runs to thirteen volumes). It tells the story of the conquest of the land of India and in so doing provides instruction for the various rules of life. It offers a guide to life in all its dimensions, including religion, philosophy, social science, politics, and even medicine. The single most influential part of the *Mahabharata* is the *Bhagavad Gita*, "The Song of the Great One." The *Gita* explains the nature of man and the universe, and from the explanation of matter and spirit are derived ways of life which will enable one to achieve the ultimately good life.

The *Ramayana*, a beautiful poem in four volumes, presents ideals for womanhood and manhood in the persons and lives of Sita, and her husband, Rama. The epic suggests an ideal order for society as a whole, and also an ideal ordering of the life of the individual.

During this period treatises on justice and righteousness—the *Dharma Shastras*—were compiled. These treatises were concerned primarily with regulating the life of the individual and the society in respect to specific codes of actions, which were presented along with their justification in the literature on *dharma*. The *Artha Shastra* of Kautilya justifies the need for and the importance of the various means of life and shows how they may be obtained. The *Manu Shastra* shows how justice and order may be secured in society by the king and the institutions of government. The *Shastra* of Yajnavalkya emphasizes justice and order in the life of the individual. The *Kama Shastra* (sometimes translated as *Kama Sutra*) of Vatsyayana deals with the attainment of pleasure. These are among the more influential of these treatises.

No doubt it was also during this time that the beginnings of the various systems of philosophy were established, for there are references in the *Mahabharata* to certain of the systems. But these systems did not receive definitive form until near the end of the Epic period.

THE SUTRA PERIOD: Toward the end of the Epic period, the beginnings of several systematic philosophical explanations of the world and man were established. These systems represent the first purely philosophical effort in India, for not only did they attempt to explain the fundamentals of life and the world, but they did so self-consciously and self-critically, arguing for the correctness of the answers suggested on the basis of reason.

The *Sutras*, or aphorisms, of Buddhism, Jainism, and Carvaka are designated *nastika*, or unorthodox, because their authors did not accept the pronouncements of the Vedas as true and final. Neither did they endeavor to justify their analyses and solutions by showing them to be in accord with the Vedas. The aphorisms expressing the philosophies of the Schools of Nyaya, Vaishesika, Samkhya, Yoga, Mimamsa, and Vedanta, on the other hand, all accept the authority of the Vedas.

Forest-dwelling Sages. *Reprinted by kind permission of Nancy Wilson Ross from* THREE WAYS OF ASIAN WISDOM (*Simon and Schuster, New York*).

These schools are all concerned to show that their analyses and solutions do indeed agree with the pronouncements of the Vedas. Consequently varying "orthodox" interpretations of the Vedas came about; each school's claim for its views was demonstrated by agreement with the "correct" interpretation of those teachings. These divisive claims especially affected the Vedanta philosophies.

The major division, however, is between Carvaka and the others: Carvaka is a completely materialistic system: all the others allow for spirituality—Nyaya is concerned primarily with a logical analysis of the means of knowing: Vaishesika analyzes the kinds of things that are known: Samkhya seeks to relate the self to the external world: Yoga analyzes the nature of the self and explains how the pure Self can be realized: Mimamsa concentrates on the criteria for the self-validity of knowledge, attempting thereby to establish the truth of the Vedic pronouncements: Vedanta begins with the conclusions of the Upanishads and attempts to show that a rational analysis of knowledge and reality will support those conclusions.

PERIOD OF THE GREAT COMMENTARIES: As generations of seers and scholars studied and examined the *sutras* of the various schools, they occasionally wrote commentaries on them. In this way the great commentaries of Guadapada (sixth cent. A.D.), Shamkara (eighth cent. A.D.), Bhaskara (ninth cent. A.D.), Yamuna (tenth cent. A.D.), Ramanuja (eleventh cent. A.D.), Nimbarka (twelfth cent. A.D.), Madhva (thirteenth cent. A.D.), and Vallabha (fifteenth cent. A.D.), came to be written on the Vedanta *Sutras* of Badarayana.

THE RENAISSANCE PERIOD: As a result of outside influences, especially the contact with the West, Indian philosophers began to reexamine their philosophical traditions. Beginning with the studies, translations, and commentaries of Ram Mohun Roy in the nineteenth century, the examinations have recently been carried on in especially notable fashion by Radhakrishnan and Aurobindo among others.

CHAPTER 3

RELIGION AND PHILOSOPHY—
THE VEDAS AND UPANISHADS

THE earliest recorded speculations about the nature of the world
and the nature of man are found in the *Rig-Veda*. In the *Rig-Veda*
there is no distinction between religion and philosophy, but the questions which give rise to both are asked at this time, and provide the
structuring theme of the Vedic literature. Some of these questions—
What makes the wind blow? Why does the monsoon come? Who put
the sun, giver of warmth and light, in the heavens? and, How is it that
broad-bosomed earth brings forth these myriad life forms?—would,
according to present day classifications, belong to the sciences rather
than to philosophy. Other questions such as, Who will save me from
death? Who will protect me in time of danger? and, How will I be saved
from the evils and misfortunes of life? might be thought to belong to
religion. But six thousand years ago these distinctions did not exist, and
all of these questions were the philosopher's concern. And there were
yet other questions asked, questions that even according to today's
classifications would be considered philosophical. These included such
questions as, What is there beyond the gods? What, if any, is the relation
between actions and their consequences? What knowledge, if any, does
man have of himself?

Early attempts to satisfy curiosity about man's environment resulted
in attributing all the wonderful and terrible things in it to the gods.
The reason for this was simple: the questions *How? Why?* and *With*

what? are appropriate when applied to human activity. Consequently, when these questions were asked of *natural* activity rather than *human* activity it was easy to assume personal forces behind the natural activities; then the questions were like questions about human activity and were answerable. Of course these personal forces were not thought of as similar to ordinary persons; they were regarded as "super" persons, or gods. The activity of fire was attributed to a god of fire, the activity of wind to a god of wind, etc. Nature, when thought of as a human person, was at least partially removed from the realm of the mysterious.

To the extent that the answers attributing natural activities to various gods were conceived to be ultimate answers, men endeavored less to understand nature than to control it. If the vital questions about nature, *How* and *Why*, were answerable in terms of *Who*, it is not surprising that men sought to control nature by influencing the gods with prayers, rituals, and sacrifices. Consequently it is not surprising that major portions of the Vedas are preoccupied with ritual and sacrifice.

But not all of the seers of the *Rig-Veda* were satisfied with religion as the way of understanding and controlling nature and man. Some could say;

> Who knows for certain? Who shall here declare it? Whence was it born, and whence came this creation? The gods were born after this world's creation: Then who can know from whence it has arisen? None knoweth whence this creation has arisen; And whether He has or has not produced it: He who surveys it in the highest heaven, He only knows, or perhaps even he may know not.[1]

They were the seekers of wisdom who searched beyond the gods to the rule that governs even the gods, to the reality that exists beyond the gods. They recognized that behind the regularities of nature and the gods stands an eternal and immutable law of order and justice. They called it *Rita*. In addition to providing for orderliness, this eternal law represented the unity of reality and man, for not only the activities of nature but also of man proceed from and according to *Rita*. *Rita* stands as order and justice directing the whole play of the cosmos; nothing happens except as directed by that eternal law.

Even the religious thinkers, however, concerned with ritual and sacrifice, could not be content with the assumption that nature was controlled by the gods, who in turn were subject to the appeals of prayer and sacrifice. The questions of how the gods controlled nature,

[1] *Rig-Veda*, X.129.6,7. Reprinted in Sarvepalli Radhakrishnan and Charles A. Moore, eds., *A Source Book in Indian Philosophy* (Princeton: Princeton University Press, 1957), pp. 23, 24.

and how man could influence the gods, resulted in theologies whereby these things were explained. While for the most part these explanations (which constitute the *Brahmana* portions of the Veda) were simply concerned with the elaboration of details of religious worship, occasionally they transcended the limits of the given answers and sought to explain the efficacy of sacrifice in terms of primordial principles more basic than the gods. In the *Shatapatha Brahmana*, the seer speculates as follows:

> Verily, in the beginning this (universe) was the *Brahman* [neut.]. It created the gods; and, having created the gods, it made them ascend these worlds: Agni this (terrestrial) world, Vāyu the air, and Sūrya the sky.... Then the *Brahman* itself went up to the sphere beyond. Having gone up to the sphere beyond, it considered, "How can I descend again into these worlds?" It then descended again by means of these two, Form and Name.... These, (Name and Form) indeed, are the two great forces of *Brahman*; and verily, he who knows these two great forces of *Brahman* becomes himself a great force.[2]

This is obviously an attempt to explain the religious in terms of the philosophical, transcending the religion of the time.

The Aranyakas, composed later than the Brahmanas, represent a move away from the ritualism of an earlier period and toward free intellectual inquiry into the nature of reality. Even though they accept the religious way, they tend to substitute meditation on aspects of nature for sacrificial objects. Gradually the meditation led to free speculation, and the contemplation which permeates the Upanishads came to replace ritualism. But the fact remains that while the early portions of the Veda—the *Samhitas*, *Brahmanas*, and *Aranyakas*—contain some philosophy, for the most part they are religious in content.

It is not a simple matter to distinguish between religion and philosophy. In the main, it can be said that philosophical thought is free. It is free to take man in whatever direction his total experience leads him, free from the restrictions of predetermined truth. The early portions of the Veda were philosophical to the extent that the Persons' experiences and reflections led them to conclude that natural activities were due to the gods. But when this answer came to be regarded as absolute and final, men were no longer free to continue the quest: they were limited to the framework imposed by the attitude which regarded earlier answers as definitive.

[2] *Shatapatha Brahmana*, XI.2.2, trans. by Julius Eggeling, *Sacred Books of the East*, XLIV (Oxford: The Clarendon Press, 1900), pp. 27, 28.

Another feature of philosophical thought is that it is self-critical, ever aware that claimed answers depend for their truth upon the justifying evidence produced. Here again, the bulk of early Vedic thought appears non-philosophical, for the question of evidence for the truth of the various claims upon which the religious practices rested did not, for the most part, arise. And when the question did arise, men began to seek evidence through contemplation of and speculation upon nature and man, rather than through the way of ritual.

Another generic feature of philosophical thought is that it is concerned with fundamental and primary principles of existence and action; concerned not only with suppositions, but also with presuppositions. Thus, a great bulk of the early Vedic literature, which was devoted to descriptions of and elaborations upon rituals, could hardly be said to be philosophical.

The concluding portions of the Veda, the Upanishads, are much more philosophical than the preceding portions, for they are free from the restrictions of predetermined truth. They contain a recognition of the need to supply evidence for their claims, and they are concerned with the fundamental principles of existence. Nevertheless, even they are not fully philosophical in the current sense of that term, for they proceed without any formal analysis of the criteria of truth and the relation between truth and evidence. For the most part, personal experience of what is claimed is taken as sufficient evidence for the truth of the claim, but there is no attempt to show how it is that certain kinds of experience can count as evidence for claims about reality. And while there is general recognition that self-contradictory views cannot be true, it would be going too far to suggest that reason determined the truth or falsity of views, for there were no principles of logic or reason worked out. Consequently, the Upanishads tend to emphasize the content of the vision of the seer more that the means whereby the vision can be justified. The claims in the Upanishads are taken to be the reports of the experience of the seers, and not philosophical theories waiting to be justified. It is the experience of the seers that provides the evidence for the truth of the claims being made.

When man confronts his existence face to face and meditates on its beginning and end in an attempt to discover its meaning and value, he comes up against certain basic questions concerning the reality surrounding him. What is the nature of fundamental reality? How was the universe created? How is it controlled and regulated? How is it sustained? These are among the questions that gave rise to the speculations of the Vedas.

It was noted earlier that the first attempts to answer questions about the nature of external reality led to belief in the various gods of nature. Gradually the number of these gods decreased, as the functions of several lesser deities were attributed to a more powerful god. By this process it came to be thought that there was one single deity who was the creator and controller of the universe. By the time of the Upanishads it seems to be well accepted that there is a single reality which is the source of all external existence. But now the claim that this single reality is a deity is regarded as unsatisfactory and an attempt is made to discover just what this ultimate source is. Consequently the key question of the Upanishads with respect to external reality is, What is the one source and controller of all existence?

This question presupposes that there is a difference between what *appears* to be real and what is really real; appearance is not taken as being sufficient for its own existence, but is thought to be dependent upon some higher reality. The search was not for the world of space and time filled with sound, odors, colors, etc., which *appears* to man as his world, but for the *conditions* that made possible this appearing world.

The distinction is analogous to the distinction made between the colors one sees and the conditions which make possible the seeing of colors. One might say that what one sees are the various colors of the spectrum, taking the colors to be something that exist in the world. Someone else, however, might point out that colors as seen do not *really* exist, but that they *appear* to exist when certain wave-lengths of light pass through specified media before striking the retina. To talk about colors is to talk about the conditioned; to talk about wave-lengths and media is to talk about the sources of the conditioned which enable the conditioned to exist as appearance. Here the analogy breaks down, however, for the seers of the Upanishads were not seeking the specific conditions of any particular appearances, but were seeking that which conditioned or made possible existence itself.

These seers had no clear concept of what they sought; they simply knew that there must exist that by which all other things existed and which made them great. The name given to this "something" was *Brahman*, which means "that which makes great." It was a non-descriptive name; in fact it was a non-name, for it did not name anything definite, either abstract or concrete. The search for what "*Brahman*" named is recorded in the Upanishads as the search for the ultimate external reality. At first there was an attempt to identify that "something" with religious symbols and sacrifices, with natural objects, such as the sun and the moon, and with certain psychological functions of man. The difficulty with all of these attempts to state what *Brahman* is, was that they all presupposed limits on that power. But since they were seeking the ultimate power of existence it was impossible that it should be limited, for there could be nothing beyond it to limit it. As the seers began to realize more clearly that *Brahman* could not adequately be described by appealing to their experience of the world of appearance, they attempted to define this reality in a negative way.

According to Yajnavalkya in the *Brihadaranyaka Upanishad*, *Brahman* is not conceivable, not changeable, not injurable, etc. According to the *Katha Upanishad*, *Brahman* is inaudible, invisible, indestructible, cannot be tasted, cannot be smelled, is without beginning or end, and greater than the great. *Brahman* is described negatively in the *Mundaka Upanishad* as follows:

> Invisible, incomprehensible, without genealogy, colourless, without eye or ear, without hands or feet, eternal, pervading all and over all, scarce knowable, that unchangeable one whom the wise regard as being womb.[3]

Clearly it was felt that *Brahman* was not many and not material. But these characteristics are negative. The difficulty is that after regarding *Brahman* as that which makes possible time, space, and causality it was impossible to regard it as limited by them. Being prior to space, time, and causality means being beyond the characteristics of the empirical universe, and therefore beyond positive description. That which makes possible both conception itself and the conceptualized is not to be caught with the net of the conceptualized world. But if that is the case then the nature of *Brahman* remains elusive and mysterious.

Despite the fact that for all of their concentration on *Brahman* they were unsuccessful in establishing the ultimate nature of external reality, the thinkers of the Upanishads were not completely stymied. Some of them, unlike the seers of the early portions of the Veda, were seeking an answer to a different question; a question about the ultimate nature of *man*. This second basic question of the Upanishads is the question, What am I, in my deepest existence?

This too, was a question about the conditions of appearance rather than about the appearances themselves. The question presupposes that the self is something more than meets the eye, for the bodily organism is not particularly elusive or mysterious. But the question of what

[3] *Mundaka Upanishad*, I.1.6, trans. by Paul Deussen, *The Philosophy of the Upanishads* (New York: Dover Publications, 1966), p. 148.

enables the bodily organism to exist is another matter. I may appear to be a bodily organism, but is that what I really am? Is the "I" that thinks the self to be a bodily organism also a bodily organism? And is not the "I" more properly the self than the body? These are the sorts of questions that occurred to these thinkers.

There is no doubt that the distinction between what the self appears to be and what it really is, was assumed by the thinkers of the Upanishads. Their search for the innermost essence of man is guided by the injunction:

> The Self (*atman*) which is free from evil, free from old age, free from death, free from grief, free from hunger and thirst, whose desire is the real, whose thoughts are true, he should be sought, him one should desire to understand. He who has found out and who understands that self, he obtains all worlds and desires.[4]

The question was, What is that wonderful and mysterious Self? Trying to answer that question, the seers of the *Taittiriya Upanishad* turned their attention to the various aspects and functions of the individual person as they searched for that ultimate Self. If the Self is thought to be the body then it is essentially food, they reasoned, for the body is simply digested food. But surely the Self is not to be identified with the body only, for it is something more; it is alive and moving. If the Self is not food, perhaps it is the life of food. But they saw that while this would serve to distinguish living from non-living matter it was not the ultimate Self of the person, for a person is more than simply living food. It sees, hears, feels, etc. Perhaps, the speculation continues, the Self should be thought of in terms of mind or perception. But this too seemed inadequate, for thinking and understanding are even more properly Self than perception. However, this too is rejected as inadequate, for there must be that which gives existence to thinking and understanding. As the Upanishad says, "Different from and within that which consists of the understanding is the Self consisting of bliss."[5]

This search for the ultimate Self was essentially a matter of going deeper and deeper into the foundations of human existence. Matter was regarded as covering for life, which in turn was a covering for the sensing self. And deeper than sensing was intellectual activity. But deeper still was the bliss of total consciousness. Consequently, the Self is not to be

---

[4] *Chandogya Upanishad*, VIII.7.1. In *The Principal Upanisads* ed. by Sarvepalli Radhakrishnan (London: Allen and Unwin Ltd., 1953), p. 501. Unless otherwise noted, all quotations from the Upanishads are from this work.
[5] *Taittiriya Upanishad*, II.5.1.

identified with any of the lower forms of the person exclusively, but is to be thought of as existing within the various layers of existence, giving them life while remaining distinct from them.

In the *Kena Upanishad* the search for the ultimate Self takes the form of a quest for the ultimate agent or doer of human activity. It is asked, "By whom willed and directed does the mind light on its objects? By whom commanded does life the first, move? At whose will do (people) utter this speech? And what god is it that prompts the eye and the ear?"[6]

In the very next paragraph these questions are answered by saying that there is a more basic Self that directs the eye to color, the ear to sound, the understanding to consciousness, etc. And this Self is said to be "other than the known and other than the unknown."[7] The question here is basically a matter of asking what makes possible seeing, hearing, thinking, etc. But the question is not about physiological processes; it it about the hearing subject, the seeing subject, etc. That is, I may be said to be a hearing, seeing, thinking thing; but by what do I do these things? I see the green colors in front of me when they are present to the eye; how is it that the eye is so directed? Must not there be an inner director, an agent directing the functions and activities of a person? The answer in the Upanishads is a most emphatic *yes*.

There remains, however, another question; What is that which directs all of the human activities? The answer to that question is that it cannot be known, for "there the eye goes not, speech goes not, nor the mind; we know not, we understand not how one can teach this."[8] The reason it is beyond the eye, beyond the ear, beyond the understanding, etc., is that what is seen, heard, understood, etc., is always an object known by the human subject. But the ultimate Self is the ultimate subject. Therefore it can never be an object of knowledge, and must remain beyond the grasp of ordinary knowledge. Nevertheless, since this Self is ultimate subject, it can be realized directly in total self-consciousness, where, so to speak, the knower stands illumined by its own illumination. Thus, though in one sense the ultimate Self cannot be known, in another sense, the sense of immediate experience, it can be known intimately and completely in the experience of total self-consciousness. In this sense it is known much more surely and completely than any object of knowledge. This is the certitude of one's own existence, beyond question or doubt.

---

[6] *Kena Upanishad*, I.1.   [7] *Ibid.*, I.4.   [8] *Ibid.*, I.3.

In the *Chandogya Upanishad* man's search for the ultimate Self is presented in the form of a delightful story in which Prajapati (representing the creative forces of the universe) instructs Indra (who represents the gods) and Virocana (who represents the demons) about the Self. As students seeking the wisdom possessed by the *guru*, or spiritual teacher, Indra and Virocana come, bearing fuel, to Prajapati for instruction. For thirty-two years they prepare themselves for Prajapati's teaching by practicing self-discipline. At the end of that time he tells them that the Self is what they see when they look at their reflection in a glass or a pan of water. They look and they see the physical form, clothed and adorned with jewels. Virocana, delighted with this knowledge returns to the demon-world and teaches that the body is the Self. Such is the teaching of the demons! But Indra reflects on this teaching and sees that if the Self is the same as the body, then when the body perishes so does the Self. This cannot be the immortal Self he is seeking, so he again asks Prajapati about the Self. This time Prajapati tells him that the dream-self is the real Self. But still Indra is uneasy. For although the dream-self is not absolutely dependent upon the body, nevertheless sometimes it too is subject to pain, suffering and destruction. So again he asks what the real Self is. And this time he is told that the self that is sound asleep, beyond dreams, is the real Self. At first this satisfies Indra, but before he has reached the abode of the gods he realizes that even though the deep-sleeping self is not subject to pain and destruction, nevertheless it cannot be the real Self—in deep sleep the self is not aware of itself; one might just as well be dead, he tells Prajapati. By this time Indra has spent a total of one hundred and one years disciplining and preparing himself for that highest knowledge (*paravidyam*) and now is ready to hear about the ultimate Self. Now Prajapati tells him that the Self being sought transcends all of the selves considered so far. It is true, there is a physical self, which some think to be the only self. And there is the self which is the subject that experiences dreams, a self recognized by some. And there is the self which experiences deep sleep, otherwise deep sleep would be the same as death. But the highest Self goes beyond all of these; it is that which makes possible the self of waking experience, of dreaming experience, and of deep sleep. Those selves are merely instruments of the highest Self, which is the very source of their existence.

The state in which one realizes the ultimate Self that gives existence to the selves of the waking, dreaming, and deep-sleeping selves is sometimes called the *turiya*, or fourth state. Unlike the condition of deep sleep this state is one of total self-consciousness and illumination. In the

Brihadaranyaka Upanishad it is said, "When one goes to sleep, he takes along the material of this all-containing world, himself tears it apart, himself builds it up and dreams by his own brightness, by his own light. Then this person becomes self-illuminated."[9]

Although ordinary knowledge, which presupposes the duality of object and subject, knower and known, is impossible in this fourth state, there is no doubt of the authenticity of its existence. The same Upanishad continues:

> Indeed, while he does not there know, he is indeed knowing, though he does not know [what is usually to be known]; for there is no cessation of the knowing of a knower, because of his imperishability [as a knower]. It is not, however, a second thing, other than himself and separate, which he may know.[10]

Thus, in the Upanishads, the question, What am I, in the deepest reaches of my existence? is answered by saying that the very foundation of existence is self-illuminating consciousness, which can be directly experienced by a person when one goes beyond identification with the false self of the objectified world. It is tremendously significant that the ultimate Self—the *Atman*—can be known directly and immediately as a matter of direct experience. For here there can be no doubts or lingering uncertainty. This is an answer which when realized provides for the total satisfaction of the individual.

The discovery of *Atman* is also significant in another way. The seers of the Upanishads who were seeking both the ultimate external reality (*Brahman*) and the ultimate internal reality (*Atman*) came to inquire into the relations or connections between these realities. The exciting discovery they now made was that *Atman* was none other than *Brahman*. There was only one ultimate reality which could be approached either by looking outside of man or by looking within man. Thus, though the search for the nature of external reality, or *Brahman*, had appeared to end in frustration because of the impossibility of saying anything about the ultimate object, it was now realized that *Brahman* could be known by the self-certifying experience of total conscious illumination, because *Brahman* was the ultimate Subject, or *Atman*. There was no difference between the ultimate subject and the ultimate object; ultimate subjective reality and ultimate objective reality were one and the same! It is hard to imagine a more exciting discovery. Seeking to understand what the world was and who he was, man had discovered that all

---

[9] *Brihadaranyaka Upanishad*, IV.3.9.   [10] *Brihadaranyaka Upanishad*, IV.3.30.

things existed within *Atman*; that he himself sustained all things in his deepest Self. One need only know the Self to know all. And the Self can be known in the surest way possible, for it is self-revealing in consciousness when the objects of consciousness that block out self-illumination are transcended.

The unity of *Atman* and *Brahman* is the greatest discovery made in the Upanishads. This unity above all is the mystery and sacred teaching (*upanisat*) that is so carefully guarded by the seers of the Upanishads, and that constitutes the basic message of these treatises.

The quest for the nature of *Brahman* and *Atman* and the discovery of the relation between them is well illustrated by the account of the five householders who studied with Ashvapati Kaikeya.[11]

Pracinashala Aupamanyava, Satyayajna Paulusi, Indradyumna Bhallaveya, Jana Sharkaraksya, and Budila Ashvatarashvi, famous householders, renowned for their learning and wisdom, got together to investigate what is self and what is *Brahman*. Consulting among themselves they agreed that since Uddalaka Aruni was at present studying this universal Self they would go to him.

But when they came, Uddalaka reflected; "These great householders and greatly learned in sacred lore will question me. I shall not be able to tell them all. Therefore, I shall direct them to another (teacher)." He said to them "Venerable Sirs, Ashvapati Kaikeya studies at present this universal Self, well, let us go to him." When they arrived, they announced their purpose saying, "At present, Sir, you know the universal Self. Tell us indeed about that."

Assuring himself that these persons were qualified to receive this sacred teaching, Ashvapati Kaikeya discovered that one of the householders regarded heaven as the universal Self. Another regarded the sun as the universal Self. A third considered space to be the universal Self. The fourth thought the Self was air, while the fifth householder regarded water as the universal Self. Uddalaka Aruni looked for the Self in the earth. Ashvapati Kaikeya told each householder that his knowledge was only partial and limited. He said to them, "Indeed you eat your food knowing this universal Self as if it were many. He, however, who meditates on the universal Self as of the measure of the span or as identical with the self, eats food in all worlds, in all beings, in all selves."

This teaching of Ashvapati Kaikeya is usually interpreted to mean that the universal Self is in each person and in each being without differentia-

---

11 *Chandogya Upanishad*, V.11–18.

tion. The householders should realize the universal Self in themselves, for they are not different from that universal Self.

The *Chandogya Upanishad* also contains the famous teaching of Shandilya: "Verily, this whole world is *Brahman*. . . . Containing all works, containing all desires, containing all odors, containing all tastes, encompassing this whole world, without speech, without concern, this is the Self (*Atman*) of mine within the heart; this is *Brahman*." [12]

Because of the deep-seated ignorance that results in objectification of the world, and because of the resulting multiplicity, one is inclined to think of the ultimate reality as an other. But this is a mistake, for "in the beginning all this world was *Brahman* only. Whoever thus knows, 'I am *Brahman* (*Aham Brahman asi*)' becomes this All." [13]

Thus, the teaching received by the householders is that by knowing their deepest self they will know the universal Self; they will know all. This teaching is beautifully presented in the famous passage of the *Chandogya Upanishad* in which Uddalaka teaches his son, Shvetaketu about the ultimate reality, telling him that he is that ultimate reality ("*tat tvam asi, Shvetaketu*"). [14] Shvetaketu had become a pupil at age twelve and for twelve years had studied the Vedas. At age twenty-four, thinking himself learned, he was arrogant and conceited. His father then said to him, "Shvetaketu, since you are now so greatly conceited, think yourself well-read and arrogant, did you ask for that instruction by which the unhearable becomes the heard, the unperceivable becomes perceived, the unknowable becomes known?" When Shvetaketu asks how such a teaching is even possible, his father responds, "just as, my dear, by one clod of clay all that is made of clay becomes known, the modification being only a name arising from speech while the truth is that it is just clay." The point of this is that the variety and plurality of objects in the world is only a disguise for the unified reality which underlies these objects. And that underlying reality is the reality of the Self.

The instruction then proceeds to the famous teaching:

> That which is the subtle essence, this whole world has for its Self (*Atman*). That is the true. That is the *Atman*. That art thou [*tat tvam asi*], Shvetaketu.

The "subtle essence" referred to is *Brahman*, the source of all existence. Thus, when Shvetaketu is identified with his deepest self, or *Atman*, and that in turn identified with *Brahman*, the mystic teaching has been imparted.

[12] *Chandogya Upanishad*, III.14.1,4.   [13] *Brihadaranyaka Upanishad*, I.4.10.
[14] *Chandogya Upanishad*, VI.

Of course, by understanding this teaching (in the sense of under-standing the language in which it is presented) Shvetaketu does not thereby come to know that Self, that subtle essence. His knowledge is still of objects; the teaching itself is an object of instruction, whereas what is to be known is pure subject. Yajnayalkya brings this out when he answers Uhasta Cakrayana's request for an explanation of "the *Brah-man* that is immediately present and directly perceived, that is the Self in all things," by declaring: "This is your Self that is within all things." When the question is put again, "Which is within all things?" the reply is, "You cannot see the seer of seeing, you cannot hear the hearer of hearing, you cannot think the thinker of thinking, you cannot understand the understander of understanding. He is your Self which is in all things." [15]

This is the ultimate subject which can never become an object. Con-sequently, it cannot be known in the way that objects in consciousness can be known, but must be realized directly in self-illuminating experiences.

The advantages brought to the search for the ultimate Reality by the nature of *Atman*-awareness as immediate and direct experience resulted in providing for the establishment of the indubitable existence of *Atman*. But this kind of knowledge carries with it also certain disadvan-tages. Knowledge of objects is public in a way that direct experience is not. It is open to anyone to examine the evidence for the knowledge-claims about known objects. But one's immediate experience is available only to oneself. Thus, while for the one with the experience there is nothing surer than the experience itself, for one lacking the experience there is little or no evidence for the claimed reality.

In this respect the knowledge of *Atman* is similar to the knowledge of love. Only those experiencing love know what it is. Others might make various claims about love, but they are obviously referring to certain objective human relations, whereas the person who actually loves is having subjective experience. For the person having the experience nothing could be more sure than its existence, though a person lacking this experience might very well be skeptical of the existence of love. In a similar way, those without faith or experience might be skeptical of the existence of *Atman* and the possibility of *Atman*-realization. But those who have experienced the bliss of *Atman* know no other joy—they are completely fulfilled.

---

[15] *Brihadaranyaka Upanishad*, III.4.2.

CHAPTER 4

SOCIETY AND PHILOSOPHY

SELF-REALIZATION

B ECAUSE of the experiential nature of *Atman*-knowledge, three basic attitudes toward it were possible. The skeptics simply denied the existence of any such ultimate Subject on the grounds that they did not have any experience of it. Others were prepared to accept the existence and nature of *Atman* as a philosophical hypothesis to be established on the basis of reason. Still others, probably the great majority of people in India, were willing to accept the testimony of the sages and seers as adequate evidence for their belief in the existence and experiencability of *Atman*. For these people the major concern was to find a way to this wonderful realization.

This concern was not the privilege of a select few, but was shared by nearly all the members of society. A goodly number of the persons striving for *Atman*-realization could not, for a variety of reasons, share in the esoteric teachings and disciplines of the Upanishads, but had to rely on other means of instruction and achievement. Gradually a variety of fables, tales, poems, and codes were developed which gave the common people of India guides and ideals for the kind of life that would make possible the realization of *Atman*. This literature provides the chief vehicle for the transformation of the sacred teachings of the priests of the Vedas and the seers of the Upanishads into a way of life for the people. The early Vedic emphasis on the rituals of religion came to be combined with the philosophical monism of the Upanishads, with its

33

insistence of self-discipline and knowledge, in a way which tempered both the ritualism and the philosophical abstractness.

Rather than seeing the prayer, worship, and sacrifice of earlier traditions as incompatible with the Upanishadic emphasis on knowledge of *Atman* by enlargement of consciousness, this literature tended to synthesize these tendencies.

The most significant attempt at synthesis is the *Bhagavad Gita*, "The Song of the Supreme." In the *Gita*, which is a portion of the *Mahabharata*, the identification of the individual person with *Atman* and the identification of *Atman* with the ultimate reality of the universe are taken over from the Upanishads. But the *Atman* is here symbolized by God, and the divine teacher of the *Gita*, Krishna, describes himself as a finite form of the infinite, claiming to be both the god Vishnu of the earlier Vedas and the *Brahman* of the Upanishads. There is no contradiction here, for Vishnu is simply a form of *Brahman*, the ultimate Self, or *Atman*.

It is easy to see that the abstract philosophical discourses of the Upanishads would not find a ready acceptance by the majority of people accustomed to dealing with life in the concrete. But when the abstract *Brahman* is given concrete form in the person of Krishna, access becomes possible. Feeling in the depths of their being the surging of the infinite struggling to free itself from the bonds of the finite and concrete, the majority of India's people welcomed the symbol of the infinite made finite in Krishna. Here was a ray of light and hope, for if the infinite could reach down into the finite, then the finite could also reach up to the infinite. The gap between the finite and the infinite—between the empirical self and the *Atman*—could be bridged. This was the promise held out by the *Gita*, a promise giving hope and inspiration to hundreds of millions of people for thousands of years. The concrete forms of religious worship were a means to the realization of that ultimate Self taught in the Upanishads.

The *Gita* not only offered hope and inspiration but also provided a guide to life leading to the fulfillment of that hope and inspiration. The two important questions taken up by the *Gita* are (1) What is the relation between the ordinary empirical self and the ultimate Self (*Atman*)? (Or, looked at from the objective point of view, what is the relation between the ordinary empirical reality and the ultimate reality (*Brahman*)?) and (2) By what means can one come to realize or experience that ultimate Self, or Reality?

It is significant that these questions are considered in the context of a moral decision. As the *Gita* opens, Arjuna, representing Everyman, finds himself unable to determine the right thing to do, a situation known to every man. The specific question concerns the decision to fight or not to fight to regain the kingdom which rightfully belongs to him. The answer given by Krishna, disguised as Arjuna's charioteer, is given in general terms so that it can be adapted to any specific moral choice. The answer, occupying all but one of the eighteen chapters constituting this work, turns on the nature of man and the nature of the universe, and the resulting purpose, or end, of life.

The universe is regarded as ultimately unchanging and permanent, without multiplicity or plurality. Man's ultimate nature is also permanent, one and the same with the ultimate reality. The difficulty is that man is ignorant of his true nature, and mistakes himself for one complex changing individual among many, living in a world of many changing objects. Having identified himself with the impermanent and changing self, man seeks his satisfaction in the world of changing objects and desires, always without success, because the whole quest is fundamentally misguided.

But why does man make this mistake and engage in this misguided quest? The answer given is that it is due to the dual nature of man. On the one hand man is his empirical, or *guna*-, self. This self covers and obscures the spiritual and ultimately real self—the *purusha*, or *Atman*. The *guna*-self is the psycho-physical organism which the ignorant mistake for the real self. Thus Arjuna, who was suggesting that it would be wrong to engage in this war because of the destruction and killing that would occur, is instructed by Krishna, "The dweller (the *Atman*) in the body of everyone, OBharata (Arjuna) is eternal and can never be slain."[1] The point of this instruction is that Arjuna had failed to take into consideration that the true Self, the *Atman*, or *purusha*, was essentially independent of the psycho-physical organism; he had mistaken the psycho-physical self for the ultimate Self. Consequently, he was concerned to seek satisfaction for that lower self of the *gunas*. But this is basically wrong. Krishna says "He who thinks that this slays and he who thinks that this is slain; both of them fail to perceive the truth; this one neither slays nor is slain. . . . He [the Self] is said to be unmanifest, unthinkable, and unchanging."[2]

But if the individual person mistakes himself for the *guna*-self because the real Self is obscured, how can the veil of the empirical be rent so that

---

[1] *Bhagavad Gita*, II.30, trans. by Sarvepalli Radhakrishnan (New York: Harper Bros., 1948), and contained in Radhakrishnan and Moore, eds. *A Source Book in Indian Philosophy* (Princeton: Princeton University Press, 1957), pp. 101–163.
[2] *Gita*, II.19,25.

the real Self might be seen? This is a question about the way to the realization of the *Atman*. In the *Gita* the answer rests upon the teaching that ultimately Self (*puruhsa*) and not-Self (*prakriti*) are independent. The short answer to this question is that the empirical self must be disciplined and brought under control so that it is no longer capable of confusing a person. But even though the short answer be accurate, it is insufficient, for the starting point on the path to *Atman*-realization is always occupied by the ignorant self who necessarily looks upon the empirical as real. The real task is to present ways or paths to the ultimate knowledge which begin where the individual actually is, but progressively lead him to higher and higher understanding, until gradually he is freed entirely from ignorance.

Thus, in the *Gita*, Krishna does not tell Arjuna that since activity proceeds from the world of the *gunas*, the not-Self, it should be abandoned. In fact he teaches that action is necessary, "for no one can remain even for a moment without doing work; every one is made to act helplessly by the impulses born of nature."[3] The crucial discipline is to engage in activity without becoming attached to the activity or to the results of the activity.

The *guna*-self is a combination of three different tendencies which combine in varying proportions. These tendencies, or *gunas*, are: *sattva*, which inclines one to intellectual activity; *rajas*, which inclines one to vigorous action; and *tamas*, which inclines one to devotional activity. These three *gunas*, in their varying combinations, account for the different personality types found among persons. The crucial thing, however, is that the personality type belongs to the psychophysical self, the self of *prakriti*, and as such constitutes the binding fetters of the true Self. Even though different persons are bound by different tendencies and personality types, nevertheless, they are all bound. Now, if individual A is bound by the chains of *sattva*, it is useless to try to achieve freedom by concentrating on the bonds of *rajas*, or *tamas*. And, individual B must concentrate on freeing himself from the bonds of *rajas* if this *guna* predominates in him, etc. Accordingly, the way of discipline will vary with the type of person.

The recognition that different individuals are bound by different forces led to the distinction of three basically different paths, or ways, that would take one to the realization of *Atman*. These three paths, which correspond to the *gunas sattva*, *rajas*, and *tamas*, were the paths of discipline in knowledge, discipline in work, and discipline in devotion re-

[3] *Gita*, III.5.

spectively. What is common to the three paths is discipline, which is a matter of progressively freeing the real Self from the *guna*-self. These are the three famous disciplines, or *yogas*, taught in the *Gita*; the *yoga* of knowledge, the *yoga* of works, and the *yoga* of devotion. Because of the nature of the *guna*-self one cannot avoid engaging in activity. But it is possible to discipline oneself, no matter what kind of activity is involved, so that one can disassociate from the activity itself, which belongs to the *guna*-world. This is the essence of the non-attachment taught in the *Gita*.

According to the *Gita*, the two basic principles underlying the teaching of these three different paths of discipline are: (1) it is possible to realize one's essential independence of the *gunas*, and (2) in order to free oneself from the *guna*-self it is necessary to cooperate with and work through that *guna*-self, progressively transcending it.

This second principle, which is primarily an answer to the question of how an individual can realize *Atman* despite the *guna*-self, underlies a variety of practices and ideals characterizing the practical social life of the individual. Obviously, if the *guna*-self is capable of ensnaring the *Atman*, then the *guna*-self must be taken seriously if the attempt to realize *Atman* is taken seriously. And if this is the case, then the life of the empirical self in society must be taken seriously, for the kind of life the individual lives will determine the progress made in the quest for *Atman*, and it is obvious that human beings cannot live independently of society. Thus, the question arises, How can the life of the individual and the institutions of society be ordered so that progress can be made toward realizing one's true and ultimate Self? The question is based on a dual recognition—that there are differences between individual persons and between the various kinds of functions that society performs for the good of all persons. A partial answer to the question is contained in the system of *varna*, or social classification.

SOCIAL CLASSES

Essentially, *varna* is a theory of social organization whereby the individuals in society are divided into different classes with different functions in society according to differing personal characteristics and different social needs. The theory is that the good of society will be furthered if there are different classes of individuals who will perform the different tasks requisite for a good life in society. Furthermore, this classification will be to the advantage of the individual in that it will prove easier to fulfill oneself and reach the true Self if one is engaging in those activities for which one is peculiarly well suited by temperament, disposition, and natural ability.

It is important to distinguish *varna*, or social class, from *caste*, or social *castes*. *Varna* refers to a system of social classification of individuals according to their qualifications, tendencies, and dispositions. This scheme of classification yields the four classes, or *varnas*, of *brahmana* (the intellectuals), *kshatriya* (military and administrators), *vaishya* (producers), and *shudra* (workers). *Caste* on the other hand, refers properly to a system of classification according to birth. There are only four classes, or *varnas*, recognized, but there are approximately two thousand *castes* in India. The castes are distinguished from each other not by qualification of the individual, but by heredity, dietary regulations, endogamy and exogamy, occupation, and place in the pecking order. The native word for caste is *jati*, which means birth. The word "caste" is modern. It is taken from "*casta*," a word the Portuguese applied to the practice of classification according to birth that they found upon coming to India. Caste, or *jati*, has existed for a long time in India, and for the most part has been regarded as an evil, except by a few persons near the top of the pecking order. *Varna*, on the other hand, is a theory of social organization that is very high ideal and has been so regarded in India.

The *brahmana varna* consists of the priests and teachers, who are, generally, the maintainers of culture. Their chief tasks have been the preservation of knowledge and culture, the satisfaction of the gods, and the safeguarding of justice and morality.

The *kshatriya varna* consists of the protectors and administrators of society. They have been the guardians of the rest of society, providing for their security, and enforcing the various rules required for the necessary social functions. According to the *Gita*, "heroism, vigour, steadiness, resourcefulness, not fleeing even in battle, generosity and leadership—these are the duties of a *kshatriya*, born of his nature."[4]

The *vaishya varna* consists of the traders and producers in society. The *Gita* says that engagement in agriculture, raising cattle, and trading are the duties of a *vaishya*, born of his own nature (*guna*-self).[5] His chief function is obviously to produce the various economic goods of life required in the society.

The *shudra varna* consists of the workers and servants in society. The *Gita* succinctly gives the duties of this class by saying, "the *dharma* [duty] of a *shudra*, born of his own nature, is action consisting of service."[6]

---

[4] *Gita*, XVIII,43.   [5] *Gita*, XVIII,44.   [6] *Ibid*.

According to the principle of *varna*, certain rights and duties accrue to an individual in virtue of belonging to a certain class in society. The duties and rights being determined for the four classes, the individual is in a position to be clear about his particular rights and duties in society when he determines which class he belongs to in virtue of his qualifications. The rights and duties of the four *varnas* do not exhaust the *dharma* of man, however, as there are certain privileges and responsibilities that belong to a person inasmuch as he is a human being and a member of society irrespective of class. Thus Bhisma, in the *Mahabharata*, says that all persons have the duties of controlling their anger, telling the truth, forgiving others, begetting offspring of their legitimate wife, pure conduct, avoidance of quarrels, the maintenance of dependents, and acting justly.[7] Non-hurting (*ahimsa*) and self-restraint are usually added to this list.

The duties of man as man and the duties of man as member of a particular class in society are grounded in the very order of the universe. The universe is regarded as essentially moral. Everything happens according to a rule, for the benefit of the whole. Each class of beings in the universe, by functioning as designed, contributes to the order and well-being of the whole. Man in society is no exception to this rule and therefore, in virtue of being human and occupying a particular place in the scheme of the universe, he has certain activities to engage in to maintain the well-being of the universe in general, and the well-being of society in particular. Sin and evil result when a person refuses to do those things over which he has choice and which are necessary for the well-being of the whole. The duties common to the several *varnas* are the actions one should perform or the rules of actions one should follow in order to avoid sin. The duties of the particular *varnas* issue from the rules to be followed if the social order is to be maintained, without which order man cannot make his contribution to the total order of creation, and without which man cannot realize his own nature. The content of the various duties is derived from the nature of the *gunas*. *Krishna* in the *Gita*, says, "The duties of *brahmanas*, *kshatriyas*, *vaishyas* and *shudras* have been assigned according to the *gunas* born of nature."[8]

LIFE-STAGES

Granted that the individual is to perform his duties according to his social class for the good of society, it is still possible to ask how the

[7] *Mahabharata, Shantiparva*, 60,7. (Poona: Bhandarkar Oriental Research Institute, 1927–54).
[8] *Gita*, IV,13.

individual should order his own life so that he can make the requisite contribution to the social order and also make the greatest possible progress in achieving self-fulfillment and self-realization. And in answer to this question the institution of *ashrama* was advocated. The institution of *ashrama* consists in a series of stages in life, classified according to the activities proper to each stage. The first stage is the student stage, the *brahmacarya ashrama*. The second is that of the householder in society, the *grihastha ashrama*. The third is a stage of retirement from the social world, the *vanaprastha ashrama*. After passing through these first three stages in life's journey a person enters into a life of contemplation and meditation in order that he might completely establish himself in perfection. This last stage is called *samnyasa ashrama*.

According to Manu, the stages in life are to be taken up successively, beginning with the student stage. He says, "Having studied the Vedas in accordance with the rule, having begot sons according to the sacred law, and having offered sacrifices according to his ability, he may direct his mind to final liberation. A twice-born* man who seeks final liberation without having studied the Vedas, without having begotten sons, and without having offered sacrifices sinks downward."[9]

The various duties laid down for the different *ashrama* follow from the debts contracted by birth into the world. Life in this world is regarded as an opportunity provided as a gift to man. It is an opportunity for the Self to free itself forever from the round of births and deaths. But the individual does nothing to warrant this opportunity. The gods present the gift of life in this world and therefore man has a debt to the gods. He also has a debt to his parents and ancestors, for without them life would not have been possible either. With his second birth, the birth into the world of culture and spirit, man incurs a debt to the seers and teachers who promulgate, preserve, and teach that which is worth knowing. These three debts could be satisfied by studying (debt to the seers and teachers), having children (debt to the parents and ancestors), and by offering sacrifice (debt to the gods). The three different kinds of life required to repay the debts correspond to the student, householder, and retirement stages respectively. Only upon satisfying these obliga-

---

* "Twice-born" refers to birth into the world of Spirit in addition to the world of nature. In ancient India there were elaborate rituals marking the initiation of young people into the cultural and spiritual life of the twice-born. Initiation into the ranks of the twice-born was considered a great privilege and was, at least in theory, reserved for those judged qualified.

[9] *The Laws of Manu*, 6.34–37, trans. by G. Bühler, *The Sacred Books of the East*. XXV (Oxford: Clarendon Press, 1886).

tions to society and the gods was a person free to devote himself ex-clusively to meditation and concentration in his effort to experience the ultimate reality.

This emphasis upon satisfying one's debts through various kinds of social action reveals the importance attached to life in society and social organization in India. In fact, the very principles of life-stages and social classes are justified in terms of the importance of satisfying the empirical, or the *guna*-nature of man. This is clearly brought out in the concept of *purushartha*, which provides for the philosophical justification of the various forms of social organization advocated.

BASIC HUMAN AIMS

The word *"purushartha"* literally means "aim of a person." The four *purusharthas*, or human aims, recognized as basic in India are those of (1) *dharma*, or morality, (2) *artha*, or means of life, (3) *kama*, or enjoyment of the means of life, and (4) *moksha*, or realization of the ultimate Self (*atman*). These human aims are discussed by Manu and Kautilya, and are included in the *Mahabharata*. Furthermore they are presupposed by nearly all the literature which discusses life in society. They also underlie the social principles of life-stages and classes advocated in the *Gita*, for these forms of social organization are simply means to the achieve-ment of these four human aims.

These four human aims are the aims, or goals, in life that every in-dividual has or should have. The good life is defined in terms of these aims. Granted that man is a combination of the empirical and the spiritual, it is necessary to satisfy both the empirical and the spiritual needs in order to achieve the good life. In order to achieve the spiritual goal of *moksha*, it is necessary first to satisfy the empirical needs of the individual by providing the required means of life (*artha*) and by pro-viding for the enjoyment (*kama*) of these means. For the regulation of the attainment and enjoyment of the means of life moral rules (*dharma*) are necessary.

Although the word *"dharma"* is used in a bewildering variety of ways there is a common notion of a *rule of action* running through the different senses of the term. The word is derived from the root *"dhri,"* which means "to support," or "to maintain," and the justification of a rule is that it maintains or supports. Consequently *dharma* came to mean that which one should do, for a rule of action is, essentially, a guide to action. The importance of *dharma* lies in the necessity of follow-ing rules of action in human conduct.

With respect to the individual, one's *dharma* may be one's moral duty. But with respect to society, *dharma* provides rules for settling disputes and possible conflicts between individuals, for only when conflicts of interest between individuals and groups are kept to a minimum can society be well maintained. Thus, *dharma* has a social sense and significance, for it represents possible rules for action in society which will enable the individual to fulfill himself and at the same time make a contribution to the self-fulfillment of others.

As man does not live by righteousness and justice alone, but requires also bread and bed, it is only natural that in addition to the human aim of *dharma* there should be the aims of means of life (*artha*) and enjoyment (*kama*).

Kautilya composed a treatise on *artha* as a guide to the acquisition of the means of life in the world. In it he explains the concept of *artha* as follows: "The sustenance of mankind is termed *artha*, the earth which contains mankind is termed *artha*; . . ."[10] The word "*artha*" is derived from the root "*ri*" which means literally, "that which one goes for." From this basic meaning which is, roughly, "aim" or "purpose," derives the meaning of "thing," "matter," or "affair," from which stem the meanings of "advantage," "wealth," "profit," and "prosperity."

The following statements from the *Mahabharata* and the *Panchatantra* will reveal the attitude taken toward *artha*. In the *Mahabharata* it is said, "What is here regarded as *dharma* depends entirely upon wealth [*artha*]. One who robs another of wealth robs him of his *dharma* as well. Poverty is a state of sinfulness. All kinds of meritorious acts flow from the possession of great wealth, as from wealth spring all religious acts, all pleasures, and heaven itself. Wealth brings about accession of wealth, as elephants capture elephants. Religious acts, pleasure, joy, courage, worth, and learning; all these proceed from wealth. From wealth one's merit increases. He that has no wealth has neither this world nor the next."[11]

The traditions of the common people as reflected in the collection of tales of wisdom known as the *Panchatantra* contain the following observations: "The smell of wealth [*artha*] is quite enough to wake a creature's sterner stuff. And wealth's enjoyment even more. Wealth gives constant vigour, confidence, and power. Poverty is a curse worse than death.

[10] *Kautilya Arthashastra*, 4.1, trans. by R. Shamasastry (Mysore: Sri Raguveer Press, fifth ed. 1956).
[11] *Mahabharata*, 12.8.11.

Virtue without wealth is of no consequence. The lack of money is the root of all evil."[12]

Artha, as one of the four basic aims in life, refers to whatever means are necessary for man's life. The emphasis is upon the means to biological and social life, but the means to spiritual life are not excluded, as it is recognized that biological and social life are conditions for spiritual life. The securing of material plenty is advocated as a goal in life subject only to the important restriction that no *artha* be pursued in violation of *dharma*.

Since accumulations of wealth or property are not valuable primarily for their own sake, however, but mainly for the satisfaction, pleasure, and enjoyment they make possible, the human aim of enjoyment, or *kama*, was included as one of the basic goals in life. The classic definition of *kama* is found in Vatsyayana's *Sutra*:

> Kāma is the enjoyment of the appropriate objects of the five senses of hearing, feeling, seeing, tasting, and smelling, assisted by the mind, together with the soul. The ingredient in this is a peculiar contact between the organ of sense and its object, and the consciousness of pleasure that results from the contact is called Kāma.[13]

Discussing the relations between *dharma, artha,* and *kama,* Manu says, "Some declare that the good of man consists in *dharma* and *artha*; others opine that it is to be found in *artha* and *kama*; some say that *dharma* alone will give it; the rest assert that *artha* alone is the chief good of man here below. But the correct position is that the good of man consists in the harmonious co-ordination of the three."[14]

The basic reason for regarding enjoyment as one of the basic aims in life is that the end of all activity is some presupposed good. It is the natural inclination of all things to strive after the satisfaction of the common desires for food, drink, and sex, and therefore these desires are not to be denied and frustrated, but are to be regulated and indulged. Consequently, the enjoyments of the satisfaction of regulated desires is reason for engaging in activity and is one of the basic aims in life.

The fourth basic human aim is *moksha*. The word derives from the root "*muc,*" meaning "to release," "to free." In accord with the literal meaning of the word, *moksha* means emancipation, complete freedom. This aim reflects the emphasis put on the spiritual nature of man in

---

[12] *The Panchatantra*, trans. by A. W. Ryder (Chicago: University of Chicago Press, 1925), p. 210.
[13] *The Kama Sutra of Vatsyayana*, trans. by R. Burton and F. A. Arbuthnot (London: Panther Books, 1963).
[14] *Manu*, 2.224.

India. In accord with the teachings of the Upanishads, *Atman* is regarded as the power behind the powers of the universe. It is the ultimate power in the universe and the ultimate power in man, these being one and the same. In agreement with this conception of man, the ultimate perfection of man is seen to lie in his self-realization, in identifying himself with the ultimate source and power of his being. This realization will set man free, for this power, constituting the innermost and essential portion of his being, cannot be bound or limited by any other power. It is the ultimate power. There is, therefore, no power, not even the power of death, that can limit man because he is, in his deepest being and genuine Self, the highest power. So long as a person identifies himself with the lower powers he is bound by the higher powers and the lower powers as well. Consequently, the goal is to realize that one is not merely body, not merely biological life, not merely social organism, etc. This realization, in the sense of completely identifying oneself with the ultimate power, is the realization of *Atman*, or the true Self, and results in complete freedom, or *moksha*.

Thus, the basic presupposition of *moksha* is that man has within himself the seeds of his own perfection. But potential perfection implies actual imperfection. The problem is therefore one of moving from imperfect existence to perfect existence. Because of the integral view of man taken in India, to regard man as more than a social animal was not to deny that man is biological and social. Rather it was to assert that though man is social and biological he is something more. Consequently, it was held that the fulfillment of the biological and social were necessary, though not sufficient, conditions for the fulfillment of the something higher that man also is.

JUSTIFICATION OF SOCIAL ORGANIZATION

It is clear that the basic aims of man recognized in these theories require a fairly high degree of social organization, for the aims of *dharma*, *artha*, *kama*, and *moksha* cannot be realized in isolation. And since society can be successfully organized only when all of the different functions requisite for its maintenance are fulfilled, and this can happen only when personnel are provided for the different basic functions, it is easy to see that social classification is justified by the basic aims of life.

The principle of *ashrama* also finds its justification in the concept of the *purusharthas*. An *ashrama* is really a stage in life's journey, the goal of the journey being complete freedom, or *moksha*. It is the aim of *moksha* that provides the overall direction for the journey through life, the various stages being the means devised for the realization of this goal. But it is recognized that the traveller along life's highway is so constituted that in order to attain his goal of *moksha* he must first attain the goals of *dharma*, *artha*, and *kama*. That is, he must live a social life. Accordingly, the journey is divided into stages such that each of the basic aims can be satisfied or attained most efficiently, in a way most satisfactory to the individual.

The first life-stage, the student stage, enables the individual to learn about life in all of its various aspects. There he learns about his social and spiritual life, becoming familiar with the ideals according to which he is to live his life. It is here that one learns about social classes, life-stages, human aims, etc., and is introduced to the art of self-discipline. Having learned about the theory of life, the individual passes on to the next stage in life, where he continues to practice what he has learned in the first stage.

In the householder stage the individual looks after the society that looked after him in the first stage in his life and that will look after him in the last stages of his life. Now he must maintain and support society, maintaining the mores, the economic means, cultural values, living a righteous life of enjoyment amidst wealth, begetting and supporting children, and taking care of the old and the needy.

Having fulfilled his obligations to society, and having satisfied his biological and social needs, he now turns to a period of training in spiritual life. His training in righteousness and spirituality completed, his only concern will be with the attainment of *moksha*.

Thus the division of life into stages provides for the attainment of the basic aims of man. This is its justification. The institution of life-stages, in short, is designed to advise the individual of his various goals and to assist in the attainment of these goals by ordering his life in the best possible way. The *ashramas* are the stages in life in which one progressively realizes his true nature.

Having looked at the content of the concepts of social classes, life-stages, and human aims, it will now be helpful to look at the reasons underlying these three theories.

Turning first to the theory of the basic human aims, it can be seen that the function of the *purushartha* theory is to provide direction for human activity. The *purushartha* theory may be regarded as an answer to the question, What should man seek in life? or, alternately, How should man live? The answer embodied in the theory is that man should seek to be moral, to accumulate means of life, to enjoy himself, and eventually, to free himself from whatever binds. Looked at in this way, the concepts of *dharma*, *artha*, *kama*, and *moksha* are seen to be concepts embodying rules. They are normative concepts, providing directions for life's activities.

Now, if the concepts in question are considered to be essentially normative, that is, for the purpose of guiding human behavior, then each concept can be regarded as the embodiment of a rule or rules. And since the function of a normative rule is to guide behavior, it is reasonable to assume that the theory of human aims functions as an answer to the question, How should man live? Next follows the question, How should one act? which occurs in regard to a variety of circumstances and a variety of possible courses of action, so it is reasonable that there should be a number of rules. The theory of human aims represents an attempt to divide the basic rules concerning possible courses of action into four categories. Thus, the rules concerning how one should act with respect to other persons are included under the heading of *dharma*. The rules concerning how one should act with respect to wealth and material goods are included under the heading of *artha*. The rules concerning how one should act with respect to possible pleasures and enjoyments of the world are included under the heading of *kama*. Finally, the rules concerning how one should act with respect to realization of his inner nature are grouped under the heading of *moksha*.

Looked at in this way, the human aims are essentially answers to the question of how the good life is to be lived. Granted that it is the purpose of social organization to provide for the good life, the importance of considering the *purusharthas* for understanding the theory of social organization is obvious. For without understanding what the good life consists in, it would be most difficult to appreciate the means of social organization required to implement the good life in society.

Turning now to the theory of the life-stages, it can be seen that this also is intended as an answer to a question. The question in this case is, How should the individual so organize his life to most satisfactorily realize the good life? Thus, the *ashrama* theory, which holds that the life of an individual in society should be divided into four segments, or stages, is also normative for it provides direction for human activity.

The *ashrama* theory assumes the answer that the *purushartha* theory provides to the question, In what does the good life consist? It also develops an answer to the question, How can an individual in society best realize the good life? The answer proposed by the *ashrama* theory is that man should apportion his life so that part is spent studying and learning about the nature of self, society, and the good life, and in training for useful social activity; a part is devoted to the well-being of society by performing social service, to the begetting and rearing of children, and to sustaining the various social institutions, etc.; a portion of it is spent in establishing oneself in self-control and in meditation; and a portion is spent in concerted effort to shake off any binding fetters. Each stage has its own rules for the activities one must follow in order to realize the good life.

The theory of classes is similar to the theory of life-stages in that both presuppose the answer provided by the theory of *purusharthas* to the question, In what does the good life consist? Both theories provide direction for securing the basic goals in life, the attainment of which constitutes the good life. The two theories differ basically in that whereas the *ashrama* theory answers the question of how the individual life should be organized in order that the good life be realized, the *varna* theory answers the question, How should society be organized so as to provide for the realization of the basic goals of life for each member of society? The answer the *varna* theory provides to this question is that men should so organize society that its members are classified in such a way that the functions requisite for the proper functioning of society will be performed by those individuals best suited for the tasks they have to perform. The *varna* theory advocates distributing the labor required for a properly functioning society so that whatever is required will be performed, while at the same time each person will be doing only the work for which he is best suited. In this way social activity will be directly conducive to achieving *moksha*, the ultimate goal in life which lies beyond merely social activity. The rules for each class provide direction for the activities of the members of each class so that society will prosper and the individual will have the utmost opportunity to realize the good life.

The *varna* theory, then, proposes social classification according to a division of labor, the labor being distributed according to the special qualifications of the individual to perform the labor in question. It answers the individual's question, "What should I do to realize the good life?" by directing him to those social tasks for which he is best suited and which will, in the long run, be most conducive to the realization of his innermost nature.

The principles of Indian social philosophy can be further illuminated by considering certain objections that might be raised. One objection is that people are not, in fact, neatly divided or divisible into four distinct types, as assumed by the theory of *varna*. If people do not differ from each other in such ways that they can be classified into four distinct social groups with each group or class having different functions in society, then the *varna* theory, if put into practice, will result in certain individuals being arbitrarily saddled with jobs for which they are ill-suited, and which they would rather not do. Then social classification according to *varna*, instead of providing for the well-being of society and for individual self-fulfillment, would lead to the breakdown of society and would result in forcing individuals into doing those things for which they are ill-suited and which they are not disposed to do.

This objection possesses a certain validity which cannot be easily disposed of; for if a theory of social organization leads to the suppression of the individual and thereby contributes to the malfunctioning of society, it is an unsatisfactory theory. And if distribution of social tasks is made on the basis of supposed individual differences which do not, in fact, exist, it is possible that the individual will be forced to do precisely that for which he is least qualified, and the society as well as the individual might be the worse off for this.

Despite this core of truth in the objection, one can counter by considering that no society can function well without a division of labor within the society, for there are so many different functions that must be performed in order that society be adequately maintained. Surely there must be administrators, a military force and police, producers, and laborers within any society. The *varna* theory is based on a recognition of this basic fact. It is more than a mere recognition of this fact; it is an attempt to divide the labor required to maintain society in such a way that each person will do the type of work for which he is best suited. The assumption is that there are four fundamentally different types of activities required for the maintenance of society. Unless these activities are performed society either suffers or, in the extreme, becomes impossible. Therefore, since according to traditional Indian thought the good life is not possible without society, society must be maintained. Consequently the different requisite tasks must be performed, the different tasks being given to the individuals *best* (even though not perfectly) suited for the tasks assigned them.

Since, theoretically, classification into *varnas* is done on the basis of the qualifications of the individual being classified, it is difficult to see what more could be desired. It is doubtful that any society could function well if unqualified persons were performing vital functions, and the *varna* scheme is an attempt to ensure that only qualified persons would perform the various functions required in a good society. There may be questions about actual methods of classification, but these are questions about the implementation of the theory, which amount to questions about the practice of the theory, and not about the theory as such.

A second objection is that it is not practical to divide one's life into four separate stages, or segments. The weight of this objection lies in the implicit view that life is an integral affair, and, therefore, to attempt to live it in separate stages is to try to make of life something it is not. This would be a serious objection if the theory of *ashrama* did, in fact, require that life be divided into separate compartments or stages. To so construe the theory of *ashrama* is, however, to misconstrue it. As remarked earlier, the theory of *ashrama* constitutes an answer to the question, How can an individual best organize his life in order to realize the good life? Granted that according to the dominant thought of this period the good life was held to consist in the attainment of the four goals of *dharma, artha, kama,* and *moksha,* it was not held that these ought to be attained at separate stages of life.

All of the activities of one's life ought to be aimed at realizing the four basic aims. But as there is an order among these aims, so that before the final stage of *moksha* can be achieved the other three must be realized—and the aims of *artha* and *kama* are to be attained according to *dharma*—it follows that in order to attain all of the aims, special attention must be paid to each of them. Accordingly, it is held that the first task of an individual is to establish himself in *dharma*. Then he might attend to the aims of *artha* and *kama*. But, of course, one cannot live without *artha* and *kama,* and therefore it is not possible to ignore these aims at any stage in life. It is not the case that in each *ashrama* one pursues a different aim. According to the theory one pursues all the aims in each stage, though not necessarily with the same enthusiasm for each. The theory involves not a division of life, but an ordering of the activities of life. Thus, to argue that the *ashrama* theory requires that in one stage one realizes *dharma,* at the next *artha,* at the next *kama,* and then *moksha,* is to misconstrue the theory, for all the theory holds is that in order to attain all four of these aims it is necessary to concentrate on achieving each of them.

The objection that various of the *purusharthas* might come into conflict with each other overlooks both the nature of the *purusharthas* and the function of *dharma*. The theory of the *purusarthas* is that the good life consists in the attainment of these four aims. If, therefore, these goals should so conflict that the attainment of any one would become impossible, then it could not be the case that the good life consisted in the attainment of all four. So long as it is agreed that the good life consists in the attainment of these four goals, it cannot be argued that these four can conflict with each other. Furthermore, the function of *dharma* provides for the resolution of any conflicts of action. That is, the rules that make up the concept of *dharma* are rules for settling possible conflicts between courses of action that would interfere with living the good life. So long as *dharma* is included among them, conflict among the goals is impossible.

A fourth objection is that *varna* implies social immobility, restricting the freedom of the individual. In replying to this objection it is useful to distinguish between practice and theory. It may be that in trying to classify society according to *varna* there might occur a certain social immobility. It has often been said that this is what actually happened in India. But the question of whether or not the social classes of India did or did not become closed and whether they resulted in general social immobility is philosophically uninteresting. The interesting philosophical question is whether or not the theory of *varna* entails or implies closed classes and social immobility. The historical phenomena of India may be due to a lack of application of *varna* theory rather than to an application of it. And if the conclusion of the discussion of *varna* in this chapter be accepted, then clearly the theory of *varna* does not imply or entail closed classes or social immobility, for the principle of *varna* classification is the qualification of the individual. The individual belongs to the class for which he is best qualified and not to the class of his parents. Thus, according to the theory, an individual is free to move from one class to another if he has the requisite qualifications. There is nothing in the theory to prevent a scavenger's son from being a priest or teacher, and nothing to prevent the daughter of a priest from being a scavenger. In fact, the theory requires that if one is qualified for a certain *varna*, then that is the *varna* to which that person belongs, regardless of birth.

The objection that implementation of the *ashrama* scheme interferes with the freedom of the individual to live his life as he chooses also misses the mark. The *ashrama* scheme is essentially an arrangement to enable the individual to achieve the four goals that constitute the good life, and the individual is free to live his life as he chooses, in order to live the good life. The *ashrama* theory does not require that an individual spend a specific number of years in a given stage and then move on to the next stage, spend a specific number of years there and then move on, etc. The *ashrama* theory provides for an arrangement of life whereby the individual can, progressively, realize his potentialities; an arrangement providing for freedom rather than restricting it. One could argue that all this misses the point; if an individual is required to spend a part of his life studying and does not wish or choose to do this, then he is not free. One *could* argue that way, but then one could also argue that according to the *ashrama* theory one is being forced to live the good life, and is not free to live the bad life.

In conclusion, it might be remarked that the discussions making up this chapter reveal that traditional Indian social philosophy, as it involves the concepts of *purusharthas, varnas,* and *ashramas,* contains not only lofty, but theoretically plausible, ideals of social organization which may well serve to inspire social planners.

CHAPTER 5

SELF AND THE WORLD: SAMKHYA—YOGA

T HE ethical, social, political, and religious philosophies of the epics, *Dharma shastras*, and the *Gita* presuppose certain relationships between the empirical self that is the social organism and the ultimate Self that is pure subject. This presupposition is obvious from the emphasis placed on the various prescriptions for life in society in order to realize *Atman*. Unless there were a connection between the empirical self and the *Atman*, the activities of the empirical self would be irrelevant to *Atman*-realization. The Upanishads appear to be so full of excitement over the discovery of the *Atman* that they are not, for the most part, concerned to analyze the nature of the non-*Atman* nor to analyze the relations between what is *Atman* and what is not *Atman*. It is not surprising then, that at a later time philosophical and critical minds should inquire into these matters and attempt to show what, if any, relations existed between Self and not-Self, between the ultimate and the empirical. The underlying question is, How can one be the self of flesh and bones and desires and habits and also be the *Atman*, unchanging and identical with the ultimate reality of the universe?

SUBJECT AND OBJECT

The oldest philosophical school to take up this question of the relation between the Self and the not-Self was the school of Samkhya. The teachings of this school suggest that it grew directly out of those portions of the Upanishads emphasizing the reality of the non-*Atman*, or the non-*Brahman*. In the Upanishads, *Brahman* is said to have created the universe and then entered into it.[1] The world of objects cannot be unreal, for it consists of *Atman*, which is object as well as subject. In the *Brihadaranyaka Upanishad* it is said that *Atman* entered into the universe "up to the fingertips, as a knife is hidden in its sheath, or the all-sustaining fire in the fire-preserving wood."[2] Such passages indicate two basic realities; that of *Brahman* and that of the objective world of empirical selves and things.

There is no doubt that for the most part the tendency in the Upanishads is to regard *Brahman* as "more real" than the empirical or objective world. Nevertheless, as seen earlier, knowledge of *Brahman* is not an ordinary kind of knowledge, and exclusive of *Brahman* knowledge, one has no choice but to take seriously the reality of the empirical self and the objective world, for there is no other reality in evidence. Furthermore, the empirical and the objective must always be the starting point for any investigation of reality, which means that at this level at least, the reality of the empirical must be acknowledged.

It appears that Samkhya, disposed to accept the reality of the empirical, perhaps partially on the basis of certain realistic remarks in the Upanishads, felt keenly the need to analyze carefully the relationship between the empirical and the ultimate realities.

The felt need to establish the relationship between the empirical and the ultimate arose from two considerations. On the one hand, the Upanishads had taught that realization of *Atman* would bring an end to suffering. Therefore, to find ways to realize this *Atman* and put an end to pain and suffering, it was necessary to discover the relationship between the empirical and the *Atman*, and to determine the sorts of things that would lead to the experience of *Atman*. Ishvara Krishna begins his discourse on Samkhya with the statement: "From torment by three-fold misery arises the inquiry into the means of terminating it. . . ."[3]

The other consideration is a matter of the basic human urge to know and render intelligible all human experiences by the exhibition of certain relationships inhering in them.

[1] *Taittiriya*, II.6; *Chandogya*, VI.3.2.
[2] *Brihadaranyaka*, I.4.7.
[3] *Samkhya-Karika*, I, ed. and trans. by S. S. Suryanaranyana Sastri (Madras: University of Madras, 1935), and reprinted in *A Source Book in Indian Philosophy* (Princeton: Princeton University Press, 1957), p. 425 ff.

Focusing attention on ordinary human knowledge and the ordinary world known by such knowledge, the Samkhya philosophers argue that the entire world that can be experienced is fundamentally of the same nature. That is to say, desires, feelings, intelligence, etc., are not basically different from colors, sounds, odors, etc., all of which are fundamentally like sticks and stones. But all of this—the world that can, in principle, be experienced—is of the nature of object (or potential object), or not-self, as opposed to the Self that is always experiencer, that is ultimately and finally Subject. It would seem that the ultimate Subject is of a different nature and order than the world, since what is ultimate Subject can never become object, and what is object cannot be ultimate Subject. The difference between Self and the world is fundamentally the difference between subject and object.

The starting point for any analysis of the world and the self must be the experience of the self and the world one has available for analysis. This experience reveals the existence of a knowing self in a changing world. Nothing is more obvious than that we and the world around us are changing. It is with this obvious fact that the Samkhya philosophers begin, and from which they derive the conclusion that all experience and all that is experienced is fundamentally of the same nature, though basically different from the ultimate experiencing subject.

CAUSALITY

The orderliness and regularity of the experienced world cannot be dismissed as the result of chance. Changes are caused. Whatever is or will be, is or will be due to various causes. The first important consequence of this is that human knowledge that comes to be must be caused. It is the effect of some prior cause. But since causality is unintelligible unless the dominant features of the effect be derived from the cause, it follows that the effect must be essentially like the cause. Therefore, our knowledge must be essentially like the world that is known. Since knowledge is the result of ordering experiences, the nature of experience must be basically the same as the world. Hence the claim that experience and the experiencable are fundamentally the same.

The analysis of causality provides the main reasons for the claims made about the world and the self by Samkhya. The theory of causality adopted is called *satkaryavada*, which means that the effect preexists in the cause. Now if it is admitted that nothing can occur without a cause and also that every effect has prior existence in the cause, it follows that in an important sense the effect does not provide any new reality, for it is simply a matter of making explicit what already existed implicitly.

The Samkhya theory of the nature of causation is summed up by Ishvara Krishna when he says: "The effect is existent (pre-existent): (1) because what is non-existent cannot be produced; (2) because there is a definite relation of the cause with the effect; (3) because all is not possible; (4) because the efficient can do only that for which it is efficient; (5) because the effect is of the same essence as the cause."[4]

The reason for claiming that effects exist is that the reality of the effect can be denied only upon denial of the cause, as a cause is a cause only to the extent it produces its effects. Therefore if there are no real effects then there are no real causes. Furthermore, the effect is as real as the cause, for the effect is simply a transformation of the cause. If one were to deny the existence of both cause and effect one would be forced to deny the whole starting point of one's analysis, which would make all the conclusions contradictory. Consequently, the existence of effects cannot be denied.

The claim that the effect is of the same essence as the cause is crucially important to Samkhya, for it is the main support of the claim that all objective reality is ultimately of the same nature, the connection being that all of objective reality is simply the result of various transformations of some one ultimate stuff.

To see the force of the Samkhya argument here it is helpful to consider some of the objections that might be raised against this theory of causation. It might be objected that the effect is a new whole different from the constituent parts, and not simply a transformation of them. Evidence is provided for this objection by the fact that no effect can be known before it is produced. But if it were essentially the same as its cause it could be known by knowing the cause prior to the production of the effect. According to Samkhya this objection is not valid, for it makes no sense to say that a whole is different from its material cause. Take the case of a table. The pieces of wood, which are the material cause of the table when arranged in a certain way, are not different from the table. If it were different, one could perceive the table independently of its parts. But this is clearly impossible. And to argue that the effect and the cause are independent and separate because they

4 *Samkhya-Karika*, IX.

are perceived as separate and independent is to beg the question. The Samkhya claim is that perceiving an effect is simply perceiving the cause in transformation. To go on from this to say, "and therefore seeing the effect is seeing a new entity," is not to present an objection at all, but to beg the question.

Another objection that might be raised is that if Samkhya is right in maintaining that causality is simply a matter of transformation and not the production of something new, then the activity of the agent, or efficient cause, would be unnecessary, for the effect was already in existence. But if the effect preexisted, then no efficient cause is required to bring the effect into existence. This objection is addressed by considering the assumption that the effect does not preexist in the cause. If the effect did not preexist in the cause, then causality would be the bringing into existence of something out of nothing. (Hence the claim, "What is non-existent cannot be produced.") If we look at some non-existent things, such as square circles, it will be discovered that no amount of exertion can bring them into existence. To claim that what is can be caused by what is not is not to provide an alternative view of causation but to deny causality completely. Furthermore, if you do not admit that the effect preexists, then you have to say that it does not exist until it is caused. This is tantamount to saying that the non-existent effect belongs to the cause. But since the effect does not exist there is really nothing to belong to the cause, for a relation of belonging is possible only between existing things. Thus, if the effect can be said to belong to the cause it must be admitted that it preexists in the cause. But then what of the objection that in this case no cause is needed? The answer is that the agent or efficient cause simply manifests or makes explicit what was implicit and unmanifest, and does not create something new.

Another reply to the objection that cause and effect are distinct entities is that the preexistence of the effect can be seen from the fact that nothing can be gotten out of a cause which was not in the cause. For example, curd is gotten from milk because it preexisted in the milk. It cannot be gotten from water or oil because it did not preexist in them. If it were not the case that the effect preexisted in the cause it would be possible for any effect to proceed from any cause. But this is obviously not the case; for example, you cannot produce iron from water.

Now if it is the case that only certain causes can produce certain effects, then obviously some causes are potent with respect to some effects, but not with respect to others. But this shows that the effect preexists in the cause; otherwise it would make no sense to say that a cause is potent with respect to a given effect. The reason is that the potent cause of an effect has some power related to the effect, and without the preexistence of the effect there is nothing for the power to be related to, and then it makes no sense to talk about potent causes or potentiality.

Another objection that might be raised is that to talk about manifestation and transformation is to smuggle the notion of causality, in the sense of production of new events and objects, back into the picture in disguised form. This is answered by showing that the nature of transformation has nothing to do with the cessation of preexisting attributes nor with the coming-to-be of a pre-non-existent attribute. Rather, transformation means the manifestation of an attribute or characteristic implicitly present in the substance, and alternatively, the relapse of the manifested attribute into the unmanifest condition.

To clinch the case, the Samkhya philosopher argues that the very concept of causal possibility requires the preexistence of the effect in the cause. Non-being, the non-existent, requires no cause. So if the effect were non-existent at any time there would be no question of locating its cause. But it does make sense to talk about the possibility of effects which do not yet exist and to try to determine what will cause these effects to come into existence. This, however, makes sense only upon the assumption that the effect preexists in some sense, for that which is absolutely non-existent has no possibility of coming into existence.

The foregoing are all arguments essentially designed to support the claim that causes and effects are essentially the same. Cause is here being considered in the sense of material cause—the stuff out of which something comes to be. No effect can exist in a place different from its material cause. Hence cause and effect are numerically the same. An example given of the essential sameness of cause and effect is the tortoise going in and out of his shell. The spread-out tortoise is the effect, the contracted tortoise, the cause (and vice versa). But this does not involve the production of something new. Another example is a piece of gold which can be pressed into many shapes and pieces. But changing its shape does not make the effect something totally new. The flower made of gold is basically gold, as is the tree that is made of gold; the difference involves only name and form, and not the stuff out of which they are made.

EVOLUTION OF THE WORLD

Having established that the causality that must be assumed to exist in order to make sense out of human experience is of the nature of *satkaryavada* (meaning that the effect necessarily preexists in the cause), the Samkhya philosophers proceed to argue that this implies some one ultimate principle, which as the result of its transformations is experienced in its effects as the objective world. This claim follows once one admits that the present world exists as the result of previous changes and that change is not the production of something radically new. If this is admitted, then in order to avoid ultimate infinite regress it must be admitted that there is some one ultimate material cause, which in its various transformations or manifestations constitutes the world of experience. From this it follows that the entire world of experience is of the same fundamental nature as this ultimate material cause, for everything is basically only a transformation of this first cause. In this way Samkhya comes to the conclusion that the entire experiencable world is of the nature of *prakriti*, which is the name given to the ultimate causal principle.

This conclusion brings to the fore another question, however. How does the pluralistic world of experience derive, through a series of transformations, from this basic reality called *prakriti*? Obviously, if there are no effects except those that preexisted in the cause, then all of the effects that constitute the experienced world must have preexisted in *prakriti*. Consequently, *prakriti* itself must be composed of different tendencies, or characteristics. Accordingly, *Samkhya* posits various tendencies: *sattva*, which is the tendency responsible for the self-manifestation and self-maintenance of *prakriti*; *rajas*, the tendency of motion and action; and *tamas*, the tendency of inertia. From the psychological standpoint, *sattva*, *rajas*, and *tamas* are the principles responsible for pleasure, pain, and indifference, respectively. By various combinations of these differing principles it is possible to account for the evolution of the whole world. The varying proportions of these embodied principles account for all the diversity found in the world.

But what caused the evolution of *prakriti*? If the world is looked at as evolving it is implied that there was a logical time when the principles constituting *prakriti* were in a quiet state of equilibrium. If this is the case, it is necessary to suppose another principle of reality in the world, a principle responsible for disturbing the equilibrium of the tendencies, and thereby setting in motion the evolution of *prakriti*. This second reality is called *purusha*, and it is considered to be of the nature of pure consciousness, being ultimate Subject. It is, in fact, the Samkhya version of the Upanishadic *Atman* or *Brahman*.

It is the existence of *purusha* that accounts for the evolution of *prakriti*. It is not that *purusha* actually has anything to do with *prakriti*, but simply because of the existence and presence of *purusha*, the equilibrium of *prakriti* is upset and the evolutionary process begins.

A summation of the arguments given for the existence of *purusha* is given by Ishvara Krishna as follows: "(a) Because all composite objects are for another's use, (b) because there must be absence of the three attributes and other properties, (c) because there must be control, (d) because there must be someone to experience, and (e) because there is a tendency toward "isolation" or final beatitude, therefore, the *purusa* must be there."[5]

Arguments (a) and (b) rest on the premises that (1) all experienced objects consist of parts, these parts being ordered in such a way as to serve the purposes of other objects or beings so that the whole of nature hangs together as an ordered whole, and (2) unless there is that which is not composed of parts for the sake of which those things composed of parts exist we are caught in an infinite regress. The conclusion is that the world of *prakriti*, which is the world of objects, exists for the sake of another, proving the existence of a principle other than *prakriti*. This principle is *purusha*.

Argument (c) assumes that material objects, the objects constituting the world of *prakriti*, could not work together, each being directed to its proper end, unless there be some principle of intelligence guiding this world. The conclusion is that *purusha* must exist in order that the world be ordered as it is.

Argument (d) claims that from the psychological point of view all the objects of the world are of the nature of pleasure, pain, or indifference. But pleasure and pain cannot exist without an experiencer. The conclusion is that the world of *prakriti* must exist for some experiencer, and therefore *purusha* as the principle of experiencer must exist.

Argument (e) claims that *purusha* must exist because of the desire of the individual to transcend himself. In an ordered universe it couldn't happen that the universal tendency toward the infinite—toward self-realization—would be self-frustrating. Consequently, the *purusha* must be there to be realized, since it is being sought.

[5] *Samkhya-Karika*, XVII.

But aside from arguments, the existence of *purusha* is put beyond question or doubt by the experience of those who have transcended the world of *prakriti*.

That *purusha* is regarded as being independent of *prakriti* is clear from the claim that "from the repeated study of the truth, there results that wisdom, 'I do not exist [as *prakriti*], naught is mine, I am not [*prakriti*],' which leaves no residue to be known, is pure, being free from ignorance, and is absolute."[6]

But if *purusha* is independent of *prakriti*, are not the questions of how they are related, and how the empirical self can realize the *purusha* within, even more enigmatic than ever? The clue to the reply is contained in the above quotation according to which it is wisdom that releases the *purusha* from *prakriti*. If the *purusha* were *really* caught up in the *prakriti* and constrained by it, then to say that the *purusha* is completely different from and independent of *prakriti* would be nonsensical. But the Samkhya view is that the relation between *prakriti* and *purusha* has its basis in ignorance. In this ignorance a tragic mistake is made, and *purusha* is confused with *prakriti*.

In order to explain how an illusory connection between *purusha* and *prakriti* can cause the real evolution of *prakriti* it is necessary to see how the mere existence and presence of *purusha* affects *prakriti*. Imagine that *purusha* were a shining light and *prakriti* a pool of water reflecting the light. Without *purusha* doing anything more than shining by its own light, the reflection in *prakriti* reflects on itself. But this is not the true light of *purusha*; it is a reflection in *prakriti* and therefore essentially of the nature of *prakriti*. Now in this reflection, which is the reflection of *purusha* in *prakriti*, *purusha* is lost sight of, and *prakriti* is taken to be the ultimate reality. Due to this mistake, the illumination of the empirical self which enables a person to see, hear, feel, think, desire, etc., is not recognized to proceed from the great light that is *purusha*. Consequently, as *prakriti* continues to evolve, *purusha* is not discriminated from *prakriti* but is identified with the evolutes of *prakriti*.

The order of evolution of *prakriti* sketched in the Samkya philosophy regards the first illumination of *prakriti* by *purusha* as *Buddhi*, or *Mahat*—the "great one." This reflection becoming aware of itself is the "I-Maker" (*ahamkara*) responsible for individuation in nature. From these evolutes proceed the mind and the organs of sensation as well as the organs of actions and the essences of the things that are sensed and acted

[6] *Samkhya-Karika*, LXIV.

upon. Finally the gross objects of the world evolved. In this way the origin of all of experienced reality is accounted for by Samkhya.

SELF-DISCIPLINE

The preceding account of the nature of the empirical self and world, and their relation to the *purusha*, or ultimate Self, provides a rational basis for the techniques of dicipline known as *yoga*. The practice of *yoga* is required to achieve the wisdom whereby the ignorance wherein the *purusha* is confused with *prakriti* is alleviated and the essential nature of the Self as *purusha* is realized.

The basic question of *yoga* is, How can that wisdom be achieved wherein the *purusha*, pure subject, recognizes itself for what it is; simply the spectator of *prakriti*, not actually a part of it or connected to it? When this wisdom is achieved there is no longer suffering, for the *purusha* is no longer mistakenly attached to the changing and suffering *prakriti*. Consequently, the afflictions of *prakriti* have nothing to do with *purusha*, and cannot cause suffering.

How the relationship between *purusha* and *prakriti* results in suffering, as explained by Samkhya, can be pictured by imagining a person in a room surrounded by audio-visual devices. These devices lead the person to identify himself with a person being picked up out of the sea, wafted to the peak of a jagged cliff high over the water, and plummeted down to be dashed against the rocks below. Time after time the process is repeated; each time the broken pieces are fused together again and the process commenced anew. For the person who has mistaken this image for himself there is the pain and suffering of a thousand horrible deaths. Nothing could be more wonderful than to escape this horrible fate. But when the person realizes that he has identified himself with a self created out of film and sound he recognizes that nothing that happens to that self has anything to do with him and he is free of the suffering with which he had identified himself. The point is that the person was really free from suffering all of the time, but ignorance prevented this realization. It was neither the audio-visual material in itself nor the person himself that caused the suffering. It was the mistaken identification of the one with the other that led to suffering. In an analogous way, neither *purusha* nor *prakriti* themselves are capable of suffering, but a wrong identification of *purusha* with *prakriti* leads to suffering. To overcome the suffering of the self something must be done to remove the ignorance leading to the mistaken identification of the pure Self with the not-Self.

To this end the *Yoga* aphorisms of Patanjali prescribes *yoga*, or self-discipline. The first four aphorisms indicate the nature and purpose of *yoga*: "Now the exposition of *yoga*. *Yoga* is the restriction of the fluctuations of the mind-stuff (*citta*). Then the Seer [that is, the Self] abides in himself. At other times it [the Self] takes the same forms as the fluctuations [of mind stuff]."[7]

What is here called "mind-stuff" corresponds to what in Samkhya is called the *Buddhi*, or *Mahat*, the "great one." The fluctuations or movements in *Buddhi*, or mind-stuff, lead to the identification with these fluctuations which are due to the not-Self, or *prakriti*. When the changes or fluctuations of the mind-stuff cease there is no foundation for the mistaken identification of *purusha* with *prakriti* and the independence of *purusha* is realized. But when the fluctuations occur they are mistaken for the real Self, the *purusha*. It is as though the light of *purusha* is caught by the rippling dirtied waters of the pool and is therefore regarded as changing and dirty. When the pool is calmed and the dirt allowed to settle, the light is no longer obscured. Accordingly, the important feature of *yoga* is the disciplining and controlling of the mind-stuff.

The eight aids to *yoga* indicate that since the mind-stuff has already identified with the ego, the mind, the senses, and bases of action, one restricts the fluctuations through self-discipline, by bringing under control the other aspects of *prakriti* that have evolved as empirical self—the habits, desires, physical self, etc.

The eight aids to the achievement of the goal of *yoga* are listed as: (1) abstinence from injury, falsehood, theft, incontinence, and the acceptance of gifts; (2) cleanliness, contentment, self-castigation, study, and devotion to the Ishvara; (3) stable and easy posture, accompanied by the relaxation of effort, or by a state of balance; (4) restraint of breath; (5) withdrawal of the senses; (6) not allowing the mind-stuff to wander; (7) focusing the mind-stuff, or contemplation; (8) concentration, wherein the object of contemplation is transcended and duality destroyed.[8]

The first five aids are indirect or preliminary steps in that they prepare the empirical self for the discipline of the mind-stuff that is taken up in the last three steps. Essentially, the discipline of *yoga* is a matter of bringing under control the various evolutes of *prakriti* as shaped by

[7] *Yoga Sutras of Patanjali*, I, 1–4, trans. by James Haughton Woods, *Harvard Oriental Series*, XVII (Cambridge: Harvard University Press, 1914).
[8] *Yoga Sutras*, II, III.

mind-stuff, the reflected purusha. It is thus really the reverse process of the evolution of *prakriti*; the involution of *prakriti* back to the stage where the original mistake took place. When this occurs the *purusha* will no longer be regarded as constrained by matter and the Self will be realized in its pure subjectivity.

The explanation of the relation between the empirical and the ultimate by Samkhya, and the nature of the mistake causing bondage and suffering which is to be remedied by the discipline of *yoga*, is nicely summed up in an old and favorite Indian story. The story deals with a little tiger raised by wild goats who mistook himself for a goat and had to be instructed by a master and provided with the right kinds of experience in order to realize his true nature—that of a tiger.

The tiger's mother had died giving birth, and the infant was left all alone in the world. Fortunately, the goats were compassionate and adopted the little fellow, teaching him how to eat grass with his pointed teeth and how to bleat like they did. Time passed and the tiger assumed that he was just like the rest of the band of goats. But one day an old male tiger came upon this little band of goats. They all fled in terror, except for the tiger-goat, now about half-grown, who for some unknown reason felt no fear. As the savage jungle beast approached, the cub began to feel self-conscious and uncomfortable. To cover his self-consciousness he began to bleat a bit and nibble some grass. The old tiger roared at the little one in amazement and anger, asking him what he thought he was doing eating grass and bleating like a goat. But the little one was too embarrassed by all this to answer, and continued to nibble grass. Thoroughly outraged by this behavior, the jungle tiger grabbed him by the scruff of his neck and carried him to a nearby pool. Holding him over the water he told him to look at himself. "Is that the pot face of a tiger or the long face of a goat?" he roared.

The cub was still too frightened to answer, so the old tiger carried him to his cave, and thrust a huge chunk of juicy, red, raw meat between his jaws. As the juices trickled into his stomach the cub began to feel a new strength and a new power. No longer mistaking himself for a goat the little tiger lashed his tail from side to side and roared like the tiger he was. He had achieved Tiger-realization! He no longer took himself to be what he appeared to be in his ignorance, but realized his true nature, which had nothing to do with the world of goats.

CHAPTER 6

KNOWLEDGE AND REALITY: NYAYA-VAISHESHIKA

W HEREAS the Upanishads emphasized the ultimate nature of reality as an experienced unity, and the Samkhya attempted to show what reality must be like in order to make sense of both our ordinary experience and the claims of the Upanishads, the Nyaya philosophy centers on the nature of our *knowledge* of reality. The main question is not, What is reality like? but, What is our knowledge of reality like? What do we know about our knowledge? Accordingly, major portions of Nyaya philosophy are given over to consideration of the various problems of knowledge. Adopting the Nyaya analysis of the structure of human knowledge, Vaisheshika philosophy emphasized the nature of what is known, and came up with an atomistic picture of the structure of the universe.

The basic problem of knowledge is that of ascertaining whether or not what is claimed as knowledge is actually knowledge rather than just mistaken opinion. Does what is claimed as knowledge really reveal reality? Mistakes are easily made in matters of perception and inference. In the dim light the discarded rope appears to be a snake; it could cause someone to claim knowledge of a snake on the path. But if there were only a rope on the path obviously no one could have *knowledge* of a snake on the path. As examples like this are considered it becomes possible to speculate that perhaps what *appears* to us is always different from what really is there. It might be as though the eyes always present things as red, yellow, and blue, whereas all things are really orange, black, and green. The ear presents sounds differently from what they really are, and the other senses equally distort the reality with which they come in contact. Skeptical considerations of this sort push philosophers in the direction of trying to analyze what knowledge is.

In Nyaya the analysis of knowledge is taken up in terms of the knowing subject, the object to be known, the known object, and the means of coming to know the object. Analysis of claims to knowledge reveals that these four factors are involved in all knowledge, for there is no knowledge except when someone knows something. The one who knows is the subject, the something known is the object. The object is either the object to be known, or the object that is known. The whole point of coming to know things is to pass from ignorance, in which case the subject is separated from the object, to knowledge, in which case the subject, by various means, comes to be related to the object in certain ways. These relations constitute knowing the object. Consequently, anyone wishing to come to an understanding of what knowledge is must attend to (1) the knowing subject, (2) the object to be known, (3) the object as known, and (4) the means whereby the object comes to be known.

MEANS OF KNOWLEDGE

According to Nyaya, knowledge is essentially the revelation of an object, and the means of knowledge are distinguished according to the different causes responsible for the revelation of the object in knowledge. This principle of distinction yields perception, inference, analogy, and testimony as the four basic means, or sources, of knowledge. The principle for distinguishing between these sources is that a person is doing four basically different things in coming to know something in each of the different ways.

PERCEPTUAL KNOWLEDGE

Perceptual knowledge is defined as the true and determinate knowledge arising from the contact of the senses with their proper objects.[1]

---

[1] *The Nyaya Sutras of Gotama*, 1.4. trans. by Vidyabhusana in *The Sacred Books of the Hindus*, VIII (Allahabad: The Panini Office, 1930). Reprinted in *A Source Book in Indian Philosophy*, ed. by Radhakrishnan and Moore (Princeton: The Princeton University Press, 1957), pp. 358 ff.

It is known, by means of perception, that these words appear on a piece of paper, because of the contact of the eye with the marks constituting the words. If one were a considerable distance from the paper and perceived only dark spots on the paper, not knowing whether they were words, scribbles, or ants, it would not be a genuine case of perception, for the object perceived would not be determinate. If one were to mistake a rope for a snake it would not be a case of genuine perception either, for it would not be true knowledge, since there was no snake there to be perceived.

It may be asked, however, if in cases of perceptual illusions or mistakes there is not something actually perceived. It does not seem possible that the senses could reveal sensory objects without some external stimuli. Unless there were something with which the senses were making contact there would be nothing to be revealed. Furthermore, if it were the case that the senses could reveal something when there was no contact of any kind, it might turn out that all claimed perceptual experience was of this kind, and that in reality there was nothing in the world to be sensed. But this is self-contradictory, for the very claim itself rests on the assumption of real sensory contact.

But it still is necessary to explain how genuine perceptions of the kinds recognized as knowledge differ from and can be distinguished from perceptual mistakes. The Nyaya explanation of this point rests on a distinction between two kinds of perception. Determinate perception—perception of words on this paper—is preceded by indeterminate perception—sense contact with the marks on the paper prior to recognition and classification of them as words. To talk about a perceptual mistake in reference to the indeterminate perception doesn't make any sense, for there is nothing which is taken to be anything, and therefore it cannot be taken for something other than what it is. Indeterminate perception is simply the contact of the sense with its object. It is the most elementary sensory experience limited to precisely what is given by sense contact. But this is not classified as perceptual knowledge. Perceptual knowledge requires determinate perception in which basic sensory experience of the indeterminate perception is revealed as some kind of thing with various qualities and relations, being, in principle, nameable. There is thus a distinction between an immediate sensory experience and perception, though the latter always includes the former. Consequently there is also a distinction between ignorance and error. Ignorance may be due to a lack of either the immediate sensory experience or to a lack of determinate perception, but error results from mistaking what is given in immediate sensory experience for something other than what it is. In terms of the example of erroneously perceiving a snake instead of a rope, the immediate sensory experience reveals a darkish-colored, elongated and twisted color patch. But in perception this content of sensory experience is seen as a snake when it is in fact a rope and the result is the erroneous claim that a snake has been seen. From this is can be seen that true perceptual knowledge is the perception of what is perceived as it really is, and error is the perception of something other than what it really is.

But now the question may be raised as to how a particular perceptual judgment can be known to be true. Obviously it is impossible to *directly* test the correspondence between the perception and the reality being perceived, for this would mean knowing what is true knowledge by going outside of knowledge itself. But to know something outside of knowing it is impossible. If, however, the correspondence is tested within the framework of knowledge all we get is another knowledge claim about the claimed correspondence. And this can go on indefinitely without ever revealing anything about the actual correspondence between claim and reality.

Consequently Nyaya suggests that mistaken knowledge claims are detected, ultimately, in terms of the successfulness of practice. If one's perception of the finely granulated white stuff in the bowl on the table as sugar is erroneous because the bowl in reality contains salt, it will not help to take another dozen looks at it. Rather, it is necessary to take some action based on the perception and see how the action turns out. If the perception is non-erroneous a spoonful of the contents of the bowl will make the coffee a pleasant drink. If the perception is erroneous because the bowl contains salt, a spoonful in the coffee will make the contents of the cup undrinkable. Expanding this principle of verification of perceptual claims, the position is reached that whatever works—in the sense that it provides for successful activity, and eventually, human happiness and liberation—is true because it is seen to correspond to reality as attested to by the successful activity.

In this way the Nyaya philosophers define true perception in terms of correspondence to reality. But they advocate practice as the means of testing this correspondence.

Different kinds of perceptual knowledge can be distinguished according to the ways in which contact is established between the senses and their objects. Ordinary perception occurs when the eye sees color, the ear hears sound, the nose smells odors, the tongue tastes flavors, resistance is felt, or the mind comes into contact with psychical states and processes. The first five kinds of perceptual knowledge yield indeterminate perception, or merely the basic sensory experience itself. The sixth kind of perceptual knowledge, which is internal, is a matter of becoming aware of the sensory experiences and perceiving them to be something or the other. It corresponds to ordinary determinate perception.

In addition, Nyaya admits extra-ordinary perception. Analysis of our knowledge reveals that not only are there basic sensory experiences and perceptions of individual things, but also there are perceptions of natures of things. Visual experience of certain color patches is not simply perceived to be an individual thing that goes by the name of, say, Rama, but is perceived to be that *man*, Rama. Since the perception of the nature of the individual, by virtue of which the individual can be recognized as a member of a class (e.g., the class "man"), is not given in ordinary perception, it is regarded as one of the three kinds of extraordinary perception.

The second kind of extra-ordinary perception explains how what is proper to one sense organ can become the object of another sense. For example, it is often said that ice looks cold, or that flowers look soft, or fragrant. But coldness, softness, and fragrance are not the proper objects of sight. Consequently, these kinds of perceptual experiences are regarded as extra-ordinary.

The third kind of extra-ordinary perception refers to the perception of things in the past or future, or hidden, or infinitely small in size by one who possesses unusual powers generated by disciplined meditation, or *yoga*.

INFERENCE

Although perception is the basic kind of knowledge, there are three other means of knowledge recognized by Nyaya. Inference is regarded as an independent means of valid knowledge that is defined as producing a knowledge that comes after other knowledge.[2] For example, from perceptual knowledge it is possible to infer something about reality that has never actually been perceived. We know that dinosaurs existed because of certain fossil remains that have been seen. Inference proceeds from what has been perceived to something that has not been perceived by means of a third "something" called a *reason*, which functions

2 *Nyaya Sutra*, I.5.

as a middle term in syllogistic reasoning. For example, in the syllogistic inference, "There is fire on the hill because there is smoke on the hill, and wherever there is smoke there is fire," the universal connection between smoke and fire is the reason (the third "thing") for affirming fire on the hill, even though the fire was not actually perceived.

A commonly used example of inference in its ordinary syllogistic form is as follows:

1. Yonder hill has fire.
2. Because it has smoke.
3. Whatever has smoke has fire, e.g., a stove.
4. Yonder hill has smoke such as is always accompanied by fire.
5. Therefore yonder hill has fire.

Nyaya distinguishes between reasoning to convince oneself and reasoning to convince another. When reasoning to convince oneself it is not necessary to set out the steps so elaborately as above, and either the first two or the last two steps can be eliminated. But when the inference is set down formally for the consideration of another, all five steps are insisted upon. The essential part of the inference in the above example is the coming to know that there is fire on the hill on the basis of (1) the perceived smoke and (3) the reason constituted by the invariable connection between smoke and fire.

In the above example, the first proposition represents the new knowledge claim. The second proposition gives the perceptual grounds for the new claim. The third proposition asserts the reason for making the move from a claim about smoke to one about fire. It is, so to speak, the inference ticket, enabling one to move on to the conclusion constituting the inferential knowledge claim. The fourth proposition asserts that the inference ticket is good for this trip, i.e., that the reason applies in this case. The fifth proposition repeats the claim, now not as a matter for testing, but as a valid knowledge claim, as established by the reasons provided.

Clearly, the most crucial part of the inferential process is establishing the reason (3), the invariable connection between two objects or events. Grant that it was observed on one or a hundred occasions in the past that fire was accompanied by smoke. Is this a guarantee that in the next case smoke will be accompanied by fire? After all, just because the first ten or one hundred persons who walked into the UN building were males does not mean that the next person will be male.

Nyaya philosophers regard the enumeration of individual objects or events as an important part of the establishment of universal connections between events or objects. If ten black crows are seen and no non-black crows, there is some probability that there is a universal connection between being a crow and being black. But if thousands of crows have been observed, all of them black, the probability is increased. However, even if a million crows, all black, have been observed, and the next crow observed is white, the probability that there is a universal connection between being a crow and being black is zero, even though we might want to say that the probability is very high that the millionth-and-second crow will be black.

But if this is the case it would seem that no amount of confirming instances would ever establish a necessary connection between events or objects, for it would always be possible that the very next observed case would refute the necessity of the connection. In light of this possibility, even though Nyaya places much emphasis upon presence of confirming experience and absence of unconfirming experience, the matter is not left here. After all, they argue, there is a difference between claims such as "Wherever there is smoke there is fire" and "Whatever is man is mortal," on the one hand, and the claim "All crows are black," on the other. The difference is that there is nothing in the nature of a crow that requires blackness. But there is something about the nature of man that requires mortality. Usually that is expressed by saying that smoke is *caused* by fire, and mortality is *caused* by man's nature as a composite being.

Nevertheless, even if there is, in reality, a difference between these cases, the question still arises as to how it is possible to determine that in some cases the connection is universal and necessary because causal, and that in others the connection is mere coincidence without any causal basis. Since inference proceeds from perceptual knowledge, if there is to be knowledge of a universal and necessary connection between events or objects, it must be that this necessity is perceived, and not inferred. Accordingly, Nyaya includes in perceptual knowledge the perception of the class-nature in the individual. This is a kind of extraordinary perception whereby the individual is perceived not merely to be this or that particular thing or event, but as this or that particular thing *and* one of a certain *kind*, or *class*, of things, the class-nature, or essence, being perceived along with the individual characteristics of the thing or event.

Those inferences involving universal connection are of either of two kinds. Either (1) the unperceived effect can be inferred from the perceived cause, or (2) the unperceived cause can be inferred from the perceived effect. All other inferences depend upon a non-causal and non-necessary uniformity, and cannot be shown to be necessarily true.

To aid in avoiding certain common mistakes in drawing inferences, the Nyaya philosophers have listed a number of fallacies to be avoided. A fallacy is defined as that which appears to be a valid reason for inference, but which is really not a valid reason. In the inference "There is fire on the hill because there is smoke on the hill and where there is smoke there is fire," the inferred knowledge is that there is fire on the hill. The assertion "there is fire" is being made about the hill. Technically the term "fire" is called *sadhya*. The term "hill" is called *paksha*. The reason for the assertion—"There is smoke"—is called *hetu*. Unless what is taken to be a reason for connecting the *sadhya* with the *paksha* is really a reason, or *hetu*, the inference will be invalid. To insure that the given *hetu*, or reason, will really be a reason, several rules must be observed. (1) The reason, or *hetu*, must be present in the *paksha*, and in all other objects having the *sadhya* in it. (2) The reason, or *hetu*, must be absent from objects not possessing the *sadhya*. (3) The inferred proposition should not be contradicted by valid perception. (4) The reason, or *hetu*, should not make possible a conclusion contradicting the inferred proposition.

COMPARISON

The third means of valid knowledge recognized by Nyaya philosophers is knowledge by comparison based on similarity. For example, if someone knew what a cow was, and was told that a deer was like a cow in certain respects, he might come to know that the animal he met in the woods was a deer. This is different from being told what name to apply to a certain object. If, for example, one were to see a deer for the first time and he was told, "That is a deer," the knowledge would be due to testimony, not to comparison. Knowledge by means of comparison is attained when the association of the name of an unknown object is made by the knower on the basis of experiencing the similarity of the unknown object with a known object. The crucial aspect of this means of knowledge is the observation of the similarity. Nyaya thinkers hold that similarities are objective and perceivable. Accordingly, knowledge of the nature of a new object on the strength of its similarity to a known object constitutes a separate means of knowledge. While comparative

knowledge involves both perception and inference, it cannot be reduced to either of them, and therefore is to be counted as a third means of
knowledge.

TESTIMONY

The fourth means of valid knowledge recognized in Nyaya is technically called *shabda*. Literally, it means the word of a person, and it
refers to the knowledge achieved as a result of being told something by
a reliable person. Opinion is not the same thing as knowledge, for
opinion might be erroneous, but knowledge cannot. Consequently,
simply hearing the opinion of another is not a means of knowledge.
But when the knowledge claims of another are heard there is genuine
knowledge attained, if one understands the claim. The three basic
criteria of knowledge based on the testimony of another are: (1) the
person speaking must be absolutely honest and reliable with respect
to what he is saying; (2) the person speaking must actually *know* that
which he is communicating; (3) the hearer must understand exactly
what it is that he is hearing.

OBJECTS OF KNOWLEDGE

Having analyzed the means of valid knowledge, the next step is to
consider the objects of valid knowledge. Nyaya lists as objects of knowledge the self, the body, the senses and their objects, knowledge, mind,
action, mental imperfections, pleasure and pain, suffering, and freedom
from suffering.[3] These objects of knowledge all depend upon the
relation between a knowing subject and a world of objects, for they
have to do with the actions and passions of a subject. If one considers
objects of knowledge from the viewpoint of their own independent
existence they include the categories of the Vaisheshika system. These
categories are (1) substance, (2) quality, (3) motion, (4) generality, (5)
particularity, (6) inherence, and (7) nonexistence.[4]

These categories are the types of objects that correspond to the different types of perceived objects. Since perceptions are due to contact with
objects by an experiencing self, the differences in perceptual objects
must be due to different real objects. Thus, classification of objects of

---

[3] *Nyaya Sutra*, I.9.
[4] *Vaisheshika Sutra*, I.4, trans. by Nandalal Sinha, *The Sacred Books of the Hindus*, VI (Allahabad:
the Panini Office, 2nd ed. 1923), Reprinted in *Source Book in Indian Philosophy*, pp. 387 ff. Actually,
the seventh category, that of non-existence, was added centuries later than the others.

knowledge yields a classification of existing things, as differences in perception are due to differences in what is perceived.

The first kind of existing thing is substance. This refers to that which exists independently of other kinds of things, but which is the *locus* of existence for the other kinds of things. Real in itself, a substance can be thought of as the substratum of qualities and actions. The category of substance includes: (1) earth, (2) water, (3) light, (4) air, (5) ether, (6) time, (7) space, (8) self, and (9) mind. Earth, water, light, air, and ether are regarded as physical elements since each of them is known by a particular external sense; earth by smell, water by taste, light by sight, air by touch, and ether by sound.

These substances can be considered in two ways. First, they can be thought of as atomic, eternal, and indivisible. Secondly, they are the results of combinations of atoms, in which case they are temporal, composite, and destructible, being produced by the combination of atoms. That substances in the sense of composite things, such as this jar, are made up of atoms is known on the basis of inference. If the jar is broken it is reduced to several parts. Each of these parts can again be broken, being reduced to more parts. But no matter how long this process continues it is impossible that every part should be destructible, for that would mean it is composite. But if composite things exist it is necessary that their ultimate constituents be simple, or else composite things would never be produced. Therefore, the ultimate constituents of gross substances must be atomic. The substance space is inferred on the grounds that sound is perceived and since sound is a quality, there must be that in which it inheres or that to which it belongs, namely, space.

Space and time are known to exist because of our perceptions of here and there, far and near, and past, present, and future. Knowledge is a quality, and therefore it must exist in a substance called the self, which is the ground of consciousness. Mind is inferred on the grounds that feeling and willing are known, but since they are not known by the external senses they must be known by the mind. In addition there is that which directs the senses and collects their contacts into experience. That in which sense contacts reside as qualities is the substance known as mind.

The second category of known objects is that of quality. It refers to the various qualifications of the substances, and includes color, odor, contact, sound, number, measure, difference, connection, separation, long or short, far or near, knowledge, happiness, sorrow, volition, hatred, effort, heaviness, fluidity, potency, merit, and demerit. This list of qualifications is a way of saying that things or substances can be, e.g., red or blue, pungent or fragrant, touching or apart from, soft or loud, one or many, large or small, the same as or different from, separate or together, long or short, far or near, knowing or ignorant, happy or sorrowful, desiring to or desiring not to, loving or hating, trying or not trying, light or heavy, mobile or immobile, able or not able, and good or bad, respectively. There are many divisions of some of the qualities, but the above list is being taken as referring to the basic kinds of qualification of substances.

The third kind of basic and irreducible reality is motion. The different kinds of motion are (1) upward, (2) downward, (3) contraction, (4) expansion, and (5) locomotion. The kinds of motion are the kinds of reality that account for the changes substances undergo.

The fourth category is that of universal essences. It accounts for sameness found in substances, qualities, or actions. Four cows, four red objects, and four upward motions are each of them the same in that they are cows, reds, or upward motions. This sameness is regarded as objective, belonging to the individual things just as truly as do qualities. The reason that the four cows can all be recognized as cows is that they share in the same essence or nature. It is this essence which enables one to form class concepts and to classify individual things into various classes.

From a continuous field of sensing and mental activity particular objects are perceived. The ability to perceive particular and distinct objects is due to the category of particularity which belongs to the objects perceived. If things did not have the character of being different from other things there would be no reason why they should be perceived as different. But since they are perceived as different there must be some foundation for this difference in reality. Hence, particularity must exist in reality.

The category of inherence reflects the fact that different things, such as substance, quality, action, etc., appear as one whole. Thus, the size of the man, his color, his nature as man, and his particularity as this man, all appear so unified that we think of one thing appearing, rather than a collection of things appearing to us. Thus, the whole inheres in its parts; the jug in the clay, the pencil in the wood, etc. The basis for the unity of different categories must, like the other categories, have a foundation in reality, as different from other kinds of things. Otherwise it would appear as one of the other kinds of things, and not as separate. Therefore, the category of inherence is recognized as an independent kind of reality.

In addition to the above kinds of knowable objects there is non-existence. Although non-existence may seem to be a queer kind of reality it's existence cannot be questioned, for to question it is to suggest that it does not exist, which is to affirm the category of non-existence. Only by assuming non-existence does negation become possible.

In the way just outlined Nyaya and Vaisheshika come to their metaphysical view of reality. This list of the basic kinds of things that exist is a sketch of the ontological universe.

THE KNOWER

Considering the knowing subject, rather than the objects to be known, or the objects as known, Nyaya argues that the self is a unique substance. The qualifications of this substance are knowledge, feeling, and volition. Accordingly, the self is defined as the substance in which the qualities of desire, aversion, pleasure, pain, etc., inhere, for these follow upon knowing, feeling, and volition. Now, since none of these are physical qualities, since they cannot be perceived as physical qualities by any of the senses, it must be admitted that they belong to a substance other than a physical, or material, substance. Therefore the self must be distinct from physical objects, from sensations, from consciousness, and the mind, for the self experiences all of these. One may ask, who knows reality, who perceives, who is conscious, etc.? In every case the answer is given, "The self." Since everything else can become an object for the self, but objects—as objects—require a subject for which they are objects, it follows that the self cannot be an object, and therefore cannot be identical with anything that becomes an object, for it must be always subject.

Since the self is a unique substance and consciousness belongs to it as a quality, the self does not depend for its existence upon consciousness. In fact, according to Nyaya, ultimate liberation, or freedom, will also be freedom from consciousness. The reason for this is that consciousness is seen as consciousness of something or other. But that presupposes a duality between subject and object. And when there is duality there is possible suffering and bondage, for the subject can be bound by the object and caused to suffer. But to eliminate suffering and bondage duality must be eliminated. This can be done upon the elimination of consciousness. But if the self were essentially consciousness this would mean the extinction of the self. However, since consciousness is only a characteristic of the self, the self is not destroyed when consciousness is eliminated. All that can be said about the self in this state of liberation is that it simply exists as self.

CHANGE AND REALITY: VEDANTA

ALL the philosophies of India were very much influenced by the teachings of the Upanishads, including the philosophies of Jainism, Carvaka, and Buddhism, which did not accept the authority of the Veda. With the exception of these latter philosophies, all the philosophies of India took themselves to be in essential agreement with the teachings of the Upanishads. But as the canons of experience and reason were differently interpreted there came to be a variety of conclusions concerning the interpretation of the Upanishads, and some of these appeared to conflict with the conclusions of the Upanishads when these were taken literally. The Vedanta philosophers set out self-consciously to underwrite the main conclusions of the Upanishads with critical interpretations of reason and experience which did not conflict with those conclusions. As a result, the Vedanta philosophies turned out to be highly critical of some of the conclusions of the other systems. For example, the Samkhya claim that the world of the not-Self was eternally real and distinct from the Self, and the Nyaya, Vaisheshika and Mimamsa views of the world as real and pluralistic, being made up of different kinds of atoms, came in for severe criticism, since these conclusions appeared to deviate furthest from the emphasis on the sole reality of *Atman*, or *Brahman*, in the Upanishads.

The Nyaya, Vaisheshika, Samkhya, and Mimamsa systems of philosophy are unanimous in agreeing that our perceptions have a basis in reality. That basis can be expressed by saying that what is perceived exists independently of being perceived. Genuine knowledge occurs when the knower comes to see things as they really are. Philosophically, this position is known as realism, which simply indicates that the objective world revealed by experience is real and exists independently of being known. These systems also are pluralistic in that they agree that this objective reality is constituted by a variety of ultimately different objects. This view, pluralistic realism, is not a very startling view of the world. In fact, it is the view held by most people in the world. Philosophical proponents of this view have argued that whenever one's experiences are to be taken seriously as providing knowledge it is necessary that there be knowledge of *something*. If there is no something to be known there can be no knowledge. However, if something exists to be known, then there are objects that exist independently of perception even though they can be related to a knower in such a way that they come to be perceived and known. Therefore, it is logically necessary to admit the real existence of the world that is experienced unless it can be shown that there really is no knowledge. But to claim that one knows that there is no knowledge is absurd, for it is a claim that there is knowledge. And what basis other than knowledge is there for claiming that there is no knowledge of the world?

These are some of the difficulties faced by the Vedanta philosophers who felt that the realistic and pluralistic conclusions of the philosophers of the other systems were in direct opposition to the conclusions of the Upanishads. After all, the Upanishads taught the unity of reality and the identity of self with reality in passages such as the following: "All this is *Atman*."[1] "Atman being known . . . everything is known."[2] "There was only Being at the beginning, it was one without a second."[3] "All this is *Brahman*."[4] "This self is the *Brahman*."[5] "I am *Brahman*."[6]

The very fact that the unity of reality was thus taught in the Upanishads was sufficient reason for a Hindu to accept this view as true, for the Upanishads belong to the tradition of infallible literature. Nevertheless, for the critical mind it is important to show that this teaching does not conflict with reason or experience. A significant step in this direction

[1] *Chandogya Upanishad*, 7.25.2.
[2] *Brihadaranyaka Upanishad*, 4.5.6.
[3] *Chandogya Upanishad*, 6.2.1.
[4] *Mundaka Upanishad*, 2.2.11, and *Chandogya Upanishad*, 3.14.1.
[5] *Brihadaranyaka Upanishad*, 2.5.19.
[6] *Brihadaranyaka Upanishad*, 1.4.10.

could be taken simply by showing that opposing claims about reality were self-contradictory and implausible. Consequently the task of showing that the philosophies with conclusions at variance with the monistic teachings of the Upanishads were unsatisfactory became an important part of Vedanta philosophy. As a result, the critical analysis of the other philosophies came to be emphasized. But it was not sufficient simply to show that other systems were unsatisfactory. It was also necessary to show that the system of reality claimed by the Vedantic interpretation of the Upanishads was not subject to the same kinds of criticisms aimed at the other systems. In this way the Vedanta philosophies came to provide rational criticisms of the other philosophies and also to provide rational defences of their own interpretations and systems.

There are three principal schools of Vedantic philosophy, differing from each other in the way they account for the relations between persons, things, and ultimate Reality (*Brahman*). The oldest of these schools, that of non-dualism is often referred to as the Shamkarite school, being named after Shamkara, one of its important early philosophers who lived in the eighth century. The second school, that of qualified non-dualism, claims the eleventh-century philosopher Ramanuja as its principal figure, and is therefore sometimes called the Ramanuja school. The third school, the dualistic Vedanta, or Madhva, school has as its central figure the thirteenth-century philosopher named Madhva.

SHAMKARA'S NON-DUALISM

Shamkara's view of reality is that there is one absolute and independent reality which alone exists as real and unchanging. This reality is the *Brahman* of the Upanishads. This view rules out theories according to which the world is thought of as the product of material elements, or the transformation of unconscious matter that evolves, or the product of two kinds of independent reality, such as *Brahman* and matter.

According to Shamkara, *Brahman* is the reality that provides for the existence of the appearances that constitute the empirical world, but it is also beyond these appearances, not being exhausted by them. From the empirical and conceptual point of view, *Brahman* is in the world, or immanent. From the absolute point of view, *Brahman* transcends the world.

The nature and existence of *Brahman* cannot be proved from perception or reasoning, but is to be taken either on the basis of scriptural testimony (the Upanishads) or by direct and intuitive experience of the kind made possible by yogic concentration. Nevertheless, reason can be put to the use of justifying these means of knowing *Brahman*.

To reconcile the perceived plurality and objective reality of the world with the monistic conclusions of the Upanishads, Shamkara regards the world as appearance rather than reality, and perception as illusion rather than knowledge.

The individual self as pure subject, or *Atman*, is not different from *Brahman*.

By way of refuting conflicting claims about the nature of reality Shamkara considers first the Samkhya view and then the Vaisheshika view. According to Samkhya philosophy, the world is the result of the spontaneous evolution of unconscious matter, or *prakriti*, which is composed of the three *gunas—sattva*, *rajas*, and *tamas*. Samkhya includes within its view the existence of purpose in the world, for the world is such that it fits reborn selves and enables them to be liberated. But how can one suppose that the world, which is a harmonious system of related objects and ordered events as we experience it—and as claimed by Samkhya —could be the accidental result of an unconscious cause? To attribute purpose to unconscious nature is unintelligible according to Shamkara's analysis, and therefore the Samkhya view is untenable.

The Vaisheshika view is that the world is caused by the combination of atoms. But again, how can unconscious atoms produce out of their combinations the order that makes possible the moral law claimed by the Vaisheshika philosophers? Even if this objection is overlooked, Vaisheshika has not explained how or why unconscious atoms should first begin to move around and join together to produce the world. If atoms were incessantly in motion and joining together because of their very nature neither the beginning of the world nor its dissolution would be explicable. Therefore the Vaisheshika view is not satisfactory according to Shamkara's analysis, since it claims both production and destruction.

Thus, the explanations of Vaisheshika and Samkhya are seen to be inconsistent within the framework of their own assumptions. But their basic assumptions are not altogether satisfactory either. Nyaya, Vaisheshika, Samkhya, and Mimamsa all accept as a basic assumption the fact of real change and causation. That is, they all admit that various real changes occur in the world and that these changes are caused.

Concerning the relation between cause and effect only two views are possible. Either the effect preexists in the cause or it does not. If the effect does not preexist in the cause then the effect is totally new. This view is called *asatkaryavada* (non-existence of the effect). If the claim is that the effect preexists in the cause—this view is called *satkaryavada*—then two consequences may follow. On the one hand, it can be admitted that change and causality is a matter of making explicit what was implicit in the cause. Or it can be claimed that there is no difference between cause and effect. Nyaya and Vaisheshika held to *asatkaryavada*, as did some of the Mimamsa philosophers, on the grounds that effects are experienced as something totally new. Other Mimamsa philosophers and Samkhya philosophers held to *satkaryavada*, admitting change in the sense of making explicit what was implicit in the cause, but denying that effects were new realities.

Shamkara, in critically examining these views of causation, finds them both logically unacceptable. Nothing can show an effect to be different from its material cause. Clay pots are clay, gold rings are gold, etc. Furthermore the clay pot cannot exist apart from the clay, nor the gold ring apart from the gold. Consequently it is incorrect to say that an effect is something new that has been produced and that it did not exist before. In terms of its material cause it has always been there. From another point of view, it is argued that it is impossible to conceive of something totally new coming into existence. All that can ever be thought is the transformation of matter, never the coming into existence of matter.

Samkhya argues that if the effect were something new we would have the coming into existence of the non-existent. If this were possible, why not get non-existent oil out of sand? However, even though Samkhya may be right in claiming the theory of *asatkaryavada* to be unacceptable, the Samkhya philosopher does not realize that his own interpretation of *satkaryavada* is also untenable. If the effect already preexists in the cause, how can there be a genuine change of the material into the effect? If the effect is already there, then it is impossible for the material to become the effect, for that would be the coming to be of what already is, which makes no sense. If the Samkhya philosopher replies that though matter does not come into existence, the form does—a new form is produced—he is really admitting the existence of *asatkaryavada*, for he is admitting the effect as something that did not previously exist. But this contradicts his own arguments against *asatkaryavada*.

However, from the fact that the Samkhya philosopher has contradicted himself, it does not necessarily follow that something new does not come into existence. What follows is that either nothing new can come into existence, or that he was wrong in his argument and something new can come into existence. Consequently, it is still necessary for Shamkara to tend to the question of whether a change of form is a real change, for it cannot be denied that changes in form are perceived. Shamkara's solution is to show that though changes in form are perceived this does not imply a change in reality unless a form has reality of its own. But, of course, form has existence only in dependence upon matter, for there is no form except in formed matter. There is no form of a cup excepting the cup made of matter. Therefore, form has no independent reality. If a change in form were a change in reality, a person sitting down would be a different reality from a person standing up, since the form is different. But, of course, the same person standing up or sitting down is one and the same reality.

From another point of view, the argument is provided that if substances are distinct from their forms or qualities it would be impossible to explain the relation between the quality or form and the substance. If the form is distinct from the substance it cannot be related to the substance except in terms of a third reality which connects or relates them. But then, in order to relate this third distinct reality to the other two, another distinct reality is needed. And to relate this reality to the others, still another is needed. There would be no end to this process of multiplying entities to relate the form to the substance. But if there were no end to the process, then the form would be unrelated to the substance, making a change in reality impossible. If it is admitted that the form has no reality independent of matter then there is no change in reality.

ILLUSION

These arguments, if valid, lead to the conclusion that no changes are possible, for it has been shown that it is impossible for causation to bring about change. But on the other hand there is the perception of changes. Shamkara's solution to the dilemma is to suggest that since the perceived changes cannot be rationally accepted as real, they be regarded as similar to the perception of an illusory object.

If the objects constituting the furniture of the world are like the illusory objects of dreaming experience, it becomes possible to reconcile the existence of *Brahman* alone as the ultimate reality with the existence of the empirical world as unreal. The snake perceived in the dream *exists* in the dream, but is not *real*. That it exists must be admitted, for otherwise there would be no dream. But that it is real cannot be admitted for its unreality is what marks this particular experience as dreaming experience. In a similar way, the objects of the empirical world exist, for they are perceived. To deny the existence of the objects of the empirical world is to deny ordinary perceptual experience. But if there is an analogy between dream objects and the objects perceived in waking experience, then perhaps the objects of waking experience could also be said to be unreal, as compared with the experience of a greater reality. After all, as long as one is dreaming it is impossible to regard the objects of the dream as unreal. It is only possible to regard the dream objects as unreal when a different level of experience is attained. From the vantage point of waking experience the dream objects can be said to be unreal. But it may also be possible that from another level of experience—the experience of *Brahman*—the objects of ordinary waking experience could be seen to be unreal.

Thus, if the objects of ordinary waking experience were like dream objects in this respect it would be possible to reconcile the existence of the perceptual and empirical world with the sole reality of *Brahman*, in a way similar to the reconciliation of the existence of dream objects with their unreality.

If it is suggested that the whole world of ordinary experience is somehow illusory, it becomes important to understand the nature of illusion in order to see what sense this suggestion makes. An example considered in Vedanta is that of the rope that is mistakenly seen as a snake. The rope is said to be a snake because of ignorance of what really is there. If it were known that there is a rope there, there would be no illusion. But ignorance in itself is not enough to produce the illusion. After all, there are many things of which one is ignorant, but one does not say that these are snakes. The ignorance that produces an illusion must have two aspects. First, it covers up the reality actually present, e.g., the rope. Secondly, it actually distorts what is really there, representing it as something other than what it is.

Now, if the nature of the world is like an illusory object it must be that the world is also a product of ignorance, where the basic reality is not simply obscured and hidden from view, but is actually distorted into something other than what it is. In this way, the true reality, *Brahman*, as a result of ignorance, could be mistaken for the world of ordinary empirical objects. These objects are simply the concealing distortion of

Brahman, which alone is real. But, of course, it is only from the standpoint of the ignorant that there is any ignorance. It is only from this ignorance that the world proceeds, as it covers up the true nature of reality and causes us to see mistakenly something else in its place. Just as an illusion is produced when a magician makes one coin to appear to be many— though illusion exists only for the ignorant, not for the magician— similarly from the point of view of absolute reality there is no plurality of objects—no illusion. There is only the one true reality, just as for the magician there is only the one coin. For the wise, who succeed in seeing through the illusion of the magician, there do not appear many coins. Similarly, for the wise who experience *Brahman*, there does not appear a world of empirical objects as the ultimate reality.

It follows, if the empirical world is unreal, that there are no real changes in the world, for the changes have the same reality as the objects that are supposed to change. Consequently, the only theory of change possible is that of apparent change rather than real change. Real changes and causes are possible only if there are real objects and they really change. But if Shamkara is right, there can be no real changes and causes, for there are no real objects to change. This lends support to the Vedanta claims that the Nyaya-Vaisheshika and Samkhya theories of change are incorrect.

This theory of the nature of the empirical world also enable Shamkara to explain those passages in the Upanishads that speak of the world being produced out of *Brahman*. The world can be produced out of *Brahman* just as snakes are produced out of ropes and bent sticks are produced by water (by refraction). There is existence inasmuch as there are objects for experience. But there is no reality because the objects are illusory, being the result of ignorance.

This attempt on the part of Shamkara to explain the world as an appearance produced by illusory perception depends for its success largely upon showing that the analogy of illusory perception applies. This is done by analyzing carefully the notion of perceptual error.

Mimamsa philosophers argue that perceptual error is impossible. Immediate perception at least must be allowed to be valid, for it is the basis of all other knowledge. In support of their claim that perceptual error is impossible, the Mimamsa philosophers analyze alleged cases of perceptual error. They argue that in the case of perceiving a snake in a rope an error is made, but it is not a perceptual error. That erroneous knowledge is not simply one piece of knowledge, but a mixture of perception and memory, along with the failure to discriminate between the two. Thus, they argue that the perception itself is correct and the memory itself is correct, but that the two are wrongly conjoined. The error lies in failing to discriminate.

To this argument the Vedanta philosophers reply that the claim, "This is a snake," does not represent three pieces of knowledge—with the mistake being made in the third kind—but represents only one piece of knowledge. That memory is involved is not denied, but the claim that memory exists independently of the perception is challenged. Unless the memory combined with the perception to produce this one bit of knowledge there would be two claims: (1) "I perceive this," and (2) "I remember a snake." But in point of fact there is only one claim, "This is a snake." And this argues for positive identification, not merely a failure to recognize the difference between the perceived and the remembered. And, of course, if the Mimamsa reasons for their claim that no perceptual error is possible are unsatisfactory, then the claim need not be taken seriously.

The Nyaya-Vaisheshika view of error is that error is possible, but that it is really a matter of extra-ordinary perception. What happens when a snake is perceived in a rope is that this perception sets up the memory image of a snake perceived in the past so sharply that one becomes immediately aware of that image, mistaking it for the perceived object. The crucial part of this theory of error for Vedanta is the claim that error is taking something that really existed in the past for what is being perceived in the present. If this account is correct, then the notion that a perceptual illusion is possible is mistaken. The present perception of the world as an illusion makes sense only upon the assumption that a real world was perceived in the past and is being substituted now for the world presently being perceived. But this argues for the reality of the empirical world and not for the Vedantic view of the world as unreal.

The first objection to this theory of perceptual error is that it is not possible that something which existed at some other time and in some other place should be *perceived* now. What is perceived is *this*, and a memory is always of *that*, no matter how vivid. Thus, on the Nyaya account, the presence of the illusory object would be unexplainable. To suppose that a memory idea could actually transfer objects from one time and place to another is wildly implausible.

On other grounds it can be objected that the Nyaya view is unsatisfactory because what does not exist here now can appear to exist here now, and this is due to ignorance of what is here now. In the light of these objections it can be argued that a more plausible theory of error would hold that illusions are caused by the non-perception of the present object and the *construction* of another object which is substituted for the present object which is hidden by ignorance.

Of course, the illusory object must be present as an illusory object, being created by ignorance. However, it cannot be said to be real, nor can it be said to be unreal. In one sense, the snake is there: it is why one runs away and screams. It is not unreal in the way that a square circle or the son of a barren woman is unreal. But its reality lasts only as long as the ignorance lasts. When it is discovered that there is only a rope there, the snake no longer exists, so it cannot be said to be real. The difficulty of classifying the illusory object as real or unreal is comparable to Shamkara's difficulty in classifying the empirical world as real or unreal. In one sense it is real, for it is experienced. But in another sense it is unreal, for what is experienced is not what is really there but is the distortion of what is there. Just as in claiming that dream objects and events are not ultimately real one does not deny their existence, so Shamkara does not deny the existence of the empirical world, though he does deny its ultimate reality. In fact, Shamkara's analysis requires a more complicated classification of the reality of objects of experience than is usually found. On the one hand there is that which cannot exist at all, in any sense. These are the things that are logically impossible, such as square circles and children of barren women. Then there are the objects that exist in dreams and illusory perceptions, but which are repudiated by normal waking experience. Next come the objects of ordinary waking experience, which the realist takes to be the ultimate things of the universe. These objects are or can be repudiated by experience of *Brahman*. Lastly, there is pure existence, *Atman* alone, the ultimate reality which in no way is unreal.

Thus, Shamkara does not really propose an alteration of our ordinary view of the world that consists in repudiating the existence of the universe. He does not suggest that the existence of any objects of experience be denied. Rather, he extends the nature of reality by claiming that in addition to the objects existing in dreams and in waking consciousness there is an ultimate reality. Whatever reality objects have they have; no one, not even Shamkara, can take that away. But to recognize that there is a higher view is to add a significant dimension to our notion of reality. It is only from this higher view that the rest of existence can be seen to be ultimately unreal. In this respect the matter is similar to waking and dreaming. Unless one wakes up it is impossible to regard dreaming objects as unreal. Within the dream they can only be regarded as real. But when one wakes up, the existence of dream objects is not denied. One simply now recognizes that dream objects were merely dream objects. They have the reality they have. Only now it is seen that there is a higher level or reality, namely, waking reality. In a similar way, one might wake up to the higher reality of enlightenment and discover that until now one has been having merely ordinary waking experience and not enlightened experience (*Atman*-realization).

Shamkara's view of the nature of reality provides explanations for both the reconciliation of the perceived plurality in the world with its absolute oneness and the identity of the self with this absolute oneness. He can say, "All this is that," when the "this" refers to the empirical world, and the "that" refers to *Brahman*, because the world is merely the misperception and the misconception of *Brahman*. It is like saying that the many coins of the magician are really the one coin displayed before performing the trick. But due to our ignorance we mistake the one coin for many, and *Brahman* for the world.

In an analogous way we mistake the psycho-physical self to be the true reality, whereas in fact that self is ultimately illusory and unreal. To say, "thou art that," is to say that "thou"—the self one takes oneself to be in ignorance—is, not in its appearance, but in its very basis, that *Brahman*. For the ignorant, of course, the self is only potentially *Brahman*, and this potentiality is realized by overcoming the ignorance. From the viewpoint of *Brahman*, however, it is not possible that the self is only potentially *Brahman*. It is one thing for the ignorant to regard the snake as potentially a rope, and quite another thing to suppose that from the viewpoint of what things really are a snake is a rope.

What happens in ignorance is that the individual self, which is really a composite of self and not-self, becomes the experience of the world because of this confusion. Experience is a strange phenomenon, because it requires that in a way the self become the other, though it must also remain the self and the other must remain the other. But unless other and self become one there is no experience. This shows that for experience to be possible, there must be a combination of the self and the not-self. But from the fact that the subject always remains subject—the self having the experience—it follows that the subject, or the self, is essentially independent of the object, or the not-self. Of course, this ultimate Self cannot be *looked* at as the true self, for to look at anything (either perceptually or conceptually) requires that it be an object of experience. But since the supposition is that the self is pure subject it follows that it cannot be known in any objective way.

The question might arise as to how this ultimate Self, which is identical with *Brahman*, is related to the empirical self, which is a combination of self and other. According to Shamkara, the self, or the "I," is so opposed to the not-self that they cannot really be related to each other. It is not a logically expressible relationship, for the not-self exists in ignorance, and the object of ignorance cannot be said to be either real or not real.

In this view becoming *Brahman* is a matter of the removal of ignorance which results in mistaking the appearance of the not-self for the reality of the Self. The fact of reality is the sole reality of *Brahman* and the identity of Self, or *Atman*, with *Brahman*. Ignorance veils this truth, but a practical realization of the ultimate Self will destroy the ignorance. There is no question of the theoretical knowledge of the ultimate reality. Such knowledge is ruled out by the fact that the ultimate reality is pure subject, one without a second. Knowledge of *Brahman* is practical knowledge; it is a matter of direct and immediate personal experience. Since ultimately the universe is identical with the Self, realizing *Brahman* is a matter of being completely oneself, and experiencing one's ultimate reality.

The real Self, the *Atman*, is not an appearance and is therefore not subject to the laws of appearances. The laws of causation apply to the world of appearance, not to the world of reality, or *Brahman*. There is consequently no saying that the Self is related to the appearance, for it is neither cause nor effect, these relations belonging only to the lower level of appearances. And if the *Atman* is not related to the appearances constituting the empirical world in any ways which are knowable, it becomes impossible to know *Brahman* except by an intimate experience that will be ineffable and incommunicable. This realization that one is the Self of pure consciousness, free from change and suffering, is certified by its own illumination. As Shamkara asks, "How can one contest the fact of another possessing the knowledge of Brahman, vouched as it is by his heart's conviction?"[7]

In conclusion, it can be said that for Shamkara the empirical world and the empirical self exist, but they are not ultimately real. The very basis of their existence is a higher reality than their appearance. This basis is pure existence, the very ground of experience and appearance. Consequently, when the individual takes the empirical world and the empirical self to be the ultimate reality he is confused, mistaking the appearance for the reality on which the existing appearance depends.

[7] *Shamkara Bhashya*, IV.1.15 trans. by George Thibaut in *The Sacred Books of the East*, vol. XXXVIII (Oxford: Oxford University Press, 1904).

That there is something beyond the existence that is perceived empirically can be seen by the fact that empirical things come into and pass out
of existence, but their possibility of existence does not itself come into
being and pass out of being. Of existence itself there is no coming into
being or passing out of being, since it is prior to change, and presupposed by change.

QUALIFIED MONISM

Ramanuja agrees with Shamkara that ultimate reality is one rather
than many. But he disagrees concerning the nature of his one. Ramanuja's
view is that *Brahman* as the ultimate reality is not distinct from the empirical world, but that this world is a constituent part of *Brahman*.
Brahman is a unity made up of the differences that constitute the experienced world as well as its basis. There is thus no distinction between
Brahman on the one hand and the world on the other.

Basically, Ramanuja's differences with Shamkara are due to the
former's position that pure identity is an abstract nothing. Identity and
difference are correlative, and in existence are dependent upon each
other. To posit one without the other is to posit an empty nothing. Unity
or identity is the unity of different things; identity is an identity of
parts. When the different things or parts are denied there can be no
unity or identity. Consequently, the unity constituting *Brahman* is the
union of the different selves and things making up the world. The
identity is the identity of these parts in their substrata as existing.

Also, Ramanuja argues the self cannot be identified with knowledge,
for knowledge requires a known and a knower. Where there is no
known there is no knower, and so to regard the self as pure knower
without a known is to regard the self into nothingness. Rather, it should
be said that consciousness is the substratum of the self, wherein the self
can come to know the unity of reality.

Thus, Ramanuja's view is that *Brahman* is an organic unity constituted
by the identity of the parts. It is not abstract, but concrete, being made
up of the various objects of consciousness as well as consciousness itself.
This organic unity Ramanuja calls *Brahman*, or the Lord (*Ishvara*).

His view is that things and selves are distinct from *Brahman* in the way
the body of a person is distinct from the self of a person. On this view
unity of reality is maintained because the person is one thing, but
plurality is also maintained because a person consists of both self and
body. Furthermore, on this analogy *Brahman* is superior to selves and

things just as a person's self is superior to his body, the body belonging to the self as the self's qualifications. The position is stated by Ramanuja as follows: "The supreme *Brahman* is the self of all. The sentient and non-sentient entities constitute its body. The body is an entity and has being only by virtue of its being the mode of the soul of which it is the body. The body and the soul, though characterized by different attributes do not get mixed up. From all this follows the central teaching that *Brahman*, with all the non-sentient and sentient entities as its modes, is the ultimate."[8]

According to this explanation reality is one, like a person, with the many things and selves in the universe constituting the body of reality, and *Brahman* constituting the self of reality. The body is real, although real not independently, but as a mode of *Brahman's* being. Thus, individual selves and individual things are the real qualities or modes of *Brahman*.

According to the metaphysics underlying this account of the relation of *Brahman* to selves and things, substance alone is independently real, and whatever exists as a characteristic or quality of a substance exists as a mode of that substance and can be identified with the substance of which it is a mode. The teaching "All is *Brahman*" should not be taken to affirm the existence of *Brahman* alone without qualification, for on that interpretation there is no "All" which can be identified with *Brahman*. Rather, the "All" should be taken to refer to the various things and selves in the world, because these are the real qualifications of *Brahman*. The mode of their existence is that of the body of *Brahman*. Just as a body does not exist except as the body of a self, so things and selves do not exist except as belonging to *Brahman*.

This view is supported by a theory of meaning according to which the terms referring to the qualities of a substance refer also to the substance which the qualities qualify. For example, if we say, "The teacher is white-haired," "white-haired" refers to the color of the teacher's hair, but it also refers to the teacher whose hair is white, for having white hair qualifies the teacher. But the reference does not stop there, for being a teacher is a qualification of the person who is the teacher, and thus "white-haired teacher" refers to a qualification of a person and to the person who is so qualified. Being a person, in turn is a qualification of matter and self, and so the term "white-haired-teaching-person" refers beyond merely the person to that of which

[8] *Vedarthasamgraha of Shri Ramanujacarya*, Para. 81, trans. by S. S. Raghavachar (Mysore: Sri Ramakrishna Ashrama, 1956), p. 67.

person is a qualification. Continuing in this way, the term "white-haired" is seen to ultimately refer to the absolute reality upon which everything else is dependent for its existence. This is, of course, *Brahman*, and therefore all terms refer ultimately to *Brahman*. If *Brahman* did not exist as the ultimate reality to which all terms refer there would be nothing for terms to refer to, just as if there were no ultimate substance there would be nothing of which qualifications would be qualifications of, and then there would be no qualifications. Thus, if there are qualifications—and this cannot be denied for qualities are the primary objects of perception upon which knowledge rests—there must also be *Brahman* as the possessor of these qualities. Ramanuja puts the point this way: "This is the fundamental relationship between the Supreme and the universe of individual selves and physical entities. It is the relationship of soul and body, . . . That which, in its entirety depends upon, is controlled by and subserves another and is therefore its inseparable mode, is called the body of the latter. Such is the relation between the individual self and its body. Such being the relationship, the supreme Self, having all as its body, is denoted by all terms."[9]

In this way Ramanuja maintains the reality of both selves and *Brahman* by admitting differences within the identity that is *Brahman*. Selves are real as differentiations *within* (rather than *from*) the ultimate reality.

DUALISTIC VEDANTA

A third school of Vedanta, that of Madhva, differs from the positions of the Shamkara and Ramanuja schools in claiming a fundamental dualism in the world. The world as empirically experienced, and its foundation as *Brahman*, are eternally and fundamentally distinct. The Self is regarded as distinct from both *Brahman* and the material things constituting the empirical world. The basic argument for this position is that perception is essentially a matter of becoming aware of the uniqueness of something. Since perception is the basis of all knowledge, and it depends upon realizing differences, to claim non-existence of differences is to repudiate the very basis of the arguments for the non-existence of difference. Objects are perceived as distinct from the self, and the basis of things and self is conceived to be different from either the things or the self. There is no possible evidence that these perceived differences are mistaken, as they constitute the very possibility of knowledge. Therefore these basic differences must be admitted.

[9] *Vedarthasamgraha*, Para. 95.

Furthermore, individual selves must be distinguished from *Brahman* if they are said to be caught up in suffering and bondage. Since it is with the individual suffering self that every attempt to achieve liberation must begin, the existence of individual selves cannot be denied. But if they are admitted, they must be admitted as different from *Brahman*. It will not do to say that as *suffering* the individual is different from *Brahman*, but that as released from suffering it is identical with *Brahman*, for two things that are really different cannot at *any* time be said to be the same. Being released from suffering does not change the nature of something, making it a something else. But if this is the case, and an initial difference is postulated, then individual selves and *Brahman* must remain eternally different. Madhva argues in the same way for the eternal difference between *Brahman* and matter. Along the same lines, arguing also for a real difference between selves and matter, between one self and another, and between one thing and another, he arrives at his "five differences." These are the differences between (1) *Brahman* and matter, (2) *Brahman* and selves, (3) selves and matter, (4) one self and another, and (5) one thing and another.

The epistemological basis for Madhva's claim that these five basic differences exist consists in his analysis of knowing as a simultaneous revealing of both the subject who knows and the object that is known. According to this analysis there is no denying that subject is different from object, for knowledge is always knowledge *of* something, and it is always knowledge *for* someone. Furthermore, to know one particular thing is to know it as that thing rather than another, and this is to be aware of its differences from other things. But if this is true, and the differences between subject and object and between one object and another are *known*, they must be revealed in knowledge. Thus, knowledge in its very nature reveals differences in reality. These differences cannot be called into question without calling into question the very basis and nature of knowledge. And if this is attempted within the limits of knowledge the attempt is self-defeating, for it requires rejecting that upon which a stand must be taken in order to do the rejecting.

Since knowledge reveals things to be different from each other and different from the self, and since it is acknowledged that both selves and things depend upon *Brahman* for their existence, Madhva maintains eternal difference between *Brahman*, selves, and things. Unlike Ramanuja, these differences are not accounted for in terms of the qualifications of *Brahman*, thereby maintaining the unity of reality, but are regarded as different substances. But if these are maintained to be different substances it is hard to see how things and selves—as ultimate substances —could be dependent upon a third substance, for a substance is complete in itself and independent. In fact, it is difficult to see why a third substance would be postulated as the ultimate reality. Of course, Madhva is reluctant to give up the dependency of selves upon *Brahman*, for then all traditional teachings about salvation must be given up. And if he gives up not only dependency, but also *Brahman* as the ultimate reality, he has given up the whole tradition!

These three schools of Vedanta represent the three basic ways of looking at the relations between the world and *Brahman*, and thus constitute the three basic interpretations of the Upanishads. According to Shamkara, *Brahman* alone is real, the world being mere appearance. Ramanuja claims that the world is real, but is not different from *Brahman*, since *Brahman* is the unity of differences that constitute the world. Madhva argues that the world and *Brahman* are eternally distinct. Reality is of the dual nature of *Brahman* plus the world, with *Brahman* always remaining distinct and different from the world of selves and things.

CHAPTER 8

CONCLUDING REMARKS

A<small>T</small> the beginning of this discussion of the Hindu systems it was said that a dominant characteristic of Indian philosophical thought was its practical character. This practical character was said to derive from the basic aim of philosophical activity which was to overcome suffering. Having followed the claims and arguments of the different philosophical schools and having noticed the heavy emphasis on logical consistency the reader may at this stage be skeptical of that original claim. However, the requirement of logical consistency does not rule out practicality. It might rule out every whim and fancy containing within itself the seeds of its own self-contradiction, but it does not rule out sound practice. Every one of the philosophical schools considered begins by observing that knowledge (of man and the universe) is required in the effort to improve life.

The Nyaya system, though primarily concerned with an analysis of the means of valid knowledge, begins by noting, in the first *Sutra* of Gautama, that supreme happiness follows upon the attainment of true knowledge of the various categories. Right knowledge will bring about the cessation of pain and death. The Vaisheshika system concentrates on analyzing the kinds of things that exist, but the *Sutras* of Kanada begin with the observation: "Now, therefore, we shall explain *dharma* (righteousness). *Dharma* (is) that from which (results) the accomplishment of exaltation and the supreme good." The Samkhya system, which provides an analysis of causality and a theory of the evolution of the world from a first cause, has for its first *Sutra* the statement: "From torment by the three-fold misery arises the inquiry into the means of terminating it: . . ." Yoga, concerned to show the true nature of the Self and to explain the functioning of the empirical self, has for its aim complete liberation. The concluding *Sutra* of Patanjali is: "Absolute freedom comes when the qualities, becoming devoid of the object of the *purusha* [Self], become latent; or the power of consciousness becomes established in its own nature." The Mimamsa *Sutras*, concerned to show the validity of the Veda, begins as follows: "Next, therefore, comes the enquiry into *dharma* (duty). *Dharma* is that which is indicated by means of the Veda as conducive to the highest good." Shamkara, in his commentary on the first statement in the *Brahma-Sutra*, observes that the enquiry into *Brahman* has for its fruit eternal bliss.

But not just any theory of the nature of man and the universe counts as right knowledge. And to find out which theories are inadequate it is useful to measure them against the yardstick of logic, which means, ultimately, against self-contradiction. It may be that reality, in its foundations, is beyond the reach of the logical net and that in the last analysis logic is irrelevant. But from the viewpoint of ordinary knowledge, expressible in conceptual and linguistic terms, it is nonsensical to say that logic is irrelevant. Logic is a basic presupposition of language and conceptual thought, and to dispense with it is quite impossible. What is self-contradictory cannot be known and—from the conceptual point of view (the only point of view from which self-contradiction is possible)—cannot exist. Philosophy is, at least in part, a conceptual matter, and insofar as it is a conceptual matter, respect for the principle of non-contradiction is an absolutely necessary condition of philosophical activity. Consequently, it is necessary to test theories of man and the universe against the measure of logic. What does not measure up must fall into the refuse pit of nonsense and self-contradictions. But, of course, measuring up to the yardstick of logic and being logically consistent does not guarantee the truth of the theory. For this it is necessary to go beyond the linguistic and logical to direct and immediate experience. Shamkara, for example, could regard his essential philosophical task as showing that claims about the nature of man and reality in opposition to the conclusions of the Upanishads were self-contradictory. After all, the claims of the Upanishads were the result of direct and immediate experience of man and reality and therefore could not be wrong.

It is not difficult to see how systems of thought can be practical insofar as they aim at eliminating suffering, and also be logically subtle and abstract. The various systems of philosophy can be seen as critical attempts to remove error from theories about the nature of man and the world by showing that the implications and assumptions of those theories lead to nonsense and self-contradiction. This is essentially an activity of logic and argument, though it is undertaken in order to secure a practical aim. This combination of respect for logic and respect for the testament of immediate experience has resulted in finding a place in philosophical theories for the practical and the ideal, the material and the spiritual. It would be a curious phenomenon for a culture to have no skeptics and materialists at all, but in India the view that knowledge and understanding is impossible, that there is nothing in existence except material things, and that the highest aim in life is pleasure, was considered so unsatisfactory that, though it was espoused by various individuals, it did not generate enough support to develop into one of the philosophical systems. The difficulty with materialism as a philosophy is that it ignores the demands of both logic and immediate experience. Consequently, the ground for this kind of philosophizing in India proved to be stony and barren.

The two most significant Indian philosophers in our time, Radhakrishnan and Aurobindo, looked to the ancient traditions for wisdom to guide modern man. Each emphasized the need for philosophy to encompass both logic and experience, the material and the spiritual.

RADHAKRISHNAN

Sarvepalli Radhakrishnan, the recent president of India, who had written scores of philosophical articles and dozens of philosophical books, was a champion and interpreter of the Shamkara school of Vedanta. He agrees with Shamkara that the empirical is not the ultimate reality, but he is aware that just as the criteria of logic and experience demand that philosophy admit an ultimate reality, so also do they require inclusion of the empirical and practical. For him there is no inconsistency in a philosopher actively participating in social and political affairs, for these are appearances of *Brahman*, and thus are means to be utilized in the effort to achieve the experience of the ultimate reality.

Recognizing that the experience of ultimate reality—*Atman*-realization—is the goal of human life, and seeing religion as the chief vehicle employed in man's quest for the absolute ground of all reality, Radhakrishnan's main philosophical problem consisted in working out a satisfactory philosophy of religion. The task of philosophy of religion is to develop a theory of the nature of things in the world, selves, and the ultimate ground of things and selves, that will exhibit the inter-relations between these three realities. This theory must account for the facts of religious experience and at the same time accommodate reason, for no attempt at explanation which is self-contradictory can be satisfactory. Consistency may not be enough, but it is a minimal necessity for any philosophy. Granted rational consistency, the theory must have its basis in religious experience itself. The experience and statements of religious persons must be explained—not repudiated or ignored—by a philosophy of religion.

Radhakrishnan's view of religion allows that theology, dogma, ritual, and various institutions are the external trappings of religion, not its essence. The essence of religion is the attempt to discover the ideal possibilities of human life. This quest is personal and necessarily involves the whole person. Experience which involves merely an aspect of a person, such as feeling, thinking, or volition, is not religious. What distinguishes religious experience from aesthetics, science, philosophy, and morals is that these are guided primarily by feeling, reason, and volition, respectively. Religion includes feeling, reason, and volition, but it goes beyond them to the innermost center of the person to the very source of these aspects of humanity, integrating these faculties and directing them from the wholeness that is their source, using it to transform the life of the person into something complete and whole.

This inner self which is the very source of the various limited aspects and faculties of man is referred to as Spirit, and the substance and essence of religion is experience of the life of the Spirit—not just as it is in man, or as it is in the world, but Spirit as it joins together self and other in a whole that is complete and perfect in itself, though utterly inexpressible. But though the experience itself is deeply inner and inexpressible there are clues to its character, for this experience takes form in the manifestations of spiritual encounter which constitutes the essence of all religious life, and as such is attended by ritual, dogma, interpretation, and the varying institutions which provide forms that allow the expression of contact with the Spirit in an intelligible and understandable way, and which serve to guide other persons to the direct experience of spiritual encounter.

These forms of religion may all change as culture and civilization change. In fact, as the forms of culture and civilization change, the forms of religion must change if they are to adequately manifest the immediate experience of spiritual encounter. Radhakrishnan says: "Theory, speculation, dogma, change from time to time as the facts become better understood. *Their value is acquired from their adequacy to experience.* When forms dissolve and the interpretations are doubted, it is a call to get back to the experience itself and reformulate its content in more suitable terms."[1]

Although a philosopher of religion could hardly proceed except by giving primacy to religious experience—that is, by considering the data of religious experience to be the basic material out of which one fashions a theory of religion—to do so is exceedingly complicated because of the great difficulty in describing religious experience. Religious experience is unlike the ordinary experience that provides the foundations for thinking and talking about ourselves and the reality around us. Our ordinary experience presupposes that the something experienced is always distinct from the experiencer; the subject is never the object, and vice versa. A person sees a stone or hears a bird; a person's reason is aware of a certain feeling consequent upon encountering a work of art, or one's feeling is aware of one's reason at work. In these cases we maintain the distinction between subject and object. But in religious experience the whole person is involved: there is nothing outside of the person, so the experience is radically different from ordinary experience. Because of this radical difference the distinctions that are usually made or presupposed between subject and object, between one faculty and another, are left behind and the claim is made that in religious experience the subject and object merge, becoming one, and the whole person, rather than just certain aspects of his being, is involved in the experience. But when the subject-object distinction is overcome all ordinary distinctions presupposed by thought are also left behind. Past, present, and future become so many abstractions that have no reality—there is only the *Now*, perfectly dimensionless. And there is no room for various locations in space; there is only the *Here*, without location.

Radhakrishnan explains religious experience as follows:

> It is a type of experience which is not clearly differentiated into a subject-object state, an integral, undivided consciousness in which not merely this or that side of man's nature but his whole being seems to find itself. It is a condition of consciousness in which feelings are fused, ideas melt into one another, boundaries broken and ordinary distinctions transcended. Past and present fade away in a sense of timeless being. Consciousness and being are

[1] *An Idealist View of Life*, Ch. 3 (London: George Allen & Unwin Ltd., 1929), and reprinted in *A Source Book in Indian Philosophy*, ed. by Radhakrishnan and Moore (Princeton: Princeton University Press, 1957), p. 616. Italics added.

there not different from each other. All being is consciousness and all consciousness being. Thought and reality coalesce and a creative merging of subject and object results. Life grows conscious of its incredible depths. In this fullness of felt life and freedom, the distinction of the knower and the known disappears. The privacy of the individual self is broken and invaded by a universal self which the individual feels as his own.[2]

Granted this view of religion and religious experience, what kind of theory of selves, things, and ultimate reality will serve to adequately accomodate, in a rationally acceptable way, the facts of religion? If the ultimate reality—*Brahman*—is taken to be alone real it is difficult to see how religion is possible, for the self struggling to realize *Brahman* would have to be regarded as unreal. And without a self struggling to achieve ultimate reality there can be no religion. On the other hand, if selves and *Brahman* are taken to be distinct and different realities, it is difficult to to see how the self could ever successfully identify itself with *Brahman*, without self-repudiation or self-annihilation.

Radhakrishnan's solution to this dilemma is to interpret *Brahman* not as static but as dynamic being. *Brahman* is the absolute reality, providing the ground of all existence and giving the universe unity. All things are united in *Brahman* which is the source and ground of all being. As the source and ground of all being *Brahman* is ever active, by its function expressing its substantial nature. It is this functioning of *Brahman*, which is not different from its existence, that manifests itself in the various things and processes that make up the universe of selves and things. Thus, things and selves are not unreal, for they are the expression of *Brahman's* functions. But as expressions of *Brahman* they are not totally distinct and separate from *Brahman* either. This explanation provides for distinctions between individual things and selves, for the functions of *Brahman* are dynamic, ever new. Since no one of *Brahman's* functions (nor aspect of the functioning of *Brahman*) totally exhausts the nature of *Brahman*, any given expression of *Brahman's* function lacks the total reality of *Brahman* wherein all functions and all expressions of those functions are united.

Proceeding with this interpretation of *Brahman*, Radhakrishnan goes on to regard man as the locus where *Brahman*, as absolute Spirit, and the world, as the functioning of this absolute Spirit, come together, for the person combines Spirit with matter. He makes this point by distinguishing between the empirical or lower self and the higher or spiritual self, which in its purity is one with the absolute Spirit. The

---

[2] *Idealist View of Life*, Ch. 3, reprinted in *Source Book in Indian Philosophy*, p. 618.

essence of the religious quest is now interpreted to be the lower self struggling to return to its source in the higher self. It is the movement toward transformation of self—never the annihilation or repudiation of self—in identification with its source, *Atman-Brahman*.

In explaining the relations between selves and things and both of these to *Brahman*, Radhakrishnan abandons the static substance view of reality according to which the world is thought to be made up of a great many independent beings or substances, each attended to by a greater or lesser number of characteristics or qualities. Instead, he views the world as constituted by processes. The structure of reality is not due to the relations qualities have to their substances, but to the inner structure of the activities making up reality. Thus, the world is essentially dynamic with all of the various processes interconnected. The various processes can be distinguished from each other according to the structure of their functioning. In this way, for example, living "things" can be distinguished from non-living, conscious from non-conscious, etc. They are similar in that they are of the nature of process, being essentially activities, but they differ according to the structure of the activities involved.

In explanation of the diverse structures found in the processes corresponding to the various gradations of existence, Radhakrishnan postulates unceasing activity of the absolute Spirit. Spirit is the source and ground of all the various grades of existence encountered on the empirical level. But these various distinctions do not imply absolute differences; they merely serve to mark out modes of spiritual activity. Even matter, finally, is spiritual activity. It is merely a different mode of the Spirit than consciousness or life. But regardless of the mode of manifestation, Spirit remains Spirit, and insofar as it is Spirit there is no denial of its reality. The various grades of matter and life are real and are expressions of *Brahman*, the absolute Spirit. But no one mode in itself is the totality of *Brahman*, and cannot be equated with the absolute reality.

Against this background, the main purpose of religion is to help a person realize that he can rise above the limits imposed by matter or life or consciousness to the realization that in his innermost being he is identical with the absolute Spirit and is in truth completely free from the limitations inherent in identification with simply one particular mode or function of Spirit. This realization is possible only in terms of practical activity; an activity of being rather than knowledge. It is the spiritual realization of Uddalaka's teaching to his son, Shvetaketu, "Thou art that [*Brahman*]."

Sri Aurobindo, the great philosopher-yogi of Pondicherry, studied and commented upon the ancient texts of the Veda and, in the early part of this century, was the leader of the movement for Indian independence. Emphasizing the ultimate spirituality of man, Sri Aurobindo recognized as the great problem of our times the transformation of the present lowly and ignorant man into the great spiritual being that he is potentially. To this end he worked out a theory of social organization not radically different from the ideals contained in the theories of *purusharthas*, *varnas*, and *ashramas*. His major works, *The Life Divine*, and *Synthesis of Yoga*, are attempts to show the type of life man can achieve by a total and comprehensive discipline, or *yoga*. The "life divine" is, of course, the life lived in full realization of *Brahman*, and the *yoga* is the means to this life. Sri Aurobindo emphasizes that the *yoga* must be practiced by present man in his present condition as a means to changing this condition, for therein lies the secret of the transformation into the Ideal Man.

Aurobindo's conception of the task of philosophy and the nature of reality is indicated in the following statement:

> The problem of thought therefore is to find out the right idea and the right way of harmony; to restate the ancient and eternal spiritual truth of the Self, so that it shall re-embrace, permeate and dominate the mental and physical life; to develop the most profound and vital methods of psychological self-discipline and self-development so that the mental and psychical life of man may express the spiritual life of man through the utmost possible expansion of its own richness, power and complexity; and to seek for the means and motives by which his external life, his society and his institutions may remould themselves progressively in the truth of the spirit and develop towards the utmost possible harmony of individual freedom and social unity.[3]

According to this view, the reality constituted by things and selves is the manifested power of the spirit. Spirit provides the unity of reality, and the manifested power of spirit provides the manifoldness of the universe. The various levels of existence—matter, life, mental life, supramental life—are distinguished insofar as the fullness of spirit emerges through these manifestations of its powers.

The main problem for Aurobindo is that of explaining how all the many things experienced—both at the conscious level of the empirical

[3] *Arya*, July 15, 1918, pp. 764-5; reprinted in *Source Book in Indian Philosophy*, p. 577.

and the rational, and at the supra-conscious level of mystic intuition—came to be, and why they are different. His solution is to explain that the absolute existence which makes it possible for anything whatsoever to exist is itself pure existence, complete and perfect. This existence—*Brahman*—for no reason whatever, simply out of the sheer exuberance of its being, manifests its *maya*, or power, in the manner of sport or play. The manifestations of this power constitute the universe of existing things. The universe exists therefore, as the play of pure existence. But it is not simply capricious, for this play is directed by the Being-Consciousness-Joy (*sat-chit-ananda*) that constitutes the absolute Spirit of the universe. The evolution of the universe as a whole and of particular species within the universe is seen as the returning of the manifested powers of *Brahman* to their source. As these powers move toward their source, evolution moves to higher and higher forms of life and consciousness.

According to this explanation, the differences between levels of reality are due to the evolution of spirit. As the spirit evolves higher life-forms come into existence. But this is not the evolution of one *kind* of thing to another *kind* of thing, such as matter becoming spirit. Rather, it is the evolution of one thing—Spirit—from its many lower forms and manifestations to its higher forms, the aim being to reach the fullness of being, consciousness, and joy that constitutes Spirit. The usual problems attending evolutionary accounts of existence, the problem of blind matter groping impossibly to evolve beyond itself, into something quite other than itself, and the problem of blind matter being lifted beyond itself by some other reality without any effort on its own part, do not arise for Aurobindo. According to his explanation the lower is ever evolving into the higher, but these are not absolutely different. The higher is making itself felt in the lower, and the lower is struggling to express itself according to the higher laws of the spirit within, and this is the mutual effort that constitutes the play of *Brahman* manifesting itself through its powers, but always remaining *Brahman*.

Seeing evolution as involving the mutual activity of both the lower and higher forms of Spirit has important consequences for the life of man, for it means not only that it is possible for man to evolve to a higher kind of being than he now is, but also that he can, at least in part, direct this evolution. The aim of man's existence—in its self-consciousness higher than the existence of matter and non-conscious life-forms—is not to remain at its present level, but to transcend itself, moving on to higher levels of existence just as previously lower levels of existence moved up to the level of human existence. This is possible, Aurobindo points out,

> for the evolution proceeded in past by the upsurging, at each critical state, of a concealed power from its evolution in the inconscient, but also by a descent from above, from its own plane, of that power already self-realized in its own higher natural province. . . .[4]

How is man to direct his own evolution? Aurobindo's answer is that he must practice self-discipline (*yoga*) that is all inclusive, not ignoring any part of his being, and integrating the various aspects and faculties of his being, so that the lower comes under the control and direction of the higher, allowing man to gradually come to live according to the laws of the spirit dwelling within him, at the very center of his being. This requires, among other things, the material and social conditions that will enable man in his present state to successfully reach beyond himself, elevating his existence until it becomes the "Life Divine."

In his social philosophy, Aurobindo argued that justice and freedom are to be provided for and guaranteed by society as necessary conditions for the higher evolution of man. His view of the object of all society is:

> first to provide the conditions of life and growth by which individual Man— not isolated men according to their capacity—and the race through the growth of its individuals, may travel towards its divine perfection. It must be secondly, as mankind generally more and more grows near to some figure of it—for the cycles are many and each cycle has its own figure of the Divine in man—to express in the general life of mankind, the light, the power, the beauty, the harmony, the joy of the Self that has been attained and that pours itself out in a freer and nobler humanity.[5]

Clearly, in both Radhakrishnan and Aurobindo, as in the Vedas and Upanishads, the aim of philosophical activity is to make possible the realization of the Self that dwells within all beings.

[4] *Life Divine*, p. 859, reprinted in *Source Book in Indian Philosophy*, p. 604.
[5] *The Human Cycle* (Pondicherry: Sri Aurobindo Ashram, 1962), pp. 83–84.

PART TWO

Buddhist Philosophies

Serene Buddha. *The Indian Museum, Calcutta*

CHAPTER 9

BUDDHISM AND SUFFERING: BASIC TEACHINGS

No ONE who has lived in the world can be untouched by human suffering. Either in his own life or in the lives of those with whom he comes in contact there has entered injury, illness, misery, anxiety, death, or some other form of unwholesomeness and evil. Human existence is far from perfect. Even the most fortunate, the happiest people in the world have to admit a measure of unhappiness. Most people, in fact, recognize that life is not perfect. Either they simply shrug their shoulders and exclaim, "That is the way life is," or else they set about trying to reduce the imperfections in life. Ordinarily, when the latter attitude is adopted, effort is directed toward reducing poverty by increasing available wealth, reducing illness and premature deaths by extending sanitation or by promoting the practice of medicine, etc. But seldom is there a person who carefully and systematically directs his attention to the fundamental *causes* of suffering and the ways for the elimination of these causes. Gautama Siddhartha, the Buddha, was such a person, and the religious philosophy that issued from his teachings presents a systematic analysis of the nature and causes of suffering and provides a manifold of means for the overcoming of suffering.

Buddhism as a *Way of Wisdom* taught and practiced for the sake of improving the quality of life by removing the sources of suffering is, in its details, a complicated phenomenon incorporating a great many historical changes, but in its essence, as taught by the Buddha, it is a relatively simple teaching to grasp. One must hasten to point out, however, that understanding the outlines of a Way of Wisdom is quite different from following that Way. Following the Way is difficult. It is, indeed, so difficult that it has not yet been mastered by the discipline and self-control of the majority of mankind. Consequently, it should be kept in mind that there is all the difference in the world between *following* the Way and *talking* about following the Way. To follow the Way there is no substitute for practice. In fact, without practicing the Way, it is unlikely that one will even achieve a satisfactory intellectual understanding of what the Way is. Nevertheless, it is possible to achieve considerable knowledge about Buddhism by studying and analyzing the main features that constitute this Way of life.

THE BUDDHA

According to widely accepted legends concerning the life of the historical Buddha, Gautama received the immediate impetus for meditation and concentration on the problem of suffering by dramatic encounters with sickness, old age, death, and renunciation. His father, the ruler of a prosperous principality, had been told that if his son became acquainted with the evils of the world he would renounce his father's kingdom and become a great ascetic and teacher of men. Not wanting to lose his son in this way, the father resolved that everything would be done to seclude him from the cruel world. Accordingly the king provided him with all of the wealth and pleasures of life available to man—palaces, young and comely servants, entertainers, a beautiful wife—to protect him from experiencing the suffering of the world. The father was determined that Gautama should remain ignorant of the sorrows that beset mankind.

But one day, when the young Gautama was out riding in his chariot, the young lord saw an old man,

> as bent as a roof gable, decrepit, leaning on a staff, tottering as he walked, afflicted and long past his prime.[1]

Upon seeing him Gautama asked his charioteer why that man was not like the other men. The driver informed him that the man was old,

[1] This account of Gautama's encounter with suffering is found in *Digha Nikaya*, XIV. The quotations are taken from *Buddhism: A Religion of Infinite Compassion*, ed. by Clarence H. Hamilton (Indianapolis: Bobbs-Merrill, c. 1952), pp. 6–10.

but this word Gautama did not understand. He had no experience with old age. The driver explained that this man was nearly finished, he was soon to die. As understanding began to trouble his spirit, the young lord asked,

> "But then, good charioteer, am I too subject to old age, one who has not got passed old age?"

The answer horrified Gautama; and from this time he began to think about the suffering of old age:

> "You, my lord, and we too, we all are of a kind to grow old; we have not got past old age."

Many days after this, he was once again setting out for the park, when Gautama encountered "a sick man, suffering and very ill, fallen and weltering in his own water, by some being lifted up, by others being dressed."

Upon seeing this, Gautama asked his charioteer what this man had done that he was not like other men. The driver explained that the man was ill, and that this meant that he was not far from being finished, that he might not recover. Gautama asked again,

> "But am I too then, good charioteer, subject to fall ill; have I not got out of the reach of illness?"

The answer that sent him back to his palace meditating on illness was,

> "You my lord, and we too, we all are subject to fall ill; we have not got beyond the reach of illness."

Many days later, when Gautama was again driving to the park, he saw "a great concourse of people clad in garments of different colors constructing a funeral pyre. And seeing this, he asked his charioteer, 'Why now are all those people come together in garments of different colors and making that pile?'"

Upon being told that this was because someone had died, Gautama demanded to view the corpse to discover what this thing called "death" was all about. When he had been told about death, he asked, as before,

> "But am I too then subject to death, have I not got beyond reach of death? Will neither the *raja*, [king] nor *ranee*, [queen] nor any other of my kin see me more, or shall I again see them?"

And once more the answer was,

> "You my lord, and we too, we all are subject to death; we have not passed beyond the reach of death."

Many days after seeing the dead man, Gautama was once again driving to the park. On the way he saw a shaven-headed man, a recluse, wearing the yellow robe. Upon learning from the driver that this recluse is one who is said to have "gone forth," Guatama was curious to learn what this meant. Approaching the recluse, he asked,

> "You, master, what have you done that your head is not as other men's heads, nor your clothes as those of other men?" "I, my lord, am one who has gone forth." "What, master, does that mean?" "It means, my lord, being thorough in the religious life, thorough in the peaceful life, thorough in good actions, thorough in meritorious conduct, thorough in harmlessness, thorough in kindness to all creatures."

Upon hearing this the lord Gautama bade his charioteer return him to his palace, saying,

> "But I will even here cut off my hair, and don the yellow robe, and go forth from the house into the homeless state."

Having been thus duly impressed with the *fact* of suffering, Gautama meditated on that *fact*, concentrating on discovering a way to the cessation of all suffering. After years of effort and discipline, including the most severe forms of asceticism, Gautama resolved that neither the extreme of over-indulgence in pleasures nor the extreme of excessive asceticism was conducive to extinguishing suffering. Adopting then a middle path between these extremes, Gautama, self-disciplined and purified, concentrated all of his energies on discovering the causes of suffering. As he concentrated the causes of suffering were revealed, and Gautama Siddhartha became the Buddha—the Enlightened One. Enlightenment as to the causes and the cessation of suffering were now his.

THE FOUR NOBLE TRUTHS

The content of this enlightenment constitutes the basic message of Buddhism. This message, in simplest form, consists in the Four Noble Truths and the Noble Eightfold Path. These truths are: (1) There is suffering; (2) Suffering is caused; (3) Suffering can be extinguished by eliminating the causes of suffering; (4) The way to extinguish the causes of suffering is to follow the Middle Way constituted by the Noble Eightfold path.

This teaching constituted the Buddha's first sermon after his enlightenment, delivered in the Deer Park at Benares. It was the teaching of the middle path,

> which leads to insight, which leads to wisdom; which conduces to calm, to knowledge, to perfect enlightenment, to Nibbāna [Nirvāna].

Concerning the First Noble Truth Gautama taught as follows:

> This, monks, is the Noble Truth of Suffering; birth is suffering; decay is suffering; illness is suffering; death is suffering; presence of objects we hate is suffering; separation from objects we love is suffering; not to obtain what we desire is suffering. In brief, the five aggregates which spring from grasping, they are painful.

Explaining the Second Noble Truth, Gautama taught that suffering

> originates in that craving which causes the renewals of becomings, is accompanied by sensual delight, and seeks satisfaction now here, now there; that is to say, craving for pleasures, craving for becoming, craving for not becoming.

Taking up the Third Noble Truth, he explained as follows:

> This, monks, is the Noble Truth concerning the Cessation of Suffering; verily, it is passionless, cessation without remainder of this very craving; the laying aside of, the giving up, the being free from, the harboring no longer of, this craving.

Coming now to the Fourth Noble Truth concerning the Path which leads to the cessation of suffering, he taught:

> It is this Noble Eightfold Path, that is to say, right views, right intent, right speech, right conduct, right means of livelihood, right endeavor, right mindfulness, and right meditation."

Having thus taught the essential truths about the fact of suffering, the Buddha concluded his first sermon by saying:

> This Noble Truth concerning Suffering I have understood. Thus, monks, in things which formerly had not been heard of have I obtained insight, knowledge, understanding, widsom and intuition.[2]

The First Truth, concerned with the existence of suffering, lists seven areas of suffering familiar to everyone. But these seven areas should not be taken as a definition of suffering; they are simply examples of suffering, examples obvious to anyone who has lived in the world. Suffering goes much deeper than those examples. It must be recognized that the

[2] The foregoing account is taken from Hamilton, *op. cit.* p. 29.

pleasures of one person are often the pains of another. And the pains of others are disturbing to one's own contentment. Thus, though it would seem that the wealthy captain of industry who has all of the goods of society at his disposal should be happy, this may not be the case. If he is truly a sensitive human being, the poverty of those workers in industry which is the direct counterpart of the captain's wealth might very well be the bitter dressing spoiling the enjoyment of all his wealth. To be aware that one's pleasures come at another person's expense is not to bring suffering only to the other; it is also to bring suffering to oneself.

In addition, even in those cases where one's pleasures are not tied to the sufferings of anyone else, they still are fraught with suffering. The pleasures that one enjoys bring with them an attachment to the objects and activities enjoyed. The anxiety resulting from the possibility of separation from the objects or activities in question is a hidden cancer in the pleasures, and thus a source of suffering.

Another feature of the suffering underlying the various pleasures of life concerns the fact that they are not only self-perpetuating, but that they are self-accelerating. Deriving pleasure from an activity or object does not diminish the drive for that pleasure, but rather serves to strengthen the drive. One becomes more closely tied to the conditions that provide pleasure as he derives more pleasure from his activities. The more pleasures one achieves the more he seeks. This cycle goes on unendingly, catching one up in its increasing tempo, with seemingly no escape. Granted that the achievement of pleasure does not bring complete happiness and contentment, but rather leaves one even more dissatisfied and unhappy, it appears that one is being led to even greater unhappiness by grasping at the pleasures of life.

This last point is tied in with a basic assumption of Buddhism which holds that the drive for pleasure is too shallow and insignificant to fulfill a person and bring true happiness. In the *Dhammapada* it is said, "One is the path that leads to worldly gain; and quite another that leads to *Nibbana*."[3] If this is the case, then the pleasures that one finds in the world, being shallow, are really factors producing unhappiness. In recognition of this, the observation in the *Dhammapada* noted just above, is followed by the advice:

> Understanding this, let not the Bhikku, the disciple of the Awakened One, delight in worldly honour but develop detachment instead.[4]

[3] *Dhammapada*, V. 75, trans. by Acharya Buddharakhita Thera (Bangalore, India: Buddha Vaccna Trust, 1966).
[4] *Ibid.*

Thus, not only do those seven examples given by the Buddha in his first sermon belong to suffering, but even those examples that would be given of the "good" side of existence are, at bottom, only disguised suffering. The basic illness that is responsible for suffering goes deeper than the examples given; it is the grasping of the aggregates or constituents of self.

The Second Noble Truth is the truth that suffering originates in craving. In one sense, suffering is caused by craving what one cannot have or craving to avoid what cannot be avoided. Thus, craving money when one is poor leads to suffering; craving health when one is ill leads to suffering; craving immortality in the face of the inevitability of death leads to suffering; craving extinction faced with the continuity of the stuff of which life is made leads to suffering, etc. But there is a deeper sense of craving. This is craving in the sense of a *blind compulsion to be or have a self.*

If the obvious forms of suffering are analyzed it will be seen that there are two basic factors involved. First, there is what might be called the existence of certain objective factors in the world. There is the fact that Jones has no money, that Smith's child just died, or that Singh's leg was cut off. But these objective facts in the world do not of themselves involve suffering. After all, who suffers when a boulder is split in two? Who suffers when a branch is cut from the tree? Who suffers when a young oak is broken in the wind? Probably no one would ever think of ascribing suffering to the boulder, or the trunk of the tree, or the "parent" oak. But probably everyone would attribute suffering to Jones, Smith, and Singh. The difference between these cases is obvious. Trees and boulders do not have selves; hence there is no one to suffer. But Jones, Smith, and Singh have, each of them, a self. And this self is aware of the suffering caused it by objective factors in the world. We think it makes sense for Jones, or Smith, or Singh to say, "I have lost my money, or child, or leg," but it does not make sense to think of the tree or boulder as saying, "I lost my part, or branch, or child." If this latter did make sense we should very well impute suffering to boulders and trees as well as to persons.

This points to the second factor involved in suffering; the existence of a self. There is no suffering until objective factors in the world are related to a self. When these objective factors are related to a self this self may crave them or crave to avoid them. And when what is craved is not had there is suffering.

But what is this self which constitutes the second basic factor involved in suffering? And does it make sense to attribute a self to a person?

What is this "I" to which reference is made when a person claims, "I have lost my child?" The truth of the origin of suffering is that *it is the craving of a self that gives rise to suffering*. Blindly, a person craves a self that though separate is attached to the factors constituting the person. This craving leads to the invention and projection of a self. This self, being attached to the factors making up a person, suffers when the identification is threatened by changes in the factors to which it is attached, whether these be the factors of that person, other persons, or other objects and activities in the world.

Analysis of a person reveals the existence of (1) the activities constituting what we call the bodily, or physical, self; (2) activities of sensing; (3) activities of perceiving; (4) impulses to action; and (5) activities of consciousness. But in addition to these five groups of activities nothing more is to be found. The self, as that to which the groups of activities belong, is a fiction, a fiction created by ignorant craving. And it is the craving for this fictitious self that underlies all suffering.

The third Noble Truth, that suffering can be extinguished, follows upon analysis of the causes of suffering. If selfish craving is the cause of suffering, then the cessation of suffering lies in the extinction of that craving. This is precisely what the Buddha recommended. In fact, the very goal of the Buddhist—*Nirvana*—has the meaning "be blown out." What is blown out—like a lamp—or extinguished, is selfish craving. When selfish craving is extinguished, suffering is pulled up by the root. Thus, the truth of the cessation of suffering is the truth that the extinction of craving will bring about the cessation of suffering.

It is a long way, however, from the recognition of what will bring about the cessation of suffering to the actual accomplishment of that cessation. And the Buddha, good physician that he was, did not stop with an analysis and diagnosis of the malady nor with the recognition of what was required for cure, but he prescribed a method of treatment which would destroy the illness. The prescription constitutes the Fourth Noble Truth, which teaches the famous "Middle Way" of Buddhism.

THE NOBLE EIGHTFOLD PATH

This Middle Way, which sums up the way of life that characterizes Buddhism as a practical philosophy, is built upon the eight principles constituting the Fourth Noble Truth. These principles are as follows:

1. Right views (*Samma ditthi*)
2. Right resolution (*Samma sankappa*)
3. Right speech (*Samma vaca*)
4. Right action (*Samma kammanta*)
5. Right livelihood (*Samma ajiva*)
6. Right effort (*Samma vayama*)
7. Right mindfulness (*Samma sati*)
8. Right concentration (*Samma samadhi*)

The various actions of life prompted by and expressing these eight principles should proceed more or less simultaneously, the aim being to achieve a completely integrated life of the highest order. The relationships between actions of life and the principles that underlie these actions can be seen by considering the three axioms of Ethical Conduct, Mental Discipline, and Wisdom, which underlie all principles and actions. The axiom of Ethical Conduct includes right speech, right action, and right livelihood. The axiom of Discipline includes right effort, right mindfulness, and right concentration. The axiom of Wisdom includes right views, and right resolution. The purpose of Ethical Conduct is to check the inflow of additional cravings. Concentration aims at destroying the already present cravings, and Wisdom is prescribed for living a sufferingless existence.

Understanding ourselves and the universe in which we live, action will be based upon a universal love and compassion. Accordingly, Ethical Conduct is based on love and compassion and springs from wisdom, or an enlightened mind. But to achieve wisdom and to cultivate love and compassion, discipline of the self is required. Thus, Ethical Conduct, Discipline, and Wisdom are the three axioms of the Good Life.

Wisdom includes both the correct understanding of things as they are and the resolution to act in accord with this understanding. Having right views consists in seeing things as they are. This includes, on a lower level, intellectual understanding of things. But intellectual knowledge takes place within a system, or network, of concepts and principles which reflect necessarily limited perspectives as underlying assumptions. Accordingly, intellectual knowledge is conditioned by the concepts and principles of the system and its truth is relative to the truth of the system in which it takes place. Consequently, intellectual knowledge is considered a lower kind of understanding than the understanding that results from seeing things just as they are by a direct

Wheel of Becoming. *Information Service of India. Photograph courtesy of Professor Grace E. Cairns. Reprinted from* RELIGIONS OF THE WORLD *by McCasland, Cairns and Yu.*

penetration. This direct seeing is the complete illumination of things just as they are in themselves and not as limited by concepts and labels. It is this direct penetration of things that is properly called Wisdom. It reveals the relative and conditioned nature of all things and shows suffering to be caused by selfish grasping.

Wisdom reveals the nature of things and the causes of suffering, but does not stop there. It also expresses itself in the resolution to overcome suffering by leaving aside all selfish cravings. This involves the resolve to cultivate a love universal in depth and scope that reveals itself in compassion and non-hurting. Selfish desires, ill-will, hatred, and violence are entirely given up when Wisdom is achieved.

Wisdom cannot be achieved without discipline, and therefore one practices right effort, right mindfulness, and right concentration. Practicing right effort includes (1) preventing evil and unwholesome states of mind from arising, (2) getting rid of such evil and unwholesome states of mind that may already exist, (3) bringing about good and wholesome states of mind, and (4) developing and perfecting good and wholesome states of mind already present.

Right mindfulness consists in being aware of and attentive to one's activities. This includes the activities of (1) the body, (2) sensing and feeling, (3) perceiving, and (4) thinking and consciousness.

To be aware of and attentive to one's activities means understanding what these activities are, how they arise, how they disappear, how they are developed, controlled, gotten rid of, linked together, and what they are in themselves.

Right concentration is essentially a matter of recreating oneself as an enlightened person. Ignorance and enlightenment and suffering and happiness have their root in one's mental activities. It is said in the *Dhammapada*:

> mind precedes all unwholesome states and is their chief; they are all mind-wrought. If with an impure mind a person speaks or acts, misery follows him like the wheel that dogs the foot of the ox. Mind precedes all wholesome states and is their chief; they are all mindwrought. If with a pure mind a person speaks or acts, happiness follows him like his never-departing shadow.[5]

If this is the case, it is entirely plausible to concentrate on purifying one's mental activities as a means of achieving happiness.

Ordinarily four stages of concentration are distinguished. In the first stage one concentrates on getting rid of lust, ill-will, laziness, worry, anxiety, and doubt. These unwholesome mental activities are replaced by feelings of joy and happiness. In the second stage one concentrates on seeing through and getting beyond all mental activities,

[5] *Dhammapada*, 1, 2.

although retaining an awareness of joy and happiness. In the third stage one goes beyond the mental activity responsible for the feeling of joy, and achieves an equanimity pervaded by happiness. In the fourth and final stage of concentration there is complete equanimity and total awareness, beyond both happiness and unhappiness.

Ethical Conduct is both a reflection of, and a condition for, Wisdom and Discipline. Only a wise person can be good, and only a good person can be wise. And both wisdom and goodness require discipline. Accordingly, one begins and ends with all three simultaneously. To act ethically means to be correct in speech, action, and means of earning a living.

Right speech means generally to avoid all talk that will lead to unhappiness and to use speech to bring about happiness. Its negative application includes: (1) no lying; (2) no slander, or character assassination, or talk that might bring about hatred, jealousy, enmity, or discord among other; (3) no harsh or rude talk, no malicious talk, no impolite or abusive language; and (4) no idle or malicious gossip, or foolish chatter. Its positive application teaches that one should tell the truth, speak in a kindly and friendly way, use language meaningfully and usefully. This includes knowing the time and place for which certain talk is appropriate. This implies that sometimes one should maintain "noble silence."

Right action means avoiding killing or hurting, and precludes stealing, cheating, and immoral sexual activity. Positively, it means that one's actions should aim at promoting peace and happiness for others and respecting the well-being of all living beings.

Right livelihood extends the principle of right action to one's chosen profession throughout one's life. Accordingly, it precludes professions that would harm others, such as trading in firearms, liquors, drugs, poisons, killing, sexual procurement, etc. Only those means of earning a living which promote peace and well-being are in accord with this principle.

It is obvious how the axiom of Ethical Conduct rests upon compassion and love for others. But further, this compassion and love is the natural result of a recognition of the conditionedness and relativity of things. If no things have independent being (*svabhava*), then all are dependent upon each other. But this leaves no foothold for selfishness. Consequently, ignorance and selfishness must be replaced by wisdom and compassion.

CHAPTER 10

HISTORICAL CONSIDERATIONS

THE last chapter was concerned with the ethical-religious teachings which constitute the basic core of Buddhism as a way of life, and which probably reflect the main teachings of the historical Gautama. These teachings, aimed at inculcating the discipline and compassion that characterize the life and attitudes of a Buddhist, are not basically different today than they were twenty-five hundred years ago. On the other hand, the philosophies of Buddhism, which reflect the intellectual attempts to systematize the Buddhist way of life and to provide a rational basis for these ethical-religious teachings, have undergone considerable change and development.

The distinction between Buddhism as a way of life and Buddhist philosophies is the distinction between a way of living and the attempted justifications for that way. Thus, though Buddhists through the ages could agree on how to live, they could also disagree on the question of *why* they should live that way. If one is a Buddhist it follows that the Buddhist Way is accepted as the best way of life, for no person chooses an inferior way of life when he knows a superior way. But the question of justifying this acceptance is still open. Buddhism is sufficiently tough-minded and empirically inclined to rule out justification of the Middle Way by appeal to the fact that the Buddha said it was superior. In fact, appeal to faith as the only justification of the Middle Way was ruled out by the Buddha himself, as he encouraged his followers to examine the doctrine for themselves. Aside from an appeal to faith one could appeal

to the consequences of following the Noble Eightfold Path. If this kind
of life provided for goodness and happiness it could hardly be said to be
an inferior way of life. But granting this kind of justification, and granting
even that in a very important sense the results of a certain kind of life
are the only justification for that kind of life, it is possible to raise the
question of *why* that kind of life leads one out of suffering and provides
for peace and contentment. It is this question that serves as a starting
point for the *philosophies* of Buddhism. In the different answers to this
question the different philosophies of Buddhism are to be found.

By way of providing a basic orientation to the cultural phenomenon
of Buddhism and of seeing the historical relations between the religion
and the philosophies of Buddhism, this chapter will be devoted to a
brief historical account of the development of Buddhism.

PRE-BUDDHIST INDIA

The philosophical atmosphere of India in which Buddhism took its
place in the sixth and fifth centuries B.C. was dominated by three attitudes. First of all there was the attitude that ritual and sacrifice were the
principal effective means of securing whatever was desired. This attitude
was connected with the belief—probably thousands of years old already
by this time—that the creation and functioning of the world was due
to, and controlled by, the effects of sacrifices and rites. The second attitude, reflected in the Upanishads, regarded the observable world and
the observable self as mere "name and form." What was mere name
and form was only temporary and passing, possessing no abiding reality.
What was of abiding reality was the unchanging Self and the unchanging
Real. This attitude was connected with belief in *Atman* as the abiding
inner reality and *Brahman* as the abiding external reality, and with the
identity of *Atman* and *Brahman*. The third attitude was skeptical. It was
probably associated principally with the denial of the principal beliefs
underlying the other two attitudes. Judging by various criticisms of the
skeptical philosophy, it would appear that its adherents were the
materialists, who denied physical, moral, and sacrificial causality, and
who denied the possibility of knowledge.

The skeptical attitude obviously offered men no help in their struggles
to overcome suffering because it consisted chiefly in denying the possibilities suggested by the other attitudes. The sacrificial and ritualistic
attitude was at this time so involved with magic and taboos and with the
cult and corruption of the priests that it also failed to offer any real

hope in the perennial struggle against suffering. While the attitude reflected in the Upanishads was not as obviously helpless as the other two, its associations with philosophical abstractness and the underlying belief in the unchanging nature of the Real made it appear relatively unserviceable as the basis for a way to overcome or lessen suffering. Consequently, when the Buddha appeared teaching the causes of suffering and the way for ending suffering he found a ready acceptance.

BEGINNINGS OF BUDDHISM

Gautama Siddhartha was born about 563 B.C. at Kapilavastu, in what is today Nepal. Shielded by his father from the ugly scenes of suffering to be found all around, and happily married to a beautiful girl, Gautama led the easy pleasure-filled life of a prince of leisure until he was twenty-nine years old. Then, having been exposed to the sufferings of old age, sickness, and death, and having reflected that it would be well to discover some means for overcoming suffering, he left his palaces and family and took up the life of an ascetic. For six years he practiced the most extreme forms of self-discipline and self-denial. All to no avail. Finally, on the brink of death, he determined that the truth of the cause and cessation of suffering was not to be achieved by following the extreme of asceticism. Resolved now to follow a middle way between indulgence and asceticism, he soon achieved the enlightenment he was seeking. For the next forty years of his life the Buddha traveled around India teaching the Four Noble Truths and the Noble Eightfold Path. During these years of teaching the Buddha attracted many followers, and the Order of Buddhist Monks was already of good size when he died, in about the year 483 B.C.

The history of Buddhism after the death of the Buddha is a very complicated subject. Its early history can be viewed in terms of the changes in the Order prior to its split into two main movements, the more conservative movement characterized in the literature of the Theravada School, and the more liberal movement known as Mahayana. From that point on, Buddhist history is a matter of changes within each of these movements.[1]

[1] It must be noted that historical accounts of Buddhism are, for the most part, tentative because of insufficient evidence. The reader interested in the historical development of Buddhism would do well to turn to E. J. Thomas' *The History of Buddhist Thought* (London: Routledge & Kegan Paul Ltd., 2nd ed. 1951), which very carefully points out the kinds and amounts of evidence available for the various historical claims made. The reader is advised to construe this historical account as no more than "a likely account" of what took place historically.

The content of early Buddhism was contained not only in the actual teachings of the Buddha about suffering and its cessation, but also in the rules for living developed by the Order of Monks. In fact, it appears that clashes of opinion within the Order over interpretation of disciplinary rules occurred earlier than differences of opinion over the religious-philosophical teachings. Furthermore, these differences of opinion over disciplinary rules were considered more serious than other differences of opinion. So important was the matter of discipline that the early divisions in Buddhism and the formation of different schools were primarily the result of arguments over these matters. This is not surprising, of course, for after all the Buddha was concerned chiefly with getting rid of suffering. And getting rid of suffering is more closely tied up with how one lives than with theoretical teachings. Thus, the first three Buddhist councils were held for the purpose of discussing and resolving differences of opinion concerning interpretations of disciplinary rules.

The first council of Buddhists was held shortly after the death of the Buddha at Rajagaha. This council, attended by five hundred monks, resolved—in the face of a suggestion that since the Master was dead the monks could do as they chose—that the rules were to be kept as exactly as the Buddha prescribed, without either addition or deletion.

Probably about a hundred years after the first council there was a second council—the council of Vesali. Again the occasion of the council was a dispute over discipline. But this time it appears that the number of monks wanting a relaxation of the rules was relatively large. It was either at this second council or at the next council, that of Pataliputta, that the first main division took place. This division resulted in the Mahasanghika school being formed. It was followed by a series of further splits, both in the old order and within the Mahasanghika school. This development of differing schools can be pictured as in the diagram on the following page.

THERAVADA AND MAHAYANA

The exact teachings of each of these various schools, however, is a matter of considerable uncertainty. No doubt, these schools differed from each other on matters both of doctrine and disciplinary rules. But the exact nature of these differences is not known. Partially, the uncertainty in this area is due to the fact that by the fifth century of Buddhism, the major division was not that into these twenty schools, but

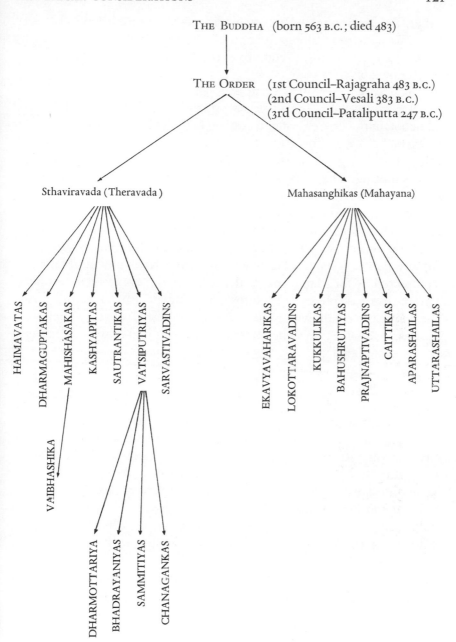

THE BUDDHA   (born 563 B.C.; died 483)

THE ORDER   (1st Council–Rajagraha 483 B.C.)
             (2nd Council–Vesali 383 B.C.)
             (3rd Council–Pataliputta 247 B.C.)

Sthaviravada (Theravada)   Mahasanghikas (Mahayana)

HAIMAVATAS
DHARMAGUPTAKAS
MAHISHĀSAKAS
KASHYAPITAS
SAUTRANTIKAS
VATSIPUTRIYAS
SARVASTIVADINS

EKAVYAVAHARIKAS
LOKOTTARAVADINS
KUKKULIKAS
BAHUSHRUTIYAS
PRAJNAPTIVADINS
CAITTIKAS
APARASHAILAS
UTTARASHAILAS

VAIBHASHIKA

DHARMOTTARIYA
BHADRAYANIYAS
SAMMITIYAS
CHANAGANKAS

EARLY HISTORICAL SKETCH OF THE DEVELOPMENT OF
BUDDHIST SCHOOLS

rather, the division into the Theravada and Mahayana schools, or sects. This was a division along religious lines, the chief differences being concerned with the interpretations of the Buddha's teachings concerning the attaining of *Nirvana*.

In Theravada there was great emphasis on self-discipline and individual achievement. The goal was *arhat*-ship, which symbolized the extinction of the fires of lust and craving in the individual, brought about by his or her own efforts. In Mahayana the goal was to become a *Bodhisattava*—a being whose only concern was with helping others extinguish suffering. The compassion shown by the historical Buddha was emphasized greatly, and as a result there came to be less reliance on individual effort and self-discipline, and more reliance on faith in the Buddha and *Bodhisattavas* who would provide assistance in overcoming suffering. In time these two different emphases in Buddhism came to be supported by different metaphysics. The emphasis on universal salvation represented by the Mahayana ideal of the *Bodhisattava* came to be underwritten by metaphysics of philosophical skepticism and absolutism. The emphasis on individual salvation represented by the Theravada ideal of the *arhat* came to be underwritten by a metaphysics of realistic flux, as formulated in the doctrine of momentariness.

PHILOSOPHICAL SCHOOLS

Thus, whereas from the religious perspective, the main division was into Mahayana and Theravada, from the philosophical perspective the division was into philosophies of realism as opposed to philosophies of idealism and absolutism. The philosophies of realism, which tend to be identified with Theravada Buddhism, are represented by the Vaibhashika and Sautrantika schools. The philosophies identified with Mahayana are (1) the "suchness" absolutism of Ashvaghosa, (2) the relativism of the Madhyamika school, and (3) the idealistic absolutism of the Yogacara school.

Before continuing with an historical outline of Buddhist schools of philosophy it must be pointed out that a division of Buddhism into religious and philosophical schools is somewhat arbitrary, and it is necessary to emphasize that the division is possible only from a certain perspective. In this case it is a perspective assumed primarily on the basis of the distinctions ordinarily made between religions and philosophies of the West. Buddhism as the living cultural phenomenon of the Orient is neither philosophy nor religion; nor is it really both religion and philosophy. It is simply Buddhism. The above distinctions do not apply. It might well be said that to look for philosophy in Buddhism is like looking for the tracks of birds in the air. Buddhism is essentially a way of life; it is not a philosophy about life. But granting this, it does not follow that Buddhism, as a way of life, does not presuppose a philosophy, or have an implicit philosophy. To be sure, it does rest upon certain views of man and the world, despite the common attitude that the philosophical analysis of those views is not essential to a Buddhist way of life. Nevertheless, the fact that Buddhism presupposes certain philosophical views means that one path to the understanding of Buddhism is through an analysis of these views. Thus, it is important not to mistake the metaphysical views found in the philosophies of Buddhism for the "Essence of Buddhism." The "Essence of Buddhism" consists in understanding and getting rid of suffering; not in theoretical views of man and the world. But an understanding of the views implicit in Buddhism can lead one to recognize the logical foundations of Buddhism and make possible a philosophical estimate of these basic foundations.

Probably the earliest of the philosophical schools was the Vaibhashika, as all of the other schools refer to the teachings of this school. The criticisms found in other Buddhist schools as well as in the Hindu schools reveal that the Vaibhashika held that the world is made up of atoms in continuous motion and also that this world can be directly perceived as it exists. But the individual philosophers belonging to this school are unknown.

The Sautrantika school may also be older than the schools belonging to the Mahayana, but the individual philosophers who are known to be connected with this school are contemporary with Madhyamika and Yogacara philosophers. Kumaralabdha, a contemporary of Nagarjuna, probably lived in the second century A.D. Probably he is not the first philosopher of this school, but he is the earliest known to us today. Other philosophers connected with this school are Vasubandhu, who composed the famous *Abhidharmakosha* as a summary of realistic philosophy, probably sometime in the fifth century A.D., and Yasomitra, who wrote a commentary on this work. One of the logicians of this school, Dharmottara, lived in the ninth century A.D.

The Madhyamika and Yogacara philosophies probably developed out of the insights present in the philosophies of Ashvaghosa and the

Lankavtara Sutra. Ashvaghosa formulated his philosophy of the "Thusness" of reality sometime in the first century A.D. This philosophy emphasized the role of consciousness in knowledge and understanding and pointed to the ultimate unknowability of reality. The *Lankavatara Sutra*, also emphasizing the activity of the mind in experience, is probably earlier than Ashvaghosa.

The Madhyamika school concentrates on the ultimate unknowability of reality by conceptual and perceptual means. It is thus a school of philosophical skepticism. It is not, however, a school of unqualified skepticism, for conceptual reality and conceptual activity are not regarded as the ultimate reality. The earliest and greatest of the Madhyamika philosophers was Nagarjuna, who should probably be placed in the middle of the second century A.D. His pupil, Aryadeva, commented on some of his works. Later philosophers of this school who attracted the attention of other philosophers in India and China were Kumarajiva, who lived in the fourth century A.D., and Buddhapalita and Candrakirti, both of whom flourished around the middle of the sixth century A.D.

The Yogacara school represents many of the tenets of the *Lankavatara Sutra*, as it emphasizes the activity of mind to the exclusion of everything else. It is the "Mind-only" doctrine of Vasubandhu of this school that attracted the most criticism from philosophers outside of this school. This is the same Vasubandhu who summarized the realistic philosophy of the Sautrantikas. He was converted from Sautrantika to Yogacara by his older brother, Asanga. And even prior to Asanga, there is a philosopher named Maitreyanatha, who belonged to this school.

With Dinnaga, a pupil of Vasubandhu, Yogacara philosophy took on an emphasis on logic that brought it closer to the Sautrantika school. Dinnaga, Dharmakirti, and Dharmottara are all logicians who seem to have a philosophy midway between Sautrantika and Yogacara. Sometimes this philosophy is referred to as Svatantra Yogacara. Later Yogacara philosophers are Shantarakshita and Kamashila.

After the ninth century A.D. Buddhist philosophies began to disappear from India. Although Buddhist philosophical activity did not disappear as Buddhism spread to China and other parts of Asia, there was never again to be the intense and critical philosophical activity in connection with Buddhism that was found during the first thirteen centuries of the Buddhist era in India. Whether it was because of a widespread feeling that the inadequacies of intellect for solving problems about ultimate reality had been so clearly shown by this time that no one wished to devote his life to the intellectual activity of philosophizing, or whether it was due to the more practical inclinations of the Oriental mind outside India, is hard to say. But though Buddhism as a way of life was as strong or stronger than ever, the heyday of Buddhist philosophy in India was over by 1000 A.D.

CHAPTER 11

THE NATURE OF THE SELF

The main philosophical implications of the ethical-religious teachings of Buddhism are contained in the doctrines of no-self (*anatta*) and impermanence (*anicca*). Both of these doctrines in turn are underwritten by the principle of dependent origination (*paticca samuppada*). The chief difference between the doctrines of *anatta* and *anicca* is that the former refers to the non-substantiality of the self, whereas the latter refers to the non-substantiality of things in the world. Both doctrines presuppose the theory of dependent origination.

As Buddhism developed, the principle of dependent origination underwent different interpretations. These different interpretations were then used to underwrite different theories of the non-substantiality of things and the self. The basic Buddhist philosophies can be studied by considering first the theories concerning the self, and then the theories concerning the nature of things in the world. In this chapter different views of the self will be considered.

BASIC PRINCIPLES

The Buddha's prescription for curing the ills of life follows upon his analysis of the causes of these ills. The Noble Eightfold Path was prescribed because it was what was needed to uproot the causes of suffering. No doubt, the religious genius of the Buddha is what made possible his diagnosis of the causes of suffering and the prescription for its cure. But both the discovery of the causes of suffering and the prescription for its cure are dependent upon the Second Noble Truth—that suffering is caused.

The recognition that suffering is caused reflects an understanding of the relations between events and things in the world. The Buddhist understanding of these relations is reflected in the theory of dependent origination (*paticca samuppada*) which holds, roughly, that whatever is, is dependent upon something else. The formulation of the theory is as follows: (1) If this is, that comes to be; (2) From the arising of this, that arises; (3) If this is not, that does not come to be; (4) From the stopping of this, that stops.

There are several features of this view of dependent origination that need to be noted before applying the theory to an analysis of the self. First, if whatever is, is dependent upon another, then any kind of "straight line" causality is ruled out. There are no independent beings who are responsible for the existence of dependent beings. For example, the theistic notion that one absolutely independent being—God— created the rest of what exists, and that this created universe depends for its existence upon God, makes no sense in the Buddhist view of dependent origination. Rather, whatever creates is also created, and the processes of creating and being created go on simultaneously without beginning or end.

Secondly, as a consequence of the mutual dependence of all beings, it follows that no beings are solely "other-created," but that all are mutually self-creating. The ongoing processes that make up the universe are co-dependent and mutually influencing. Each aspect of the process shares in the creation and the continuation of the other aspects of the process.

Thirdly, ordinary notions of space and time are ruled out by the Buddhist theory of dependent origination. Ordinary notions of space and time depend upon the location and duration of independent beings. Spatial characteristics are derived from the comparison of the location of one being relative to another. Temporal characteristics are derived by comparing the duration of one being to another. But according to the theory of dependent origination there are no beings independent of each other. There are only ongoing processes of mutually dependent factors. Reality is of the nature of process; *things* are merely abstractions. But ordinary notions of space and time depend upon these abstractions, and hence must also fall into the category of abstractions rather than realities. There are no beings; there are only becomings. And since a completion of becoming is never attained, being is never reached.

Fourthly, adequate definitions are impossible. If the universe is thought to consist of things, relatively complete and independent, it is possible to adequately define the things making up the universe. But when the universe is considered to be of the nature of process, definitions are not possible, for whatever might be defined would belong to past stages of the process and never to the present reality of the process.

DEPENDENT ORIGINATION AND THE WHEEL OF BECOMING

Avoiding linear notions of time and space, Buddhists ingeniously diagram the endless continuum of processes constituting reality by using the figure of a wheel. The wheel of becoming (*bhavacakra*) represents the major aspects of the continuous processes constituting what we ordinarily call a person. It is essentially an application of the theory of dependent origination to the processes constituting the self and represents an attempt to exhibit the causes of suffering. The stages of becoming constituting the suffering person are usually represented as in the diagram on the following page.

In the cycle of life depicted by the wheel, the suffering (*dukkha*) of man is symbolized by old age and death. It is not that *dukkha* is thought to consist solely in becoming old and dying, but rather, since these are two of the ills that are especially dreaded, they serve well as representatives of all the ills of life. Now it is asked, Upon what do old age and death depend? The answer is that it is upon the arising of birth that there is death, for death follows birth as surely as night follows day. Without birth there would be no death; and birth would not occur if there were no "becoming forces" (*bhava*) available to be born. In turn, the "becoming forces" depend for their existence upon grasping and clinging to life; grasping and clinging could not exist without desire; desires depend upon perception; perception follows upon sense impressions, which would not be possible without the six sense organs. The sense organs, in turn, depend upon the mind and body (*nama-rupa*), but the functioning of mind and body is dependent upon consciousness. And consciousness is dependent upon the impulses to action, for consciousness is clearly an activity, and without an impulse to action there could be no consciousness. All of these phases of the processes and activities constituting the life of the individual can belong to the self only upon the presence of ignorance. And ignorance, in turn, depends upon the preceding factors in the cycle. And so the cycle goes, without beginning and without end. Each phase or factor is relentlessly brought about by others, which in turn are brought about by still others; the

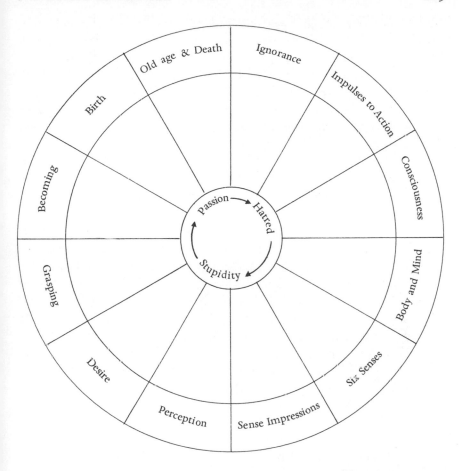

THE WHEEL OF BECOMING (*BHAVACAKRA*)

arising and the falling of the various factors of existence constitutes the unending continuum of process that makes up reality. In this cycle man is caught up, being born, suffering, and dying; being born, suffering, and dying, *ad dukkham*. Life brings death and death brings life, as these are no more than phases in the eternal process.

Although all of the factors constituting a being are intertwined and interdependent, constituting one ongoing process, the factor of ignorance is usually taken as the root-cause of the processes causing suffering. Accordingly, the wheel of becoming can also be interpreted by starting with suffering and then examining it in forward order. When this is done the reflections are as follows: ignorance makes possible the impulses to action, which make possible consciousness; these factors together make possible the mind and body organism; given the mind and body, sensing is possible; and when sensing is provided for, then sense impressions are possible. Following upon sense impressions there is perception; when there is perception there is desire to achieve or avoid what is perceived. Desiring, in turn, makes possible grasping at and clinging to life in its various aspects; this, in turn, provides for the force of becoming, without which there would be no birth. And without birth of a self there would be no self to be suffering.

It is customary when commenting upon and explaining the wheel of life to divide the factors into those concerned with the present life, those concerned with the past, and those concerned with the future, so that ignorance and the impulses to action are regarded as the causes from the past, and birth and old age and death are regarded as effects to occur in the future, with the other factors making up the present existence of the individual. But this division into past, present, and future is somewhat misleading. After all, if the self is really of the nature of process, then there are no sharp lines between past, present, and future. Past, present, and future merely proceed from certain arbitrary perspectives which result from emphasizing the *thingness* rather than the process nature of reality. This can easily be seen by considering that what we call a person is no sooner born than he is dying; the process of aging which culminates in death is going on already at conception. But by the same token, the process of aging and dying is also part of the process of conception and birth. In fact, if a considerable over-simplification is allowed, it might be said that basically it is this ignorance of process and the consequent cutting of this process into segments, which are regarded as independent of each other, that underlies the grasping and clinging that inevitably leads to suffering. It means that the individual is constantly out of tune with reality.

The divisions of past, present, and future result from taking an arbitrary point of view which looks at reality as if it were cut up into distinct and separate pieces or things, rather than seeing it as an integral process. But the division of becoming into the twelve factors represented by the wheel of becoming also represents an arbitrary point of view, for in reality there are an unlimited number of factors that could be distinguished in the processes constituting an individual, with no clear lines of demarcation between them. Consequently this list of factors should not be taken as a true and complete list of the factors of reality.

Instead, it should be regarded as an attempt to effect a transition from an attitude which cuts up reality and makes possible clinging and grasping, to an attitude which is consonant with the flow of reality. The latter attitude cannot itself be adequately represented conceptually, for the whole conceptual approach rests upon the attitude that reality is of the nature of being rather than process. Concepts can adequately reveal only a static reality. However, they can point to (though not express) a different kind of reality.

Taking care that the picture of reality represented by the wheel of becoming is not taken to be the last word and truth about the subject, there are other traps one must avoid when reflecting on this symbol of the wheel. It would be easy to be misled into thinking that Buddhism is basically nihilistic if one seized a wrong interpretation of the causes of suffering and the way to their removal. If old age and death follow upon being born, and if birth were stopped, then old age and death would be stopped. And isn't this precisely what the Buddha taught? "Locate the factors upon which suffering is dependent and remove them, and this will bring about the elimination of suffering." It is true that the Buddha taught that removal of the causes of suffering will eliminate suffering. But it does not follow from this that he maintained that non-existence was the way to non-suffering. On the very face of it, the teaching that only non-existence would lead to non-suffering is absurd, for who could subscribe to this teaching as a way of deliverance? And history reveals that Buddhism has been embraced as a saving teaching by hundreds of thousands of persons for many, many centuries. If the Buddha did not teach nihilism, then what did he teach? Upon the non-existence of what would there be non-existence of suffering? To answer this question it is necessary to reflect on the Buddhist notion of what a person is.

STOPPING THE WHEEL OF BECOMING

Ordinarily when we talk about what a person is, especially when we talk about what we ourselves are, we assume that in addition to the bodily and mental characteristics constituting the individual there is also a self, an "I." Thus we say, "*I* will do that, *I* am doing this," etc. And the claim is made that various things, including our bodies and minds, belong to the person. We say, "It's *his* body." Or, "I'm improving *my* mind." It is this ego-self—this "I"—to whom suffering is attributed, as for example when we say, "It's terrible, the doctor just told me that

I am dying of cancer, and this is why I am suffering so." Clearly, if there were no ego-self, or "I", there could be no suffering, for suffering is always the suffering of a self; it always belongs to someone.

What foundation is there for the ordinary belief in the existence of an ego-self? This is the question underlying the Buddhist analysis of the self, undertaken to uproot the conditions upon which suffering depends. It is to the non-existence of the ego-self that the theory of *anatta* refers, and it is in overcoming attachment to the "I" that release from suffering is found. As the Buddha said,

> Therefore say I that the Tathagata has attained deliverance and is free from attachment, inasmuch as all imaginings, or agitations, or proud thought concerning an Ego or anything pertaining to an Ego, have perished, have faded away, have ceased, have been given up and relinquished.[1]

But surely it is paradoxical for anyone to claim that he does not exist. To say "I do not exist" obviously is not to make any claim at all, as the remark negates itself, since a non-existent being could not make the claim and an existing being would be asserting his own existence in making the claim. Consequently, the Buddhist claim that the self does not exist could not be a claim that there is no individual existence, that the person is non-existent. It seems more reasonable to regard a remark such as "I do not exist," as an attempt to get attention for another claim that is to be made. For instance, it might reasonably be claimed that I do not exist as a substance independent of the processes that constitute me. This is not a claim about my existence *per se*, but a claim about my existence as a "such and such." And these are quite different matters. The Buddhist claim about the non-existence of the self is a claim about the non-existence of the self as a being *in addition to*, or *apart from*, the various factors that are ordinarily said to belong to the self. It clearly is not a claim about the non-existence of the factors that make up the individual person. This is evident from the Buddha's reply to Vacchagotta's question concerning whether the Tathagata had any theories of his own (concerning the nature of the self). His reply was as follows:

> The Tathāgata, O Vaccha, is free from all theories; but this, Vaccha, does the Tathāgata know,—the nature of form, and how form arises, and how form perishes; the nature of sensation, and how sensation arises, and how sensation perishes; the nature of perception, and how perception arises,

---

[1] *Majjhima Nikaya, Sutta 72*, in H. C. Warren, *Buddhism in Translations* (New York: Atheneum, 1963) p. 125.

and how perception perishes; the nature of the pre-dispositions, and how the pre-dispositions arise, and how the pre-dispositions perish; the nature of consciousness, and how consciousness arises, and how consciousness perishes.[2]

This answer reveals that rather than considering various theories of the substantiality of the self, the Buddha took a long hard look at what a person is, and found no extra-mental or extra-physical thing to which the word "self" might refer. Rather, upon analysis it became evident that a person is constituted by a large number of processes. These processes can be grouped together, for the sake of convenience, in the way indicated by the Buddha's answer to Vachagotta's question. Schematically, this analysis of a person can be represented as follows:

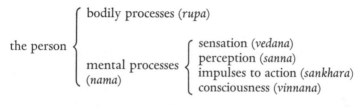

All of the various things that can be said of a person are about one or another of these processes. No person ever engages in any activities that do not belong to one or another of these five groups. But if the analysis of a person does not reveal anything other than these five groups of processes, then what foundation is there for claiming the existence of another component, namely, the self or the "I"? Ordinarily we say that the body, or the habits, or the thoughts of a person *belong* to a self, and thus suggest that there is, in addition to what is owned, also an owner of the processes. It is clear upon analysis, however, that this is simply a way of speaking, and cannot be taken as evidence that there exists a self in addition to the groups that make up a person.

It is now possible to become clearer about exactly what is meant by the theory of *anatta*, which denies the substantiality of the self. The *anatta* theory denies the existence of a self only when the word "self" is taken to refer to some thing in addition to the groups of factors making up a person. The *anatta* theory does not deny the existence of a self when the word "self" is taken to refer to only the five groups of processes constituting the person. Thus, it is the view that the self is a substance independent of the processes making up a person that is denied by the doctrine of *anatta*.

[2] *Majjhima Nikaya, Sutta* 72. Warren, p. 125.

With this explanation of the *anatta* theory in mind it is possible to see that the theory of dependent origination applied to the rise and fall of suffering in the wheel of becoming has nothing to do with nihilism. The ignorance that must be destroyed is the ignorance that consists in living as though the self exists over and above the groups of processes. The conviction that there is a substantial self is the root-cause of suffering, for this results in the attitude that underlies and makes possible the attachment of the various processes to a self. It is this ignorance that allows the attachment and thereby makes possible suffering.

It is important to note that the processes in themselves are not capable of suffering; it is only a self that suffers. Because of ignorance, a self is considered to exist and is attached to the groups. And now, when the groups change in relation to the self, there is suffering.

On the other hand, if the ego is not born there can be no attachment to the groups. The groups will continue their flow in conformity with the process nature of reality; there is no stopping this flow, even if one wished to do so. But the ego—the "I"—need not be born; it need not arise. It is from the arising of this ego that suffering arises. And upon stopping that ego from arising, the suffering will stop.

With this in mind, the wheel of becoming can be meditated upon as follows: old age and death come to a self because the self is born; a self is born because there is attachment to the becoming forces; there is attachment to the becoming forces because there is grasping; and there is grasping because there is desiring. Feeling leads to desiring. Feeling is possible because of attachment to the sense impressions; and because there is attachment to the sense organs impressions are received. Attachment to the sense organs follows upon attachment to the mind and body; this in turn follows upon attachment to consciousness, which follows from attachment to impulses to actions, which proceeds from ignorance.

Meditating on the wheel in forward order, reflection reveals that without ignorance there would be no attachment to the impulses to action, no attachment to the processes of consciousness, no attachment to mind and body, to the sense organs, to the sense impressions, to the feelings, to the cravings, to the grasping and clinging, to the becoming forces; and there would then be no ego to be born and no self to grow old and die.

It is important to notice that the various processes would go on without interruption; the removal of ignorance would not alter that. But the processes cause suffering only because of a wrong attitude toward them; an attitude that mistakes them for something other than what they are by cutting up reality and attaching this cut-up reality to a self which in ignorance is thought to exist. It is *attachment* to the groups and not the groups themselves that brings about suffering.

The difference between groups of processes and attachment groups is explained by Buddhaghosa (400 A.D.) as follows:

> "Groups" is a general term; while the term "attachment groups" specifies those which are coupled with depravity and attachment.[3]

Then, after indicating his intention to teach the difference between the five groups and the five attachment groups, he goes on to say:

> All form whatsoever . . . belongs to the form-group. All sensations whatsoever, . . . all perception whatsoever, . . . all predispositions [impulses to action] whatsoever, . . . all consciousness whatsoever, ... These, O priests, are called the five groups.

Distinguishing between the groups as such and the groups as attached to an ego he says,

> . . . those groups which are in the grasp of attachment are attachment groups.[4]

Clarifying the distinction between the groups and the attachment groups, Buddhaghosa goes on to say:

> When there is form, O priests, then through attachment to form, through engrossment in form, the persuasion arises, "This is mine; this am I; this is my ego." When there is sensation, . . . when there is perception, . . . where there are predispositions, . . . when there is consciousness, O priests, then through attachment to consciousness, through engrossment in consciousness, the persuasion arises, "This is mine; this am I; this is my ego."[5]

This distinction between the groups of existence and the attachment groups (attachment to the groups of existence) makes clear why the Buddhist teaching that to get rid of suffering the self must be rooted out has nothing to do with nihilism, but has to do only with the destruction of the product of ignorance. The groups of processes constituting existence are not to be destroyed. Only the falsely imagined self is to be destroyed. The reason why this false self is to be destroyed is that it is what makes possible the attachment to the groups which underlies all forms of suffering. Without this false ego-self, which is only a creation

[3] *Visuddhi-Magga*, Ch. 14, in Warren, *Buddhism In translations*, p. 155.
[4] *Visuddhi-Magga*, Ch. 14, in Warren. pp. 155, 156.
[5] *Ibid*. Warren, p. 157.

of ignorance, there would be no looking to the past, bemoaning what has been lost, and no looking forward to the future lamenting over what has not yet come about. Without this ego-self life could be lived in the full richness of the present moment, without distinction, division, or attachment. Consequently, once this ignorance is removed life will be found complete and perfect just as it is.

This realization of the completeness and perfectness of life is beautifully expressed in a remark by a twenty-five year old girl by the name of Yaeko Iwasaki, who achieved enlightenment after only five years of discipline and meditation. In a letter to her master, Harada-*Roshi*, dated December 27, 1935, she said:

> You can appreciate how enormously satisfying it is for me to discover at last, through full realization, that just as I am I lack nothing.[6]

The incompleteness and the insecurity and the feelings of aloneness and estrangement that characterize the basic anxiety underlying the mental suffering of most people proceed from the activity of the ego attaching itself to various processes, clinging and grasping in a desperate effort to claim existence. It is undeniably the mark of the ego that it is a struggling-to-be; it is not a being already complete. Nor is it simply an aspect of process. It is a striving-to-be and grasping-to-be which seeks to collect and dominate all of reality. No wonder then that the realization that the ego is unreal, that it is simply the product of ignorance, frees one from the basic causes of suffering. And this is why the doctrine of *anatta* is one of the fundamental principles of Buddhism, for the belief in the reality of a self is incompatible with the extinction of suffering at which Buddhism aims.

THEORIES OF THE NON-SELF

Despite agreement among Buddhist schools that the doctrine of *anatta* was basic to the Buddha's teaching and central to the message of Buddhism, there was considerable controversy concerning precisely what it was that this doctrine of non-self did allow and what it did not allow. Since the doctrine of *anatta* was, at least formally, a negative theory denying a theory of self, and since a variety of theories of the self are possible, it is not surprising that there should be disagreement concerning just which theories of the self it was that the *anatta* doctrine denied, and which theories it did not deny.

[6] The letter from which this is taken, along with seven other inspiring letters, are contained in Philip Kapleau, *The Three Pillars of Zen* (New York: Harper and Row, 1967), pp. 269–291.

Consequently, even though Buddhists agreed that the doctrine of *anatta* was a basic and true teaching of the Buddha, there came to be considerable disagreement over who it was that could be saved by following the Way. The location of the five groups constituting the empirical individual, and the rejection of the supposed existence of a substance in addition to the groups, left open the question of what distinguished one set of five groups from another, and what connection there was between treading the Path and becoming enlightened. The problem presented itself as especially acute to the Buddhist mind, for unless there was a means of distinguishing one set of groups from another, there would be no basis for differentiating between one person to be saved and another. Furthermore, there would be no basis for distinguishing between the ignorant and the enlightened person unless there were some kind of identity or continuity within each set of groups. And if the latter distinction could not be made, it would follow that the Buddha is no different from the ignorant and suffering people to whom he addressed himself. And such a conclusion about the Enlightened One is not acceptable to any Buddhist.

SELF ANALYZED IN TERMS OF ELEMENTS

The earliest systematic reflections about the *dharma*, or teachings of the Buddha, are contained in the third portion of the orthodox collection (Pali canon) of Buddhist works known as the "*Abhidharma* basket." The main concern of the Abhidharma writers was not with the question of whether or not there were substances, or selves. They assumed that existence was not of the nature of substance, but rather consisted in the continuous flow of elements, called by the Abhidharmists, *dharmas*. The problem for the Abhidharmists was one of classifying these *dharmas* and of establishing their interrelations.

The basic Abhidharmist teaching on the nature of the self holds that at the core of individual existence, instead of a permanent and unchanging substance, or soul, there is a stream of continuously flowing discrete elements of sensation, consciousness, feeling, activity impulses, and bodily processes. These continuously moving elements give rise to the appearance of an enduring self. But this appearance is to be disregarded, for the individual is never anything more than these various elements in motion. Over and above these elements, which even though conditioned and transitory are regarded by the Abhidharmists as ultimately real, there is the element of *Nirvana*, which is held to be unconditioned and non-transitory. *Nirvana* is universally regarded as beyond description and definition, but when, from time to time, philosophers have felt constrained to say something about it, they have called it the indefinable essence of the various conditioned elements in a quiescent condition. The reasoning behind this is readily understandable even if the characterization is unintelligible; the teaching of the Buddha provides for the "quieting" of the elements of existence, and since it is impossible to regard total extinction as any kind of salvation, the philosophers postulated that salvation, or *Nirvana*, must consist in the quiescence of the conditioned elements.

There are numerous lists of the basic elements given in the Abhidharma literature showing the interrelations between them. The lists occasionally disagree with each other, and frequently overlap, but the lists all indicate that the fundamental elements, or *dharmas*, are of the nature of elemental forces rather than elemental substances. Using an analogy, it could be said that the *dharmas* are likened to elemental energy charges rather than to minute bits of solid matter; though devoid of spatial and temporal characteristics themselves, by their motions and combinations they give rise to the compounded elements or processes which can be located spatially and temporally. The individual is simply a combination of these impersonal forces in motion.

Concerning what the self is, the Abhidharma question is, How are the fundamental *dharmas* constituting the individual to be classified? Five groups, or *skandhas*, are taken as basic categories of the empirical self. These categories are then analyzed into constituent components, or *dharmas*. In this way lists such as the following are derived: (1) the group comprising the bodily processes (*rupa*) are constituted by the *dharmas* of eye, ear, nose, tongue, and skin, and the corresponding *dharmas* of color, sound, odor, flavor, and resistance; (2) the group comprising the processes involved in feeling (*vedana*) and, (3) the processes constituting perception, are left undivided at this point, but (4) the processes constituting the conscious and unconscious impulses to action (*sankharas*) are divided in such a way as to reveal the *dharmas* constituting perception and feeling as well. This division is as follows: (A) *constituents of mental activity present in consciousness*: feeling, perception, will, immediate sensation, desire, understanding, memory, attention, inclination, and concentration; (B) *constituents of virtue*: faith, courage, equanimity, modesty, disgust at objectionable things, non-greed, nonhatred, compassion, and mindfulness; (C) *constituents of vice*: dullness, doubt, sloth, carelessness, immodesty, anger, hypocrisy, envy, jealousy, deceit, trickery, hatred, and pride. (5) The group consisting of the activities of consciousness is divided into the elements, or *dharmas*, responsible for the three categories of consciousness: pure, impure, and indeterminate (capable of being either pure or impure). Altogether, these three categories of consciousness include eighty-nine elements, or *dharmas*, when they are associated with the various processes constituting the *sankharas*.

However, the division of the five groups of processes constituting the individual into these *dharmas* is not the end of the story, for all of these *dharmas* are conditioned, or made—that is, they are not independent; they have no existence in their own right, and are dependent for their being upon something else. So the question can be asked, Of what are these *dharmas* made? When this question is taken seriously, the *dharmas* themselves come to be divided into an indefinite (and potentially un-limited) number of components, or moments, which are regarded as the ultimate *dharmas* of existence. Each of these ultimate *dharmas* is by itself without characteristics of mass or duration, but all together they are responsible for the characteristics of things in the world.

What this analysis of the self accomplishes is to make human exist-ence a purely impersonal thing. Nowhere is there found a trace of ego, or self. Only impersonal elements are found, in constant con-junction and process, giving rise to the appearance of an enduring self. While this Abhidharma doctrine is in conformity with the Buddha's teaching that nowhere is there a self to be found, that all *dharmas* are without self,[7] and that enlightenment requires giving up all attachment to an ego,[8] it offered little assistance in understanding the continuity of the individual. Nor did it provide for an explanation of how the effects of actions of one person could possibly affect that person at a later time; but unless this were possible, the teaching that individual persons could overcome suffering would be wholly irrelevant. Now, it is true that a nominal explanation had been provided for these points in that it was held that the grouping of elements provided individual continuities. These individual continuities served the purpose of ex-plaining the enduring characteristic of the person by providing for endurance without permanence; they also provided for the distinction of one continuity from another. The difficulty with this view of personal continuities, however, is that there is no reason why the processes should

[7] *Dhammapada*, XX. 7, trans. by Acharya Buddharakkhita Thera (Bangalore, India: Buddha Vaccna Trust, 1966).
[8] *Majjhima Nikaya, Sutta 72, op. cit.*

form such continuities. Unless the *dharmas* contain something other than discrete impersonal forces, it is not necessary that these forces should combine into these personal continuities.

THE PERSONALIST VIEW

These difficulties with the Abhidharma interpretation of the *anatta* doctrine led Buddhists in the Vatsiputriya, Sammitiya, Dharmottariya, Bhadrayaniya, and Chanaganka schools to claim that in addition to the impersonal *dharmas* there was a person (*pudgala*) to be found. These Buddhists, known as Personalists (*Pudgalavadins*), sought an explanation of the *anatta* teaching of the Buddha that would square with the common belief in a self, and at the same time not violate the basic teachings concerning the alleviation of suffering.

The "person" claimed by the Personalists was recognized as something real in its own right that an enlightened person experiences. It is this "person" that accounts for individuation of processes so that individual persons and things can be distinguished from each other. It also makes possible the continuity within one distinct and continuous process, so that the effects of one person's activities accrue to that person and not to another. It is the "person" that provides the element of connection between the ignorant and the enlightened individual. This "person" is the agent of activities, and is responsible for coordinating the activities of the various mental processes involved in knowing and acting.

Even though the addition of the "person" to the impersonal realities catalogued by the Abhidarmists made it possible to stick to familiar and commonsense ways of talking about self and experience, the Personalists could not achieve a satisfactory theory unless they could show how this "person" was related to the impersonal elements, and also that their view was in conformity with the Buddha's no-self teaching. The difficulty involved in establishing both of these points proved insurmountable for the Personalists. To avoid a wrong belief in self, they could not identify the "person" with the groups themselves. Nor could they claim that the "person" was either inside or outside of the groups. If the "person" were to be identified with the groups nothing would be gained, for the "person" would appear and disappear when the groups arise and disappear. If it is distinguished from the groups, the "person" must be attached in some way to them. But this clearly violates the teaching of non-attachment, which all Buddhists accept.

What remains as a possibility for relationship between the groups and the "person"? According to the Personalists, the relation is one of *correlation*, which they contend cannot be further explained in terms of other relations. The difficulty with this claim is that only one of the correlatives is known, for by their own admission, the "person" is undefinable in every respect. But if one of two elements held to be correlated with each other is completely unknown, there is no basis for establishing either that there is a correlation, or what the correlation is, if it exists. Trying to avoid the difficulty, the Personalists resort to an example: the "person" is like the fire that is correlated with the fuel and the flame; though they are always found together, fire has a reality of itself, evident in its nature as heat; fire is not the same thing as fuel or a series of flames.

The difficulty with examples in general is that while they may illustrate a point, they do not prove the point. The difficulty with this particular example is that it is unclear in itself and consequently does not even serve to illustrate a point. As a result the Personalist theory, which comes closest of all Buddhist theories of the self to the ordinary commonsense point of view, is really nothing more than a rather dogged insistence that since we ordinarily talk and act as though there were a "person" in addition to the groups of processes constituting the individual, that "person" must exist, even though it is not possible to say what it is or how it is related to the processes.

SELF AS "SUCHNESS"

Dissatisfaction with the Personalist theory of the self led the Mahayana philosophers to seek other ways of solving the problems of personal continuity and enlightenment without invoking a theory of substances. For Ashvaghosa, the "person," or *pudgala*, of the Personalists came to be replaced by *tathata*, or suchness. For the Madhyamika philosophers it was *shunyata*, or emptiness, that took over the role of *pudgala*. It is important to note here that *suchness* and *emptiness* were not postulated as theories to explain the empirical continuity of an individual. As the Mahayana philosophers saw it, the problem had its roots in the attempt to understand the connection between the empirical individual and the enlightened one, between the ignorant self and the one who had attained *Nirvana* by achieving *Buddhi*. No problem arose in connection with empirical identity and continuity because it was universally accepted that what was empirical was compounded; was unreal; was

transitory; was of the nature of *dukkha* (suffering); and was to be eradi-
cated, not explained. But if those persons to whom the Buddha preached
were to become enlightened, it must be the case that somehow, somewhere, within the empirical world there must be that which is not of
the nature of the compounded and is not inseparable from suffering.
It would be this—whatever it is—that would constitute the nature of
the enlightened person. The problem presenting itself here is not that
of determining the essence of the ignorant empirical self, but that of
understanding the essence of the enlightened self—the Buddha-nature
itself. The almost impossible difficulty of this problem is compounded
by the fact that it is the ignorant self who is trying to understand the
enlightened self.

No doubt it was appreciation of the magnitude of the problem created
by the ignorant self trying to understand the enlightened self that led
the Personalities to say that the "person" is completely undefinable.
But as the Mahayana philosophers point out, if this "person" is completely undefinable it ought not to be called a *person*, for a person is
something determinate and (at least roughly) describable. If the nature
of the enlightened self is beyond the empirical and conceptual it cannot
be named by the word "person" or anything else. In recognition of this,
Ashvaghosa refers to it as *tathata*—"such as it is." In other words, the
enlightened self is just what it is, and since nothing can be said of it as it
is in itself, rather than trying to make it something determinate, it is
better just to refer to it by using the non-name "suchness."

The Madhyamika philosophers also objected to attaching the name
"person," or *pudgala*, to the enlightened self. The non-name they used
for the enlightened self was *shunyata*, or emptiness. The clue to what the
Madhyamikas were getting at is made obvious by the question that
naturally follows a claim that something is empty, i.e., "Empty of what?"
What the Madhyamika philosophers were claiming was that the *pudgala postulated by the Personalists* was empty of reality. The argument
behind this claim was supported by the position that whatever is determined perceptually and conceptually is of the nature of mind and
not of reality. Perceptual and conceptual claims are based upon a cutting
up of reality, and thus do not represent reality as it is. Hence these
claims are empty of reality. The Personalist claim that there is a *pudgala*
over and above the groups of processes is just an empty claim if it is
about anything definite. On the other hand, if the *pudgala* claim is not
regarded as a claim about anything definite, it is really not a claim about

a reality. At best it could be regarded as a claim that since the theory of the groups is based on a cutting up of reality, this theory necessarily fails to establish the existence of the real self. This view would come close to the Madhyamika position, but there is no evidence that the Pudgalavadins ever advanced such a view.

The Madhyamika philosopher's own view about the nature of the enlightened self is really a non-view. Not claiming any views as his own, avoiding clinging to one theory as true and another as false, he understands that any theory of the self will be one-sided and incomplete. The achievement of enlightenment will directly reveal the peace and bliss of *Nirvana*. Thus, though he has theories about other theories, the Madhyamika has no theories about the enlightened self. In this area he remains a philosophical agnostic.

SELF AS CONSCIOUSNESS

The Yogacarins replace the Personalist's theory of a *pudgala* with the theory of *alaya-vijnana*, or "seed-consciousness." Their claim is that there is an extremely subtle and pervasive consciousness underlying ordinary consciousness, out of which ordinary consciousness evolves and into which it returns. This seed-consciousness provides the continuity between the activities of consciousness required to give continuity to the individual's mental activity. It also provides an answer to the question of the connection between treading the Path and being saved, for the essence of the self is contained in this seed-consciousness, and when everything impure and evil has been removed from this basic consciousness all *dukkha* is automatically eliminated and *Nirvana* is achieved.

That there must be a seed-consciousness can be seen by considering the nature of conscious activity, the Yogacarins argue. Building on the Abhidharma analysis, consciousness, or conscious activity, is reduced to a stream of moments, or points of consciousness. Sometimes this stream runs underground, and sometimes it surfaces, as when we are conscious of things and activities around us. Since consciousness could not come to the fore unless it were present in a latent, or seed form, it must be the case that there is a seed-consciousness. Into this seed-consciousness goes the residue of all past moments of consciousness, and from it comes the basis for the present consciousness.

This theory has the advantage of providing an explanation of *karma* (the retribution of effects of actions to the doer), rebirth (an individual is born and dies many many times), the distinction between one individual and another (different seeds), and the connection between treading the path and becoming enlightened (purification of the seed-consciousness).

The Yogacarins reject the Madhyamika criticism that all *dharmas*—including the *dharmas* of consciousness—are unreal because arrived at conceptually or perceptually by cutting up reality. Their argument is that if consciousness is taken as unreal, then the arguments whereby the Madhyamikas establish the unreality of all *dharmas* would also fall to the ground, since they are conceptual arguments, arising within consciousness. However, rejecting the unreality of all *dharmas* outside of consciousness, the Yogacarins are left without a basis for claiming the existence of other individuals, let alone distinguishing between them, since if the only reality admitted is that of my own consciousness, any other existence could be known only insofar as it existed within my own consciousness; whether there existed an objective counterpart to what was found in my consciousness would be forever unknown.

Aside from that difficulty, the Yogacarins are hard pressed to show that their theory of a seed-consciousness is correct. After all, there might be other theories that would also square with ordinary experience. It is one thing to suggest a probable theory of the self and another thing to show either that the theory is correct or that it is superior to every other theory. According to the seed-consciousness theory, ordinary consciousness arises out of, and exists in, a seed-consciousness. But out of what does the seed-consciousness arise? And in what does it exist? If something be postulated in response to these two questions, it appears that seed-consciousness is not the ultimate self, but simply an intermediary stage in the analysis. If, on the other hand, it is claimed that seed-consciousness is eternally existent and exists only in itself, it is difficult to see why the same thing could not be said about ordinary consciousness. A further and complicating difficulty is that it is only from the standpoint of ordinary consciousness that anything can be said about the seed-consciousness, and therefore claims about seed-consciousness itself are completely untestable.

The difficulties confronting these various theories of the self reveal some of the problems encountered in trying to provide a philosophically acceptable account of what a person is. It is clear that the Personalist and the Yogacarin views are both difficult to maintain without violating the principle of dependent origination. In addition, they face the various philosophical problems pointed out above. On the other hand, the views of Ashvaghosa and the Madhyamika philosophers, which provide the chief basis for the practices constituting the Mahayana Buddhist way of life, do not provide a definitive theory of the self. The Madhyamika philosophers, being complete relativists, appear to be most closely in accord with the principle of dependent origination. But this very fact prevents them from having any ultimate theory of their own, for they have no ultimates upon which to base such a theory. Even their claim that all views are relative is itself a relative claim.

It would appear that only the Madhyamikas interpreted the principle of dependent origination as applying to all conceivable existence. The realistic philosophers of the Abhidharma took the ultimate moments of existence as fundamental, or absolute, relating all other existence to these fundamental elements. The idealistic philosophers of the Yogacara school regarded the seed-consciousness as fundamental and absolute, relating all other existence to this fundamental reality.

Because they allowed exceptions to the principle of dependent origination both the realistic and the idealistic philosophers had a basis upon which to erect their theories of the self. The Madhyamika philosophers, however, did not interpret the principle in such a way that certain kinds of existence were exceptions, allowing for them to become the absolutes in a philosophical system. The price they paid for refusing to make exceptions is that they were unable to establish any view of their own, for they had no basis for any view. This, however, seemed a relatively small price to pay, for as seen above, the Buddha also professed to have no views of the self.[9] In fact, for a practicing Buddhist, having no views might well represent considerable progress along the Way, for this eliminates the possibility of clinging to purely conceptual entities, and thus marks non-attachment to the ego of ignorance that underlies suffering.

[9] See above, p. 132.

CHAPTER 12

THE NATURE OF REALITY

AN OUTLINE OF DIFFERENT VIEWS OF REALITY

Just as Buddhist theories of the self took shape according to their interpretations of the principle of dependent origination, so also different theories of the nature of external reality were influenced by this principle. As a consequence of sharing the common principle of dependent origination, Buddhist theories of the world and self have certain features in common. (1) Neither selves nor external things are of the nature of substance. (2) Both are constituted by processes of elemental forces. (3) Permanence is not found in either things or selves. (4) Space and time are not determining characteristics of either things or selves, since space and time are relative to the processes (which are already relative to each other). Nevertheless, despite this core of doctrine common to the different schools, there are many differences among their views of the nature of the external world which result from different interpretations of the principle of dependent origination.

The main differences in the teachings concerning the nature of external things can be summarized in terms of the views of the schools of Vaibhashika, Sautrantika, Madhyamika, and Yogacara. The first of these schools, the Vaibhashika, is associated with early, or Theravada, Buddhism. Its view of the world is that the elements (*dharmas*) constituting the empirical world are what make up ultimate reality. These elements are presented directly in experience as the basic content of the experience, and are held to exist as real just as presented in experience. Since it is held that there are a great number of these ultimate elements, the Vaibhashika metaphysics can be called pluralistic realism.

The Sautrantika school, though often associated with Theravada Buddhism, is really a transitional philosophy, bridging the gap between Theravada and Mahayana. At first glance it appears that the Sautrantika view of the world is quite similar to the Vaibhashika view, for both hold a view that is both pluralistic and realistic. There is an important difference, however, as the Sautrantikas reject the notion that the basic features of ordinary experience constitute the ultimate elements of things. The Sautrantika view is that the empirical is conditioned. Whatever is experienced depends for its existence not only upon the experiencer, but also upon other elements which are not directly experienced. After all, the principle of dependent origination maintains that there are no beings, but only comings-to-be. And these comings-to-be are interdependent; no one of them has an independent reality of its own. But if this is the case, then the fundamental elements of experienced reality must also lack independent reality. Consequently, the Sautrantikas teach that the fundamental elements of reality are not known directly, but lie beyond the contents of experience, giving rise to the contents of experience and being represented by them.

The Madhyamikas give up pluralistic realism completely. Agreeing with the Sautrantikas that a correct interpretation of the principle of dependent origination does not allow the directly experienced "reals" claimed by the Vaibhashikas, they went further and claimed that the fundamental elements, or *dharmas*, claimed by the Sautrantikas were as good as no elements at all. Their argument is that by removing the ultimate elements from the realm of the experiencable, the Sautrantikas had really relegated them to the realm of nothingness. Supposedly the ultimate elements of things claimed by the Sautrantikas were represented by the contents of ordinary experience. But since there was no finding out whether or not they were represented correctly or whether in fact they were represented at all, the claim that they existed was really an empty claim. Consequently, the Madhyamikas stressed the relativity of the components of things. Their reasoning is that if whatever is, is dependent upon something else, then it is not possible to postulate some existents (*dharmas*) which exist first and are independent of other existents. The quest for ultimate elements, real in themselves, was a misguided seeking of a mere chimera. It was the result of a failure to penetrate the principle of dependent origination, for it belied a clinging to the erroneous substance view. Stressing the interdependence of elements upon each other and their essential relativity, the Madhyamika philosophers became famous for their theory of *shunyata*. The word *shunyata* means "devoidness," and the theory of *shunyata* holds that all elements are devoid of ultimate reality. That is, there is no existence in and of itself; all existents are dependent upon each other, and have reality only relative to other dependent existents.

The Yogacarins agreed that pluralistic realism was incompatible with the theory of dependent origination, and that no absolute and ultimate elements of existence could be claimed to exist in the world. The Madhyamikas were, therefore, correct in pointing out the essential relativity and interdependence that characterized all external reality. But the Yogacarins felt they went too far in characterizing *all existence* as relative and therefore unreal (i.e. possessing no independent reality), for if this claim were correct, it would follow that the existence of consciousness would also be relative and unreal, and if this were the case the results of consciousness would also be relative and unreal. Since the Madhyamikas arguments were the results of conscious activity they would be relative and unreal, and there would be no way to maintain their position. Consequently, the Yogacarins insisted that consciousness must be allowed to exist in its own right; it alone is independently real, and everything else has reality only relative to consciousness.

Here the Yogacarins had come full circle from the Vaibhashika point of view. The Vaibhashikas postulated the basic elements of external reality as absolute, with everything else having reality only relative to those fundamental *dharmas*. The Yogacarins regarded those elements as relative to consciousness, giving consciousness itself the position of the fundamental and absolute reality in the system. This view—that whatever exists, exists only relative to consciousness—is known as idealism. The basic difference between realism and idealism is that realism takes the reality of external things to be ultimate, and everything else, including consciousness, is relative to external reality. Idealism takes consciousness to be ultimate; everything else, including external things, is real only relative to consciousness. The Madhyamika view— that everything is devoid of reality—differs from both realism and idealism in that it does not regard either consciousness or external reality as ultimate. It is, therefore, a complete relativism, without an absolute. Consciousness and external reality are on the same ontological footing—both are real only in relation to each other. The dictum of this school is that whatever is, is relative.

According to the interpretation of dependent origination underlying Theravada Buddhism, the processes constituting reality are comprised of an unlimited number of discrete and evanescent elements, or forces, in continuous motion. These elements, or *dharmas*, are the ultimate forces in the universe and are responsible for whatever exists. They exist independently in their own natures and everything else originates in dependence upon these ultimate elements. Though of extremely short duration, they are held to be ultimately real, for they have effects. The effects are the sticks and stones, tables and chairs, etc., that constitute the ordinary world of experience.

The relation between the fundamental *dharmas* and the world of ordinary experience is comparable to the relation between the modern scientific theory of the atomistic components of things and common sense perception. The common-sense view is that tables and chairs are stable and enduring things, as solid as you like. But the scientist informs us that what is called a table and thought to be a solid and permanent thing is really a collection of various forces and elements in constant motion. This is quite similar to the Buddhist view of *dharmas* as the ultimate constituents of things, for they too hold that the things of common sense turn out to be no more than collections of much more elementary forces in constant motion. For the Buddhist, as for the scientist, this way of looking at things does not mean the repudiation of the common sense world, nor the denial of any of its objects. The real world is out there, just as real as anybody thinks it to be. But its reality is constituted in a way different than usually imagined. It is, in fact, constituted by the combinations of discrete, evanescent elemental forces in constant motion.

In arriving at their metaphysical views the Vaibhashikas and Sautrantikas claimed the reality of the world of ordinary experience, but rejected the imposition of an abstract theory of substance on this reality. Experience is not denied. Whatever is experienced is real, otherwise it could not be experienced. However, a distinction must be made between the reality of the experienced world and the truth of a theory about that world. What common sense frequently does is to add to experience an interpretative framework. The data of experience are then clothed with the fabric of the theory, and the data of experience themselves are overlooked. The substance view of reality is a prime example of this sort of thing. Experience in and of itself never carries with it data of the identity and permanence of things. Identity and permanence, which are essential to a substance view of reality, are imposed on the data of experience as an interpretative framework. It is this framework that the Buddhist wishes to reject, for it is not given in the experience itself. The doctrine of *anicca*, or impermanence, is essentially a denial of the substance view of reality. But to deny the reality of substances in the world is not to deny the reality of the world. It is only a denial of the reality of the world *as substance*, and it leaves every other alternative open. Substituting process for substance, the Buddhist affirms the world that consists of process as real and denies only the world of substance.

The whole question of what process is, and how processes make up the world of everyday experience, is another matter. But it is clear that the reality of process is not denied. And it is because the reality of process is affirmed that the Vaibhashikas and Sautrantikas earn the name "realist." Furthermore, they are *pluralistic* realists because they hold that the processes constituting reality are made up of a great many discrete and interacting elements.

EXISTENCE

The main features of the metaphysics of the Vaibhashikas and Sautrantikas are determined by their rejection of the substance view of reality— a view that was held by many of the Hindu philosophers, especially those belonging to the Nyaya and Vaisheshika Schools. The substance view in metaphysics emphasizes the reality of being over becoming. Unchanging being is taken as fundamental, and change and becoming must be explained in relation to this reality in the best way possible. If it turns out that no theory of change can be found which is compatible with permanence and being, then change must be denied, as even more ancient thinkers of India (and Paramenides of Greece) had argued.

In order to see what metaphysics the Vaibhashikas and Sautrantikas were rejecting, it is necessary to examine the assumption inherent in the substance view. To assume a substance view of reality is to accept (1) permanence, (2) universality, (3) identity, and (4) unity as the basic characteristics of whatever really exists.

(1) Emphasizing permanence consists in stressing the stability and duration of things in the universe. In this view the unchanging rather than the changing features of reality are taken as basic. Changelessness

becomes the criterion of the real. The acceptance of permanence as a basic characteristic of existence is often accompanied by accepting the characteristic of identity.

(2) Identity refers to the sameness of things despite apparent changes in them. For example, stressing identity, one would say that though a puppy grows and becomes old, and though in the process every cell is replaced, nevertheless, it is still the same individual animal. Despite the various changes, the old dog is the same animal identical with the little puppy, except for age. The acceptance of identity is often accompanied by accepting universality.

(3) To regard existence as essentially characterized by universality is to view the difference in existing things as less basic than their similarities. For example, emphasizing similarities, various animals are lumped together into the category *dog* on the assumption that there is something important about each of them which is the same in all of them despite the differences between say, a poodle and a St. Bernard. This sameness is the essence of "dogness," and is taken to be the same for all times, in all animals, within a certain range. This essence is a universal, basically independent of space and time. Accepting universality as a basic characteristic of existence, it becomes possible to say that even though there are many different dogs, and even though the species is evolving, *what it is to be a dog* does not change. This "what it is to be a dog" is the universal found in all dogs at all times.

(4) The division of existence into distinct things which have a universal nature, which are permanent, and which are identical with themselves over a period of time, is usually accompanied also by accepting the unity of distinct things. For example, one particular thing, say, a dog, is made up of many parts. But though it is made up of many parts, it is still one thing. The assumption of many parts, or aspects, under the heading "one thing" is what is meant by the unity of a thing. Though flesh is not bone, and blood is yet a third thing, and all three of these are different from habits or appetites, and though a dog consists of all of these different things (along with many others), it is commonly assumed that they are all so related to each other that they form one thing, this dog. Sometimes this doctrine of identity is coupled with the doctrines of universality and identity, and it is held that the reason why the different parts of an organism are related in such a way that they form one thing is that they all belong to the same underlying thing, namely, the substratum of the dog. On this view the unity, identity,

and universality of things is attributed to an unperceived substratum in which the perceivable characteristics of things are thought to inhere.

Having in mind some of the main features of a substance view of existence, it is now possible to discuss the metaphysical views of the Vaibhashikas and Sautrantikas, who were, above all else, concerned to deny the substance view. Their main views are just the opposite of the permanence, unity, identity, and universality. The opposite of permanence is momentariness. The opposite of unity is conglomeration. The opposite of universality is particularity. And the opposite of identity is discreteness. In the Buddhist view, all existence is regarded as momentary, being made up of discrete particulars in various conglomerations. This view of existence is common to both Vaibhashikas and Sautrantikas. They also share the following views: (1) The discrete particulars which make up existence are "point instants" of force, or energy. (2) These "point instants" are in constant flux. (3) Arising and ceasing are inherent in existence. (4) The criterion for being real is the ability to have effects: only that can be admitted to be real which produces effects; that which does not produce effects could never be known to be real, for realities are known by their effects. (5) And of course, both of these schools accept the universal Buddhist doctrine that the order and regulation of the elements of existence is according to the principle of dependent origination (*paticca samuppada*), which is the law of arising and ceasing of elements of existence.

Before going into the arguments used to support the metaphysical views of these two schools, certain differences in their views need to be pointed out. The first difference concerns the duration of existence. The Vaibhashikas hold that the production of the succeeding moment in the sequence of becoming that constitutes reality would be impossible unless each moment existed in the past and the future as well as in the present. Unless it existed in the past it could not be affected by the moment of existence that preceded it most recently in the past. That it exists in the present is obvious. But it must also exist in the future in order to influence the next moment of existence which has not yet arisen. A considerably oversimplified picture of existence in this view would reveal each moment of existence having a small portion of its existence in the past and another small portion in the future, with the bulk of its existence in the present.

The Sautrantikas reject the view that the past and future constitute part of reality. They admit only the present as real on the grounds that

(1) *ultimate* moments of existence could not be further divided into past, future, and present moments if they were really ultimate, and (2) the past, by very definition, has passed on and no longer exists. And the future is not yet here; how then, could past and future be regarded as real?

The second difference concerns the nature of the ultimate elements, or moments, of existence. According to the Vaibhashikas these elements were the basic elements of the experienced datum. The most elementary features of the experienced datum constitute the ultimate moments of its existence. It does not appear that the Vaibhashikas distinguished between the features of the datum ("object") as it is in itself and the features of the datum as experienced. The Sautrantikas regarded the ultimate *dharmas*, or elements, as themselves not experiencable. They are outside the realm of time and space, for as constituting the basic components of existence they were the very conditions of space and time, and thus could not themselves be located in space and time. Thus, on the basis of distinguishing between the datum as perceived and the datum independent of perception, the Sautrantikas viewed the ultimate *dharmas* as the unexperienced and indescribable constituents of the perceived.

The third difference between Vaibhashikas and Sautrantikas concerns ways of knowing. The Vaibhashika is a direct realist, holding that what is, is perceived directly as it really is. Between what exists and what is perceived to exist, there is no difference. Perception conforms exactly to what is to be perceived. The Sautrantika is an indirect or representationalist realist, holding that we do not *directly* perceive things as they are in themselves, but that we perceive them only indirectly by means of certain representations. The data of experience, which are distinguished from the data experienced, are regarded as a means whereby the knower is acquainted with existence. A rough analogy can be made to a photograph. The photo is not reality itself, but it represents reality to us. If the photo is good, the datum photographed is not distorted and is presented as it really is. But nevertheless, the photo is not the reality; it is only a means for representing reality. Similarly, for the Sautrantika, the sensations and percepts of experience are only means for representing reality. Even though these are held to be adequate, in that ordinarily they do not distort reality, still reality is presented only indirectly through these means.

Turning now to the arguments used by the Vaibhashikas and Sautrantikas to support their metaphysics of flux and momentariness, we find that the overall argument is disjunctive in structure.[1] The basic assumption is that either the substance view of reality is correct, or else the opposite of that view—the flux view—is correct. Consequently, the major effort is directed toward showing the substance view to be untenable.

The arguments used to demolish the substance view of reality are arguments against (1) permanence, (2) identity, (3) unity, and (4) universals.

1. The arguments against permanence assume that the reality of something can be tested by determining whether or not it is a force capable of producing changes. Only that may be admitted to be real which can be known to have effects. The metaphysical support for this assumption is that the quest for ultimate reality is a quest for the causes of the experienced world. But since causes are causes only to the extent that they produce effects, it is not possible to have real causes that do not produce effects. Epistemologically, this assumption is supported by the fact that knowledge represents a change in the knower, and that nothing could be known which was not capable of producing a change in the knower. Therefore, it would be impossible to have knowledge of a reality which did not produce changes or have effects.

Assuming that action is the test of the real (for no changes can be caused except by bringing about a change), it remains to show that the permanent is not active. This can be done by showing that both terms of the following disjunction are false: either the action of causation is instantaneous and complete, or else it is temporally extended. The action of causation cannot be instantaneous and complete, for then all the effects would be produced at once and reality would, except for that moment, be static. Furthermore, if the action were instantaneous and complete, the question would arise as to whether or not the permanent exists after the first moment of change—if it does, then it should give rise to the same effects as it did in the first moment, and the same for each succeeding moment. But this is absurd, for it results in an infinity of complete universes. If the permanent continues to exist after the first moment of causation but not as a cause, then apparently it changed from a cause to a non-cause. But the changing is not permanent. Also, that would make the permanent two opposing things at the same time for it would have to be both cause and non-cause. Since it is not

---

[1] The following arguments are formulated historically by the Sautrantikas, but they are essentially the same as the arguments used by the Vaibhashikas. For fuller treatment of these arguments the reader might consult Th. Stcherbatsky, *Buddhist Logic* (Leningrad: Academy of Sciences of the USSR, 1932), Vol. 1, pp. 79 ff.

possible for a self-contradictory thing to exist, such a reality is not possible.

The alternative to instantaneous and complete causal action is temporally extended causal action. This view is untenable also, for if it were the case that the permanent cause produced first x, then y, and then z, etc., it could be asked whether or not y or z could have been produced while x was being produced. If the answer is affirmative, it would turn out that all the effects were producible at once, and this alternative would be indistinguishable from the first. But if the first cause could not produce effects y, z, etc. at any given time, say when x was being produced, it would be impossible for it to cause them at any later time, for what is not capable of producing a given effect at a given time cannot produce that effect at any other time, except by assuming other causal activty. For example, a barren woman cannot produce a son at this time. And for the same reason she cannot do so, she also cannot produce a son at any other time. An objection might be made to the Sautrantika argument on the grounds that while time itself does not produce a capability in the cause, nevertheless, time may allow for certain modifications to take place so that causation is possible. For example, sometimes a seed does not cause a plant, but sometimes it does. The reason is that time allows certain modifications in the conditions which enable the seed to cause a plant at one time, though not at another. But this objection begs the whole question of causation. If it is admitted that time itself does not cause things, then it cannot be admitted that time brings about modifications, for modifications are nothing other than changes or effects. Thus some other causality is required, and the same questions arise concerning the possibilities of this causation. Even if it is admitted that certain modifications in the cause are required, the Buddhist argument is successful, for this is an admission that the cause has changed. But if the cause has changed, then there are really two things; the cause prior to change and the cause after change. To admit that the substance changes as it produces effects is to deny permanence and to admit different existences at different moments. And this is in accord with the doctrine of momentariness which the Buddhists wish to support.

2. The arguments against identity proceed by trying to show that the identity of things is illusory. Advocates of a substance view of reality maintain that a thing remains identical with itself over a period of time by assuming that a thing naturally continues to exist unless destroyed or altered by outside and violent forces. But this assumption is false, for unless a thing were naturally subject to change and cessation,

nothing could bring about change and cessation with respect to that thing. For example, when forces such as a blow from a stick act upon a jar, the jar is destroyed. But one cannot say that the nature of a jar is to exist identical with itself without change unless acted upon by an outside force. After all, unless arising and ceasing belonged the the jar as part of its nature, nothing could cause or destroy a jar. If destruction was not inherent in the jar blows from sticks would mean nothing; the jar would continue to exist. But the nature of a jar is such that blows from sticks provide the occasion for its cessation. If it were not the blow from the stick then it would be some other occasion that would accompany the destruction of the jar, for the nature of a jar is not such that it can exist identical with itself forever.

The illusory quality of identity is quite clear in the case of the aging of a dog. It clearly is not the case that a dog goes along unchanging for several years, and then, at some precise time, begins to age. The process of aging begins when the puppy is conceived, and by the time it is born it has already aged considerably. Aging is simply change, which is a combination of cessation and arising of elements. The illusion of identity is based on certain arbitrary perspectives. When we fix on certain elements and notice their cessation we lament over the old age, decay, and death inherent in things. When we fix not on that ceasing of elements, but on the arising of elements, we rejoice over birth, life, and youth. But in reality, arising is always accompanied by ceasing, and ceasing is always accompanied by arising. Birth and death are parts of the same process, and it is simply the assumption of a certain attitude toward a part of the process that leads to revulsion and despair on the one hand, and to exultation and rejoicing on the other. The truth is that there is no identity. There is only the continuous arising and ceasing of elements.

3. The argument against unity is based on the impossibility of knowledge of a *whole*. According to the substance view, an object such as a table, though consisting of many parts, is held to be one whole. The Sautrantika argument against this view proceeds by showing that it is not possible to know the whole. For example, it is not possible to see the whole table. Only a small part of the table is seen. And only a small part can be touched, etc. Ordinarily this is explained by saying that it is one part of the whole table that is seen, and that by moving around to various perspectives one can consecutively come to see the whole table. But this explanation will not do, for even at best, all that would be seen would be the various *surfaces* of the table. It would not be possible

to see beyond the surface of the table, even though the table is assumed to consist of more than mere surfaces. But even if more than surfaces could be seen, the explanation would not be satisfactory, for the different visual perceptions attained from different perspectives do not of themselves also carry with them the perception that they are of the same whole. It is entirely possible that each different perception is the perception of a different thing. There is nothing in the perception itself to guarantee that it belongs to the same object as other perceptions. This being so, there is no basis other than that of fanciful mental construction for claiming that there are wholes made up of different parts. All that can be claimed is the object of perception, and since there is no valid basis for connecting these perceptions together into wholes, the supposed "oneness" of things must be illusory. Just as a movie is really no more than consecutive still pictures, so reality is no more than succeeding elements. But just as the consecutive passage of the still pictures gives rise to the appearance of one continuous whole moving picture, so does the incessant rise and fall of elements give rise to the appearance of the unity of whole things. In reality, however, the moments of existence are no more than "point-instants" of force, rising and falling in dependence upon each other.

4. The argument against universals claims the unknowability of such entities. The identity of one thing with another, such as the sameness of two tables, in virtue of their being tables, depends upon the supposition of a universal—tableness. Aside from the metaphysical difficulty of explaining how one universal entity could exist in many different entities widely separated in space and time, and be totally unaffected by what happened to the entities in which it existed, there is the problem of explaining how the universal is known. Since even the supporters of the substance view admit that perception is of particulars, the only way they can explain the perception of universals is to assume a kind of double perception, first perceiving the particular, and then perceiving the universal as a sort of timeless, spaceless duplicate of the particular. But there is no evidence of this kind of duplication in perception. Consequently the Sautrantikas take the position that the universals attributed to reality are nothing more than logical constructions placed on a reality that is in every respect particular.

In addition to arguing for their position indirectly by arguing against the opposite view, the Sautrantikas support their position by arguing that certain problems which arise as a result of trying to interpret reality systematically are more easily solved by taking a flux view of reality. Without doubt, the basic problem for a metaphysician is that of change. If change is admitted it would seem that permanence would also have to be admitted, for a change is always a change of something to something else, as when a green leaf changes into a red leaf. And the something undergoing change—the leaf—does not change, but some of its characteristics appear (red) and disappear (green).

The claim that a permanent reality exists is a difficult position to defend, as seen by the preceding arguments. On the other hand, if change is denied, the whole metaphysics is out of tune with our basic and immediate experience.

In order to maintain that reality is in complete flux, undergoing only change without any vestiges of permanence, the Buddhists obviously cannot think of change as the alteration of a permanent something underlying the various perceivable characteristics of things. In fact, they cannot accept any ordinary notions of causality, for nothing endures long enough to produce an effect. What they substitute for causality is the law of dependent origination, according to which entities and elements *replace one another rather than cause one another*. The law of dependent origination is a law of connectedness between moments, but it is not a law of causal connectedness. If it were a law of causal connectedness one moment in a sequence would be the cause of the next, and it would be necessary to attribute duration to the moments, as some of the Vaibhashikas did. But to attribute duration to the moments is to postulate a kind of permanence.

By replacing the law of causal connectedness with the law of dependent origination, the Buddhists are in a position to explain the appearance of continuity and duration that characterize the common-sense view of reality without giving up the momentariness of existence. There is continuous change without permanence because change is the *replacement* of one moment of existence by another, and not the *causing* of one moment by another. The replacement of moments occurs with a rapidity that looks like continuity and endurance—it is this false appearance that underlies the mistaken claims about permanence and identity. The mental constructions placed on the content of perceptions give rise to apparent unity and universals.

As a result of these various arguments, the Vaibhashikas and Sautrantikas hold a metaphysical position according to which reality is quite different from what those supporting the substance view claim. The substantialists hold that reality has more permanence that it appears to have: the Buddhists hold that things do not have the unity that they appear to have. The substantialists hold that there is less change in individuals than appears: the Buddhists hold that there is more. The substantialists hold that there is a greater amount of sameness (universality) in reality than appears: the Buddhists hold that there is less than appears. Thus, the Vaibhashika and the Sautrantika theory of reality is summed up in the view that reality consists of a numberless quantity of spaceless and timeless forces constantly arising and falling in dependence upon each other.

KNOWLEDGE

Turning now to the theories of knowledge underlying the metaphysical views of the Vaibhashikas and the Sautrantikas, it is found that they hold different and opposed views. Though they agree that reality can be known as it is in itself, and therefore are classified as realists rather than idealists, they disagree about how reality is known.

Concerning knowledge of reality two main views are possible. According to the first, external objects are known as they exist in themselves; there is no difference between what exists and what is known to exist. According to the other view, all that is ever known is the content of consciousness, and there is no way of showing that the contents of consciousness do or do not correspond to what really exists. This latter view, known as idealism, is rejected by the Vaibhashikas and the Sautrantikas, for they claim it allows no way of distinguishing (1) consciousness itself from the contents of consciousness, or (2) valid from erroneous consciousness.

The view that in knowledge objects are revealed as they exist in themselves has two major variations. The first variety is characterized by the claim that external reality is directly perceived to exist. The second variety is characterized by the claim that external reality is not known directly, but is inferred to exist from perceptual evidence. The first of these two views is held by the Vaibhashika, who are therefore called *direct* realists, and the second view is held by the Sautrantikas, who are therefore called *indirect* realists, or representationalists.

The Vaibhashikas support their direct realism against the Sautrantika view by arguing that representationalism is an incorrect theory. According to the representationalist view, the ultimate elements of things are never directly perceived, but are inferred to exist, as they are *represented* by the perceptual experience. It is rather as if a man who has never seen Mt. Everest, but has seen photographs of it, can infer the existence of the mountain from the existence of the photos—for if there were no mountain, photographs of it could not possibly exist. In a similar way, even though the blueness present in the visual perception of a blue object is not the same as the blueness in the object itself, nevertheless it is a kind of copy of it, and enables the viewer to infer that there is really an independent blueness existing objectively in reality.

The difficulty with this view is that if nothing is perceived directly there is never any basis for inference. It is one thing to see Mt. Everest and then to see a photo of it and consequently judge the photo to be a good or bad likeness of the mountain. But if one saw nothing but photos and never experienced a mountain in reality, it would be impossible for him to judge whether or not the photos resemble the mountains. In fact, there would be no basis for even conjecturing, let alone knowing, that anything existed other than the photos. If a person were completely unfamiliar with an external object it is not possible that any content of perceptual consciousness should appear as the sign, or the copy, or the representation of that object.

The foundation of the Vaibhashika argument is the claim that inferential knowledge is necessarily a secondary knowledge, for the essential feature of inference is that it proceeds from prior knowledge. Without the prior knowledge there would be no inference. But if all perceptual knowledge is essentially inferential, what would be the source of the required prior knowledge? Since obviously there is no knowledge prior to perceptual knowledge it cannot be the case that perceptual knowledge is inferential, and it must be admitted that at least some perceptual knowledge is direct.

One of the main reasons for the Sautrantika's rejection of direct realism is that they hold that it conflicts with the theory of momentariness. Since moments of existence are without duration it is not possible for objects to be present at the time they are perceived. By the time they are perceived these objects have given place to succeeding objects. What happens in perception, according to the Sautrantikas, is that in its instantaneous arising and ceasing, the moment of existence leaves its mark on the perceiving consciousness. This mark is converted, in consciousness, into perception of the object. But by the time this occurs the original object has ceased to be, and has been replaced by another. What happens in inference, consequently, is that from the mark left on the perceiving consciousness the prior existence of the object is inferred. This explanation may be likened to the way we see a star. Since the star is so very far away the light waves from the star may reach us only after the star itself has ceased to exist. Still, even though it was not perceived directly, but only indirectly, through the light it gave off, from the mark (light) left on the mind by the star we can correctly infer that the star did exist.

In addition, the Sautrantikas urged that the Vaibhashika view does not readily allow for perceptual error. If what is perceived is perceived directly as it is, how is error possible? According to the Sautrantika view, a representation may be mistakenly attached to an object and thus result in erroneous knowledge claims. But the Vaibhashika view does not allow such an explanation of error.

IDEALISM

According to the idealism of the Yogacara school, reality is of the nature of consciousness. The existence of an extra-conscious reality is denied and consciousness alone is maintained to be real. The basic appeal of this position derives from the difficulty of maintaining the existence of a reality outside of consciousness. Since, by definition, whatever is known is known within consciousness, it is not possible to have knowledge of an existing reality except in consciousness.

The chief obstacle in the way of accepting this view is the common tendency to suppose that consciousness is always consciousness *of* something, and unless there were objects outside of consciousness there would be nothing for consciousness to be consciousness of, and then there could be no consciousness. Since this latter view is held by the realists, the Yogacarins directed many of their arguments against the Vaibhashika and Sautrantika views of reality.

In the first place, the realist view that there are objects external to consciousness can at best be regarded as a speculative theory designed to answer questions concerning the arising of consciousness and changes in consciousness. It cannot be regarded as a *fact*, for there is no direct evidence for it. It is not possible for anyone to experience an object outside of consciousness, for to experience something means to experience it in consciousness. Consequently, all the purported evidence and proofs for the existence of extra-conscious objects must come from consciousness itself. But clearly, the existence of objects within consciousness cannot be regarded as proof that objects exist outside of consciousness.

There is no possible direct evidence for the existence of objects different from the objects of consciousness. The Yogacarins argue that this can be seen clearly by considering the example of color. Often a distinction is made between the awareness of the color blue, and the color blue itself. According to the Yogacarins, however, this distinction is without basis, for the color blue is never perceived except in awareness of something blue. And since they are never perceived independently or separately, there is no possibility of assuming that the awareness of the color blue and the color blue itself are anything other than identical with each other. But if they are identical, the distinction between them disappears. And when this happens, the basis for claiming an extra-conscious reality disappears.

A kind of intuitive objection to the conclusion of the foregoing argument maintains that there must be a difference between consciousness of an object and the object itself, because nearly everyone feels that there is a difference for ordinarily the two are distinguished. This objection is countered by the Yogacarins with the example of dreaming. Most people dream, and while they are dreaming they assume that the objects of which they are aware have objective existence outside of their dream. Now, just as the assumption within the dream that there are objects existing outside of dreams does nothing to establish the existence of such objects, just so the assumption of people in a state of ignorance that objects of consciousness have an objective existence outside of consciousness does nothing to establish the existence of such objects.

Since the realism of the Vaibhashikas and Sautrantikas is not simply a matter of obvious fact, but is a philosophical theory about the nature of the world and knowledge, the Yogacarins could attempt to defend their view of "consciousness only" by demonstrating that realism rests on an untenable basis. To this end arguments were brought forth to show the impossibility of objective existence.

If objects exist independently of consciousness they must either be simple wholes, without any parts, or else they must be wholes composed of parts. Objective existence in the sense of a simple whole is ruled out by the nature of knowledge claimed by the realist himself, according to which knowledge consists in the revelation of relations. Since there are no relations unless there are parts to be related, there could be no knowledge of simple wholes. And if it is said that it is the simple wholes that are related to each other the difficulty remains, for now all the wholes together are taken as comprising a new whole, in which the simple wholes inhere in their various relations. But this is equivalent to the atomistic view of reality, according to which objects are composed of atoms or parts. And the problem with this view is that the atoms or parts in themselves are unknowable, but are simply postulated to account for the objects of consciousness.

According to the Yogacarins, the chief difficulty with trying to prove the existence of extra-conscious objects is connected with the inseparability of the object from knowledge. There is never the least shred of evidence for the existence of an object except when the object is known. But since the object is known only in consciousness there cannot be any evidence for the existence of objects outside of consciousness.

The Yogacarins reject the argument that the very existence of consciousness constitutes a proof for the existence of independent objects, inasmuch as consciousness is constituted by the activity of relating objects to each other and to a subject. For example, it might be said that in consciousness of a chair the existence of a chair is assumed; otherwise there would be nothing to be related to the self, and there would be no consciousness. Consciousness is always consciousness of something and any proof that there is no "something" is, by the same argument, proof that there is no consciousness. And just as the attempt to prove the non-existence of consciousness by the exercise of consciousness is absurd, so also the attempt to disprove objects of consciousness is absurd.

According to the Yogacara analysis, though consciousness cannot be denied since it is self-revealing, this does not provide evidence for the existence of objects, for it is the nature of consciousness to be self-existent. That consciousness does not require an object is clear from the example of dreams, where the dream objects are by none admitted as having objective existence, but by all admitted to have existence in consciousness. If this is the case with some instances of consciousness, it proves that consciousness can exist without the assumption of extra-conscious objects. It does not, however, prove that *in fact* consciousness either does, or can, in all cases, exist without the assumption of extra-conscious objects. Granted the impossibility of proving that there are extra-conscious objects and granted the possibility of consciousness without extra-conscious objects, as evident from dreams, the Yogacarins maintain that it is more reasonable to hold that the various objects of consciousness are simply the creations and projections of consciousness. The purported difficulty of accounting for the variety of objects and modes of consciousness disappears upon recognition that consciousness is itself a dynamic unfolding of its own inherent tendencies.

Supported by the foregoing objections to realism, the Yogacara position maintains that consciousness alone is real. Ideas are real, objects are not. The distinctions that are usually made between subject and object, between things and ideas, between existence and knowledge —these are really only distinctions within consciousness, and never distinctions between what is within consciousness and what is outside of consciousness. Consequently, the central theme of this school is that whatever is experienced is mind-wrought.

This position, which is supported by the arguments against realism examined above, is based upon psychological experience. The arguments against realism are not definitive, for they are relative to those views, and not independently valid. But the direct realization of absolute consciousness as the sole reality stands as irrefutable justification of the Yogacara position. For those who have not achieved such a direct realization there is still the evidence of consciousness in trance. On the assumption that someone who has disciplined and developed his powers of meditation and has concerted all his energies to discover the ultimate reality comes closer to reality than one who is distracted and scatters his energies in countless ways, the fact that a multitude of varied forms and colors can be directly experienced in trance is convincing evidence that objects are really only manifestations of consciousness. For those without even the experience of trance there remains the faith in the reports of the Buddhas who have experienced the ultimate reality. For others, there are the various arguments against realism, and the various explanations of the nature of consciousness to lend plausibility to the "consciousness-only" view of reality.

In order to show that the realist views are unsatisfactory it is not enough simply to argue that the arguments for their positions are unconvincing, but it is also necessary to show how the plausibility of the realist view depends upon a wrong interpretation of experience. Basically, this is a matter of showing that the belief in external reality rests upon a misinterpretation of inner experience or consciousness. The misinterpretation rests upon a failure to recognize the nature and functions of consciousness.

The Yogacarins distinguish between various levels of consciousness, all of them dependent upon an absolute consciousness called *alaya-vijnana*, or "seed-consciousness." By reference to this seed-consciousness it is maintained that consciousness can exist independently, and that the various conscious activities arise from its own potentiality. Furthermore, this consciousness is entirely self-determining and self-revealing. It is this consciousness that creates the objects believed by the ignorant to exist outside of consciousness.

At one level of consciousness there is the awareness of the various objects of the senses, accounting for the six consciousnesses of eye, ear, nose, tongue, touch, and mind. But at another level there is consciousness of these six consciousnesses. This is a kind of self-consciousness which underlies the other consciousnesses and gives them unity. These two levels of consciousness are within the realm of the experiencable. The third level of consciousness is not experiencable except in ultimate enlightenment. It is the seed-consciousness, which is the ultimate reality underlying all the other levels and modes of consciousness. It is not to be confused with what is experienced in the various modes of consciousness, but is entirely undifferentiated. From this seed-consciousness originate the other activities of consciousness, and to this seed-consciousness return the effects of those other functions of consciousness.

The nature of this seed-consciousness cannot be stated literally, for it is beyond all differentiations and distinctions. As a result, the relations between this fundamental consciousness and ordinary experience are indicated only in similies. For example, in the *Lankavatara Sutra* the following illustration is given:

> Consciousness, consisting of the *skandhas* [five groups], *dhātus* [elements of being], and *āyatanas* [sense fields], which are without a self or of anything of the nature of a self, arises from ignorance, *karma*, and craving, and it functions through being attached to grasping at things by means of the eye and all the organs, and makes the presentations of its store-mind [seed-consciousness] appear as bodies and vessels, which are manifestations of its own mind [the store-consciousness].[2]

As to be expected, since all reality is regarded as mind only, or consciousness only, the ultimate reality is equated with the fundamental consciousness, or seed-consciousness. As ultimate reality it is beyond differentiation and plurality, so there is no question of its being either one or many.

What then is to be made of the many distinctions ordinarily made, and assumed by the Four Noble Truths and the Noble Eightfold Path? According to the Yogacarins, a distinction must be made between absolute reality and absolute truth, and between relative reality and relative truth. From the perspective of the unenlightened the relative reality constituting ordinary experience can be conceived of as a manifestation of the absolute reality, evolving out of the basic seed-consciousness. It is seed-consciousness itself which manifests itself as touch, mental activity, feeling, perception, and choice. And it is seed-consciousness

[2] E. J. Thomas, *The History of Buddhist Thought* (London: Routledge & Kegan Paul, 2nd ed. 1951), p. 234.

itself that manifests itself as an underlying self-consciousness, and thus makes possible the heresy of a self. But all this is only from the standpoint of the unenlightened.

In ignorance the activities proceeding from the seed-consciousness are differentiated from that consciousness and taken to exist in their own right. This gives rise to the error of externality of objects. In ignorance of the truth that both object-consciousness and self-consciousness are nothing other than manifestations of seed-consciousness, the self-consciousness distinguishes itself from object-consciousness and relates itself to object-consciousness as subject is related to object. This is manifested in the constant grasping for objects characterizing the lower levels of consciousness. The grasping, however, is without real basis, for as Vasubandhu points out:

> The various consciousnesses are but transformations. That which discriminates and that which is discriminated are, because of this, both unreal. For this reason, everything is mind only.[3]

What this absolute reality of seed-consciousness is in itself cannot be said, but must be experienced directly. As Vasubandhu says:

> To hold something before oneself, and to say that it is the reality of mind-only, is not the state of mind-only, because it is the result of grasping. But when [the objective world which is] the basis of conditioning as well as the wisdom [which does the conditioning] are both eliminated, the state of mind-only is realized, since the six-sense organs and their objects are no longer present.[4]

According to the Yogacarins, the teachings of the Buddha reflect his skillfulness in distinguishing between the levels of consciousness and the corresponding levels of reality, and adapting his teachings to the condition of the hearer. For example, the principle of dependent origination, which underlies the basic Buddhist teachings, is perfectly valid on the plane of relative reality, and it is used by the Yogacarins themselves to explain the arising and ceasing of the appearances of externality and a self out of the fundamental consciousness. But at the level of ultimate reality, the principle of dependent origination is not itself taken to be real independently of consciousness.

RELATIVISM

Whereas the Sautrantikas and Vaibhashikas took the existence of the elements of external objects as the absolute basis for their theory

[3] *Source Book in Indian Philosophy*, ed. by Radhakrishnan and Moore (Princeton: Princeton University Press, 1957), p. 336.
[4] *Ibid.*, p. 337.

of reality, and the Yogacarins took the existence of fundamental consciousness as the absolute basis for their theory of reality, the Madhyamika philosophers regarded both external reality and consciousness as
only relatively real. Because the Madhyamika philosophy recognized
nothing in the conceptual realm as ultimately or absolutely real, it
came to be known as the philosophy of *shunyata*, or relativism.

No doubt, all of the schools of Buddhism represent the attitude that
peace and wisdom are not to be found in subtle conceptual theories,
but can be realized only by a direct participation in the processes of
reality. The Buddha-nature is the ultimate reality, regardless of how
conceived, and is the ultimate basis of each person. Consequently, only
participation in that Buddha-nature will bring illumination and an
end to suffering. In Madhyamika philosophy, however, this attitude
comes to be underwritten by a critical analysis of conceptual construction.
No philosophical view escapes the criticism of the Madhyamika, and no
conceptual absolutes are tolerated. According to Nagarjuna, the principal philosopher of this school, mistaking conceptual absolutes for ultimate reality lies at the heart of man's suffering.

Nagarjuna's philosophical position appears to recognize that the
most basic and exciting fact about man is his quest to be. This quest to
be—the most fundamental of all quests—manifests itself in the activity
of creating a world out of the fundamental elements of experience.
Man sees around him only the "other." In his quest to be, he cannot
tolerate the other, for the other is not-self; it represents the being that
man seeks. To make that other—that not-self—part of one's self is the
challenge. The most obvious effort to convert the other into self occurs
in knowledge, where there is a uniting of the other with the self in the
act of knowing. In knowledge one can make the other self, for knowledge
is a unity of the self and other. The thirst for knowledge is simply one
manifestation of the quest to be, for in attempting to satisfy that thirst
one attempts to make the world his own, to make it part of his being.
In his knowledge he creates a world which is part of his own being.

The problem with this procedure is that it is temptingly easy for man
to mistake the world he has created in his knowledge, which is merely a
world of names and forms, for reality itself. When he succumbs to the
temptation he fixes on the name and form of self, that he has created in
his knowledge, as his own self. He identifies his own being with this
construction of name and form. Then the real self, burdened by the
ignorance resulting from mistaking the self of name and form and the
world of name and form for the real self and the real world, gets

overlooked in the struggle that ensues between the false self of name and form and the false world of name and form. The resulting bifurcation, which underlies this inauthentic existence in this inauthentic world, is responsible for the disease—the *dukkha*—that Buddhism wishes to overcome.

Distinguishing between reality and views of reality, Nagarjuna apparently desired to show the dangers inherent in regarding any one view of reality as being absolutely true. Views are conceptual constructions of name and form, and to claim any view as absolutely true is to refuse to recognize the insights of other views, and thus to rule out possible avenues of illumination.

The positive conception of Nagarjuna seems to be that while theories and views are constructions of name and form, and therefore could not be equated with reality itself, conceptual constructions can point to reality. Therefore a dialectic of views could provide a basis for insights into reality itself, although surely direct participation in reality is a matter beyond all views. Nevertheless, views constitute an invaluable aid to realization, if they are regarded not as absolute and independent, but as relative and complementary.

Historically, it appears that one of Nagarjuna's primary aims was to remove the sources of strife and differences found among the many different schools of Buddhism. This he attempted to do by providing a sufficiently broad base for the teachings of Gautama. Surely, since each of the schools clung to its own interpretation of the teachings of Gautama, and since Gautama clearly taught the need for non-clinging, these schools must be making a mistake. To exhibit the mistake was the job Nagarjuna set for himself. The task consisted in assuming the views (conclusions and arguments) of each Buddhist school of philosophy and showing that ultimately they were self-contradictory. The lesson drawn from the self-defeating views of the various philosophies is that a person should not cling to any one theoretical view, mistaking that view for the complete truth about reality.

The dialectic, which assumed the various conclusions and standpoints of the different philosophical systems and rigorously applied to them the canons of logic and reasoning that were accepted by their supporters, was itself not part of a philosophical system. It did not constitute or rest upon a view of reality. Rather, it was a method. Even as method it had nothing of its own to offer, for the critical analyses constituting the Madhyamika dialectic assume the principles and methods used by the supporters of the various systems. Concept after concept was taken up and shown to contain within it the seeds of its own contradiction; every system examined was shown to be inconsistent within itself. But the dialectic rested on the assumptions of the various systems and not upon assumptions accepted as true by the Madhyamikas. Every system-builder must erect his views on certain assumptions which are not, at least in his own system, questioned. The Madhyamikas, however, refused to accept any assumptions as undeniably true.

The critical aspect of Madhyamika thought, however, respresents only one side of its development within Buddhism. On the other side is found the customary Buddhist emphasis on meditation and direct realization. It is through the meditative practices that one can go beyond the emptiness of concepts and systems to the fullness of reality as it is in itself. Reasoning is a conceptual matter and always rests upon assumptions. Even though for his own methodological approach the Madhyamika philosopher does not regard the assumptions of his arguments as true, but only as accepted by his opponents, all the arguments can possibly do is to reveal something about the system in which the assumptions are located. They can never reveal the truth of things as they are in themselves, independent of conceptualization. Consequently, even the dialectic of the Madhyamika is not to be accepted as in itself valid for uncovering the nature of reality, and it too must be abandoned at some stage in favor of direct insight and realization.

Thus, even though it is Nagarjuna's view that clinging is the cause of conflict and suffering, and even though his dialectic is aimed at showing the futility of clinging to various conceptions of reality because of the complete relativity of all conceptual systems, still, in consistency with this relativity, he does not cling to relativity either. That is, it is considered just as perverse to regard relativity as the truth about reality as it is to consider any other view as the truth about reality. In fact, Nagarjuna says, "but if people then begin to cling to this very concept of Relativity, they must be called irreclaimable."[5]

Candrakirti, who wrote an extremely subtle commentary upon Nagarjuna's aphorisms, provides a quite unflattering comparison for those who insist on regarding relativity as itself absolute, and thus cling to non-clinging. "It is," he says, "as if somebody said, 'I have nothing to sell you,' and would receive the answer, 'All right, just sell me this—your absence of goods for sale!'"[6]

[5] *Madhyamika Karika*, XIII, 8, in Th. Stcherbatsky, *The Conception of Buddhist Nirvāna* (The Hague: Mouton & Co., 1965, originally published by the Academy of Sciences of the USSR, Leningrad, 1927), p. 49.
[6] Quoted by Stcherbatsky, *Ibid.*, p. 49.

On the positive side of the Madhyamika philosophy lies the conviction that through practice in non-clinging and meditation a person can realize directly the reality he seeks for his own being. The primary function of philosophy is to lead a person to this realization, clearing away the tangles of conceptual knots and one-sided views that constitute the barrier to a direct participation in the reality man seeks. Both the formulation of systems of philosophy in an attempt to delineate the nature of this reality, and the critical attempts to show the relativity and incompleteness of such systems, are tasks secondary to that of encountering the unconditioned reality itself.

It needs to be emphasized that this underlying conviction of the Madhyamika is not itself regarded as a philosophical theory which requires justification. It is regarded as a fundamental insight issuing from an experience more basic than logic and reason. Logic and reason, though of considerable usefulness when properly understood and wisely used, are lower and secondary means for the realization of the unconditioned and undivided nature of reality.

When unwisely used, however, logic and reason themselves become barriers to this ultimate realization. The truth of *shunyata* is that no theories or views in themselves are complete and absolutely true. Concepts and systems of concepts are relative to each other. Thus, whatever truth is uncovered within concepts and systems of concepts is always relative to other concepts and other systems, and is at best only partial truth. This is the essential relativity of views that Nagarjuna attempts to demonstrate with his critical dialectic. This is done, however, not for its own sake, nor for the sake of destroying confidence in the ability to achieve a genuine encounter with reality, but for the sake of preparing a person for the higher way, the way of greater wisdom— the *Prajna-paramita*—that carries him beyond the limited wisdom concerned only with the conditioned and the relative.

As seen earlier, the Vaibhashikas and Sautrantikas taught that reality is of the nature of process, or becoming, and that it is made up of atomic elements in constant flux. These atomic elements were regarded as ultimate, not dependent upon anything else for their existence since they possessed *own-being*, or *sva-bhava*. This is, however, to teach a permanent reality, for the ultimate elements themselves are regarded as uncaused and unchanging in their own being.

The Yogacara school held that mind alone is real. External reality is declared to be unreal; it lacks *sva-bhava*. Mind, however, is totally existent; in no way is it non-being. Thus, Mind is absolute existence, possessing *sva-bhava*.

According to the Madhyamika, both the realists and the idealists have made the mistake of confusing the conditioned with the unconditioned. Neither realist nor idealist takes the middle path between *is* and *is-not*. Exclusive *is* and exclusive *is-not* are both mistakes. Exclusive *is* does not avoid the pitfall of eternalism and exclusive *is-not* does not avoid the pitfall of nihilism. Both kinds of view really regard the conditioned and the relative as the unconditioned and the absolute, and this is the basic mistake. The error lies not in recognizing that there is an unconditioned or absolute reality, but in taking what is conditioned and relative to be unconditioned and absolute. The Madhyamika also recognizes that there is an absolute, an unconditioned reality. But he does not fall into the trap of mistaking the conceptual for the unconditioned. For him the unconditioned is beyond views; i.e., it is the ultimate truth which cannot be grasped conceptually and which can only be realized by direct insight. As Nagarjuna says, "The teachings of the Buddha are based on two truths, the mundane and the ultimate. Those who do not know the distinction between these two truths do not understand the profound meaning in the teaching of the Buddha."[7]

The *Madhyamika Karika* is directed to pointing out the relativism and incompleteness of the various systems and the inadequacies of the concepts put forth as elucidations of reality. The method used in the *Karika* involves showing that when the various theories about reality which have been put forth as the ultimate truth about reality are carefully analyzed, according to the very logic of their construction they are seen to be self-contradictory. The series of reductions to the absurd of the positions examined in the *Karika* should not be taken as establishing any positive view, but only as pointing out the fallacy of mistaking the conditioned and relative for the unconditioned and the absolute.

The first chapter of the *Karika* reveals the structure and the method of the work, and contains the examination of causality which underlies every theory of reality. To appreciate the fundamental importance of the analysis of causality, it must be recognized that assumptions about causality lie at the very heart of explanations of reality.

CRITICAL DIALECTIC

Every attempt to explain the nature of reality rests upon an assumption about the causal connectedness of reality. Philosophical and scientific theories are not exceptions. Unless a connectedness between events

7 *Madhyamika Karika*, XXIV, 8, 9.

in the world is assumed, there would be no basis for inferences from one observed "fact" to another. And without causal connections, knowledge would, at best, be nothing more than a chaotic collection of observations. Organization of observations presupposes a connectedness between the observations.

The inferences and deductions characteristic of both scientific and philosophical theories of reality are of a logical nature, dependent for their validity upon the nature of the concepts and theories wherein the various relations underwriting the inferences and deductions are given. The interest man takes in philosophical and scientific theories of reality rests upon the assumption that even though the inferences and deductions characterizing these theories are logical in nature, nevertheless, they have a foundation in the real world. This is the assumption that there is a correspondence between the connections made in theories about the world and connections within the world itself. This assumption must always remain an assumption, for to attempt to demonstrate its truth would only be to show the logical necessity of a theory or a concept, and would not say anything about reality (except on the chance that reality in fact corresponds to logic).

The important link between the connectedness of concepts and the supposed connectedness of reality itself is constituted by the concept of causality. Various theories of causality are possible, but they all have in common that whatever is or comes to be, is or comes to be in dependence upon something else. The search for causes is essentially the search for the conditions of the world that is experienced. Whenever the conditions upon which something depends for its existence, or coming-to-be, are known, then the conditioned—that which comes to be in dependence upon the conditions—is also known.

The assumption underlying all theories of causality is that experienced reality is not self-existent and self-explanatory. Its existence and its explanation are tied to various factors which are more fundamental than it, and these factors must be known in order to have full knowledge of the experienced reality itself. Where did it come from? Why is it shaped like this? How does it do that? etc., are questions asked by one desiring to know a reality being observed. And these are all questions about the conditions and causes of the item in question.

It is the purpose of the first chapter of the *Karika* to show that the assumptions about causality underlying the prevalent available theories of reality are shot through with inconsistencies, and are at bottom self-contradictory and untenable. If this can be done, it will have been shown—at least for the theories in question—that philosophical theories do not yield the ultimate truth about reality.

The first aphorism of the first chapter of the *Karika* states that "There absolutely are no things, nowhere and none, that arise (anew), neither out of themselves, nor out of non-self, nor out of both, nor at random."[8]

The claim being made here is that none of the four possible views of causation are tenable. These four views are: (1) whatever arises or is produced, arises or is produced out of itself; (2) whatever arises or is produced, arises or is produced out of another; (3) whatever arises or is produced, arises or is produced both out of itself and out of another; and (4) whatever arises or is produced, arises or is produced neither out of itself, nor out of another, nor out of a combination of itself and another. The first view is ruled out by the claim, "neither out of themselves." The second view is ruled out by the expression, ". . . nor out of non-self. . . ." The third view is ruled out by the claim, ". . . nor out of both. . . ." The fourth view is ruled out by the claim, ". . . nor at random."

As pointed out above, the arguments against each of these views of causality do not rest upon any claims made by the Madhyamika philosopher, but proceed by accepting the principles and conclusions adopted by the supporters of the view being examined. Consequently, the result of the argument is not to advance any independent claim about the nature of reality, but only to point out that the claim in question is untenable.

The first view of causality, that things are self-caused, is rejected on the grounds that identity of the cause and effect does not allow for causality. If things are their own cause, there is no difference between the cause and the effect. But if the cause and the effect are identical, then it does not make sense to talk of causality, for causality is possible only as a relation between two things, one of which is productive of the other. Identity, however, rules out the possibility of all relations, including the relation of causality, for it precludes real differences and genuine distinctions. Thus, to assume the complete identity of the effect and the cause is to rule out a causal relation between the supposed cause and the supposed effect. And if the cause and the effect are held to be identical only in certain respects and different in others, the problem still exists; for if they are identical in the aspects relevant to causation, the differences are irrelevant. But if they are different with respect to the aspects

8 Stcherbatsky, *The Conception of Buddhist Nirvana*, p. 71.

involved in causation, there can be no question of self-causation, for the thing as cause is held to be different from the thing as effect, and the view of causation is really one according to which things are caused not by themselves, but by another.

The second view, that things are caused by something other than themselves, is undoubtedly the ordinary view of causation. For example, when the potter is said to be the efficient (or agent) cause of the pot, and the clay is said to be the material cause, the cause is clearly being regarded as something other than the effect. This is the view according to which whenever something new is really produced, it is so because of the productive capacity and activity of other factors which are its causes. It is the view held by the Vaibhashikas and Sautrantikas, who agree that to assume self-causation is nonsensical, on the grounds that it postulates the prior existence of the thing in question and removes the basis of causation altogether by assuming the eternal existence of that thing.

Against this view of causation the Madhyamikas urge that it is the equivalent of claiming that being can be produced by non-being, which is to get something from nothing. If the cause and effect are different, what can the relation between them be? To say that they are related inasmuch as one is cause and one is effect is to beg the whole question, for the question at stake is the *reason* for calling one thing cause and another effect. Thus to say that cause and effect are completely different from each other except insofar as one is said to be cause and the other the effect is equivalent to saying that one is cause because it is called cause and the other is effect because it is called effect. But this would make sense only upon the assumption that saying that something is something else makes it that something else!

On the other hand, it has already been argued that to the extent that the effects preexisted in their causes, they were identical with their causes, and the identity of cause and effect destroys the notion of causation, as causation is a relation, and a thing cannot be in relation with itself. Thus, the realist can only argue that the cause and effect are, in all respects relevant to the question of causality, different from each other. But this means that the effect was totally non-existent before being produced. However, if production is taken to be the manifestation of a certain relation—a causal relation between cause and effect—it would seem that effects could never be produced, for what is non-existent cannot enter into relation with anything. Consequently, it is not possible for a non-existent effect to enter into a causal relation with the cause in order to be produced.

If no relation is assumed between effect and cause, it makes no sense to talk of causality, for then anything could be produced by anything else. That is, unless the causation of the sprout by the seed, or the curd by the milk, were due to certain relationships between seeds and sprouts, and milk and curd, there is no reason why gold should not be produced out of milk and sand out of seeds. The point is that the total lack of relationships between cause and effect leads inevitably to the abandonment of causality. And since the preexistence of the effect in the cause also leads to the abandonment of causality as superfluous, Nagarjuna says, "There absolutely are no things nowhere and none, that arise anew, neither out of themselves, nor out of non-self [another]. . . ."[9]

The next claim in the aphorism follows directly, for if the claim that things are produced out of themselves is untenable, and if the view that they are produced out of something else is also untenable then it follows that things cannot be produced out of both themselves and another, for the mere combination of two non-causes does not produce a cause.

The last claim of the aphorism—that things are not produced at random—requires no special refutation, because it is itself the abandonment of causality; it is a recognition of the lack of any relations between what is said to be cause and what is said to be effect.

The four views just examined represent a "strong" theory of causality according to which the cause represents a real creative power by means of which it produces the effect. The relationship between cause and effect according to this "strong" theory is rooted in this creative power of the cause. There is a weaker theory of causality according to which the relation between cause and effect is one of coordination rather than creative production. This is the view of causality Candrakirti puts into the mouths of the Buddhist realists, when he has them say,

> We are satisfied with establishing the fact that entities, such as sensation, arise in a certain coordination with (other entities), e.g., the organ of vision, etc. (This is all that we mean, when we assert that the existence of an organ of vision, etc. are the conditions under which a visual sensation, etc. can arise).[10]

According to this view there are certain conditions which are not in themselves causes, as for example, a blue flower. And there are other conditions, such as the eyes of a person, also in themselves not causes. But when these conditions are concomitant they give rise to a third

9 *The Conception of Buddhist Nirvana*, p. 170.   10 *Ibid.*

factor, the sensation of blue. When this third factor arises, the previous conditions, or factors of flower and eye, can be seen to be causes in the sense of conditions of the sensation of blue.

This weaker view of causation, or coordination, is also rejected by the Madhyamika philosophers. The difficulty with this view is that certain factors—the blue flower and the eye—are said to be conditions for the arising of a third factor—the sensation of blue. But if the sensation of blue has not yet arisen, how is it possible that it should have conditions? The eye and the blue flower would be non-conditions. But if the sensation of blue had already arisen, there would be no question of the conditions giving rise to it. So either it must be assumed that the sensation of blue always existed, or it must be assumed it came to exist dependent upon non-conditions. The former is implausible, and the latter makes nonsense out of dependent coordinations as an explanation of the arising of new factors.

The only possibility remaining is that though the factors of blue flower and visual perception are not themselves conditions for the production of the sensation of blue, they are the conditions for a concomitance which is a condition for the production of blue. This is the view that it is not the eye or the blue flower, but the concomitance of the two that is the causal condition. But to defend this view it must either be assumed that the concomitance of two things is something other than the simultaneous presence of two conditions and that this simultaneity is itself causally productive, or else that this simultaneity causes the non-conditions of blue flower and the eye to become conditions. But if simultaneity itself were a causal condition, then the concomitance of any factors should be sufficient for the production of a new factor. But the concomitance of a blue flower and an ear does not produce the third factor of a blue sensation. And if mere concomitance is not causally productive, how could it effect the change of non-causes into causes? Candrakirti puts the arguments against regarding concomitance as a causal condition as follows:

> This also won't do! Because this concomitant condition, concomitant with something which is not yet a condition, can be considered as a condition only if the other fact is (really) a condition. We are in this case faced by the same difficulty as before. Therefore this explanation cannot be accepted.[11]

If the Madhyamika attack on the examined views of causality is successful, and every view of causality is rejected, does it follow that

[11] *The Conception of Buddhist Nirvana*, p. 171.

there are no causes in the world, but only effects? Clearly, that cannot be, for effects are effects only of causes, and where there are no causes there are no effects. But if both causes and effects are denied, is not the existence of the world denied? And is this not one of the pits—the pit of nihilism—to be avoided, according to the Buddha?

The answer to this question is that it is only upon the assumption that reality is constituted by effects and causes that a denial of causes and effects implies a denial of reality. And since no sense can be made of an attempt to deny reality, it is clear that the implication of the Madhyamika arguments is to deny the assumption that reality is constituted of causes and effects. Lack of difference between cause and effect may well render the concepts of cause and effect empty and meaningless. It is a long way, however, from the emptiness of concepts to the emptiness of reality, and it is only by identification of concepts with reality that one would take the emptiness of concepts for the emptiness of reality.

The Madhyamikas distinguished between the world of concepts—a world of logical construction, a world outlined by philosophical theories of reality—and reality itself. The latter, as it is in itself, is entirely beyond views. The former cannot be the ultimate reality for it is shot through with contradiction and inconsistency. Nevertheless, the world of logical construction is based upon reality itself, even though it misrepresents it as something other than itself. It is similar to what happens in the mistaking of a shiny shell for a coin. The thing—the shell—is really there, but in ignorance the perceiver misrepresents it to himself as a coin. The coin is not real; it exists only as a construction in the mind of the perceiver. Still, it is not a construction of nothing, but is based on an existing reality—the shell—which is not seen for what it really is.

In a similar way, the world in which most people move is the world they have constructed in their mind. No doubt, there is a reality with which they come into contact and which provides a basis for the construction of the world of determinate entities and relations. But usually this reality is not seen for what it is in itself, but is mistaken for the world of names and forms which characterize the world constructed by the mind.

The constructed world created through the ignorance of its maker serves to veil the truth of the reality which underlies it. The essential furniture of this constructed world consists in (1) gross things, such as tables, chairs, persons and trees, (2) the constituent elements of the gross things, and (3) relational entities.

The gross things, such as tables and chairs, are the collections of perceptions designated by the expressions "chair," "table," etc. For example, curd is a gross thing constituted by resistance, smell, taste, and touch. Granted the combination of these entities produced by the mind in contact with something, there is produced the "thing" to which the name "curd" is applied. Curd in itself has no independent reality. It is like a forest, having no reality of itself apart from the individual things (trees) that make it up. The name "curd" is simply a conventional term applied to a collection of perceptual items in conjunction with each other. The subtle elements of existence, which are the constituents of the gross elements of the constructed world, are also conventional entities. When the perceptions of the mind, such as tables and curd, are subjected to logical analysis it is seen that they are constituted by simpler elements. The elements that are ultimate in such analysis are taken to be the subtle elements of the world, the elements taken as ultimately real by the Vaibhashikas and Sautrantikas. There is no basis, however, for regarding the results of the analysis of the conventional entities, such as curd, as themselves having any more than a conventional reality. After all, the name "subtle element" is merely imposed on what is conceived by someone to be the subtlest element constituting his experience. Since it is only by contrast with the "gross" entities that there can be "subtle" entities, and since the gross entities are seen to be merely conventional, it follows that the subtle elements, too, are merely logical constructions of the mind.

The third kind of entities in the constructed world include such things as length, weight, direction, time, and death, to name just a few. These are clearly relational entities, since they are derived by relating gross entities to each other and subtle entities to each other, and by relating the subtle elements to the gross elements. There is no length without shortness, no lightness without heaviness, no east without west, etc. The names of the relational entities are merely references to a comparison of the perceptions which give rise to the gross things of experience. There is no time except in the sense of duration of other entities. Death, too, has no being in its own right, but is simply a name given to a construction based on the comparison of certain changes to certain other changes.

The world referred to here as "the constructed world" is, of course, the world most of us take to be the real world. It is the world of ordinary things, such as people and cows, the world of the constituents of the ordinary things (such as atoms), and the world of relations between ordinary things and their constituents. But all of this is regarded by the Madhyamika as a world constructed by mind for the reasons just presented. The items in this world are constructed by the mind and analyzed by the mind. Mind is by itself incapable of dealing with anything other than what is mind-made. And what is mind-made is relational, for the nature of mental construction requires that one thing be in relation to another.

Philosophical views, just as all other items created by the mind, are constructions, and are therefore relative. There is no saying, from the perspective of any philosophical view, that what is constructed by the mind is of the nature of reality, or that it represents reality as it is in itself. Nor is there any saying that what is of the nature of the mind is unlike reality, that it distorts reality. The distinction between the relative world of mental construction and the ultimate reality of direct insight can only be based on direct insight. As in the case of mistaking the shell for a coin, it is only by seeing the coin for what it is that one can recognize that what he had perceived as a coin was in reality only a shell.

The dialectic, whereby the essential relativity of the mind-constructed world is demonstrated, reveals the non-ultimacy of the various views about this world, shows the conditionedness and dependent character of the entities of this world, and thus paves the way for a going beyond mere views of reality to a direct realization. But it does not, by itself, provide such a realization. Such a realization is necessarily entirely beyond the world of conceptualization.

With the realization of the complete relativity (*shunyata*) of the mundane world of mental construction, all basis for clinging to anything as absolute and ultimate will disappear. All distinctions, including the distinction between *Nirvana* and *samsara* (ordinary existence), will be seen to be only relative. With the abandonment of the ignorance and perverseness which insisted on taking the mind-made world as the ultimate reality, and with a direct participation in reality, it will be realized, as Nagarjuna says, "There is no difference at all between *samasara* and *Nirvana*."[12]

[12] *Karika*, XXV, 19.

CHAPTER 13

ZEN BUDDHISM

THE relativism of the Madhyamika philosophy continues to be an extremely influential philosophical persuasion right up to the present day, for it is the main philosophical conviction underlying the practices and teachings of Zen. Zen, of course, is Zen Buddhism—a way of life which has been practiced in China, Korea and Japan for the last twelve hundred years. Some of its components and aims are, no doubt, much older. The idea of *zazen*, the chief discipline of Zen, is basically the idea of *yoga*, which has a history of more than four thousand years. The idea of disciplining oneself as a sufficient means for overcoming suffering dates back to the historical Buddha, thirteen hundred years before the appearance of Zen. But these early forms of discipline and the early sects of Buddhism were not Zen, even though they contain the beginnings of this way of life. Zen (called *Ch'an* in China) appeared when scholasticized versions of Yogacara and Madhyamika which emphasized the theoretical and idealistic orientation of Buddhism met the realistic and practical mind of the Chinese. As a result of these two contributing influences, the methods and orientation of Zen tend to be characteristically Chinese, while the presuppositions underlying the practice tend to be more typically Indian.

Invariably, in discussing Zen, the question is raised as to whether it is a religion or a philosophy. Although historically the question has sometimes been answered one way and sometimes the other, I think it is a mistake to answer the question at all. If you do not accept the presuppositions that you are still smoking, or that you have just recently stopped smoking, then you will reject the question, "Have you stopped smoking yet?" rather than answer it. Analogously, if the presuppositions of the question, "Is Zen religion or is it philosophy?" are unacceptable, the question should be rejected rather than answered, for to answer the question is to accept the presuppositions of the question. In this case the presuppositions are not only that religion and philosophy can be satisfactorily defined, but that they can be clearly distinguished from each other, and that Zen must be either one or the other. Zen does not fit neatly into any of the popular definitions of a religious way of life, for it knows no gods, seeks no immortality, and has nothing to do with sin or soul. On the other hand, it does not seem to be philosophy for it is not concerned with reasons or arguments.

Not accepting the presuppositions of the question, and avoiding the categories of religion and philosophy, we can begin by characterizing Zen as a way of life. As such it incorporates certain aims, prescribes certain practices and rests upon certain presuppositions. Even though we may not, in the last analysis, be able to state what Zen is, we shall make some headway in understanding this phenomenon if we study its practices, aims and presuppositions. The first thing to note is that as a way of life, Zen is not so much a matter of beliefs, but of doing. What does a person do if he follows the Zen way? The core of his practice consists in training in the experience of seeing directly into his complete self in the fullness of the experienced moment without the mediation of intellect. Within the context of Zen experience this attempt at definition suffers the inevitable inadequacies of every attempt to comprehend things in a merely intellectual way. The reason for this is that the entire activity of conceptualization is inadequate for comprehending things as they are, because it rests upon the arbitrary and falsifying division of reality into subject and object. Zen emphasizes the integrity and completeness of the present moment of experience wherein there is no distinction between subject and object.

As opposed to the Zen emphasis on the completeness of the present moment there are other ways of life that insist on living in the moments of the past, either wishing to regain the past or to avoid it. There are also ways of life which insist on living in the future. Here the emphasis is on tomorrow. Tomorrow we will change the world by clearing the slums, invading other galaxies, unfreezing and curing yesterday's cancer patients, and so on. From the religious perspective adopted by Christianity, Islam and Judaism, tomorrow is the big event. Tomorrow will see us, if Divine providence works in our favor, enjoying the king-dom of God.

What this attitude of looking so hard to the future that the present is virtually ignored can do in the economic spheres is well known from our understanding of the Middle Ages in Europe. But what this attitude can do to the emotional and spiritual self is not so well understood. It is possible to get a glimpse of the dangers inherent in this attitude when we see the threats and fears resulting from taking seriously the claim, formulated recently by Nietzsche, that God is dead. What the death of God means in the religious sphere is that the source of life and value in the universe has disappeared, for creation and endowing value are the main functions of God. But for those who take seriously the death of God, the belief in God as the source of value and meaning in life must now be seen not only as an illusion—the fulfillment of the wish for a powerful father image—but also as a delusion, for no God exists. But if God, who created the world and bestowed value upon it, no longer exists, then what is the source and guarantee of value in the universe?

The recent answer to this question is that man himself is the source of value in the universe. But notoriously, this has left man with an uneasy feeling. He is too much aware of his own inadequacies to assume the role of God. But at the same time he is too completely caught up in the presuppositions of God's existence to be satisfied without the fulfillment of God's functions. When man relies upon himself he must face his own incapacities and inadequacies. The transformation of the world through knowledge is one of modern man's noblest ambitions. But the large gaps in his knowledge and understanding rightly leaves man with doubts and anxieties about the outcome of the transformation. The effect of the philosophies of Kant and Hume in the West, and Nagarjuna and Shamkara in the East, was to draw attention to the limitations of reason. In this century faith in the power of reason was severely shaken when it was discovered in mathematics—the very darling of reason—that the completeness of mathematical systems could not be attained. And Heisenberg's indeterminacy principle was an unpleasant dose of medicine for those confident that modern physics would completely lay bare the organized structure of the universe. In short, the universe shows no signs of being the completely rational structure in which reason would feel completely at home.

Despite the fact, however, that the inadequacies of reason are being felt at this time, the projections of life still presuppose the older goals of reason—the complete understanding of life and reason through rational means. Man has not adjusted to the inadequacies of reason. He still proceeds—though more uneasily of late—as though reason were the adequate guide to a complete and satisfying life. Thus he continues to see himself existing in one moment, but reaping the fullness of that existence in a future moment. But underneath the plans for achievement in the future lies an awareness—sometimes so dim and murky that it passes unnoticed, and sometimes so disturbingly acute that it is frightening—that there is no existence and life except in the present moment. The future moment belongs to the future, which belongs not to life, but to forms of understanding.

What Zen does, rather than postponing the complete life to that chimerical moment in the future when we will have the complete rational knowledge required to provide for that kind of life, is to make the most of the present moment, finding therein the wholeness of self and the completeness of life. It is the quality of experience here and now, and not precision of reason, that assumes paramount importance of the Zen Buddhist.

The Zen emphasis on the immediacy and completeness of the present moment shows up in the underlying principles of Zen practice, in the quality of enlightened life, and in the teachings underlying Zen. Of these three basic features of Zen—practice, enlightenment and teachings —it is practice that comes first. Enlightenment depends upon practice, and teachings support and are determined by practice and enlightenment. It is fitting, therefore, that we should turn now to a description of the practice of Zen.

Zazen, the chief discipline of Zen practice, is taken up in order to achieve the optimal conditions for seeing directly into oneself and discovering in the purity of one's own existence the true nature of all existence. This discipline requires assuming complete control and regulation of the hands, feet, legs, arms, trunk, and head. Next breathing must be regulated so that the activities of the mind can be brought under control. Through a series of special forms of concentration the activities of the mind are brought together, unified and stilled. The emotions and volitions are also brought under control and harmonized with intellect. Having attained the foregoing, it remains to cultivate what is usually called a deep or profound silence in the deepest recesses of one's being.

The question might be raised, Why engage in the discipline of *zazen*? The answer is contained in the immediate presuppositions of Zen. Zen presupposes that the ordinary person is caught up in a maze of crisscrossing ideas, theories, reflections, prejudices, feelings and emotions such that his every experience is cut up into a variety of segments. These segments are then taken as parts of experience which can be synthesized into a whole. Thus, the ordinary person does not really experience reality, but only the network of ideas and feelings he has about reality. These ideas and feelings always stand between the individual and the reality he confronts, mediating the experience. The aim of *zazen* is to free the individual from this mediating network and allow him to enter directly and fully into the reality he confronts.

There are three basic aims of *zazen*. The first is to increase the powers of concentration by getting rid of all distracting factors and all dualities. The second is the awakening of enlightenment, or the achieving of *satori*. This is the seeing into one's ultimate self and discovering the ultimate nature of reality and the completeness of existence in the realization constituting *satori*. The enlightenment may come like a flash, but it presupposes intensive training for most people. The *koans*, or problems, and the questions and answers that are commonly used in the large sessions in the monasteries and in the private sessions between master and disciple are famous as devices for triggering enlightenment. For example, the famous Zen master, Dogen, who had been doing *zazen* for many years had heard his master say on numerous occasions that in order to realize enlightenment body and mind must fall off. But one day when he heard this his mind and body dropped off and he was enlightened. That is, he had now reached the level of concentration and insight wherein he became empty of the conceptions of mind and body. The third aim of *zazen* is to incorporate the complete enlightenment of the total self into all the daily activities. Thus every action and every moment is an action and moment lived in enlightenment.

In addition to *zazen*, *koans*, or problems, are often used in practice. They serve both to teach the aspirant and to test him. Used as a test they reveal whether or not the *zazen* efforts have succeeded in reaching a given level of concentration and enlightenment. As teaching devices, *koans* represent expressions apt for leading a person beyond the bifurcations of intellect to the direct and immediate participation in the living, whole, and complete reality. One of the most famous *koans* is known, by way of the answer, as the *mu-koan*. A monk, in all seriousness, once asked master Joshu, "Has a dog a Buddha-nature?" Joshu replied, immediately, "Mu!" Now, what is ordinarily meant by Buddha-nature is that the nature of everything is such that it can become enlightened.

This is a common Mahayana teaching, and is found in many texts. But Joshu refused to say yes. No doubt he would have been right in refusing to answer affirmatively if he had suspected that the monk was thinking that there was some *thing* called the Buddha-nature, hidden somewhere within beings. Joshu's refusal to answer yes or no was more radical. He saw that the question not only presupposed the conceptions *Buddha-nature* and *dog*, but worse, in asking if a dog has or has not a Buddha-nature, it presupposes the dichotomy between *is* and *is not*—between being and non-being. This shows that the question is merely conceptual, and that the questioner has not got outside the confines of intellect. Since it is the aim of Zen to go beyond the limitations of merely intellectual understanding Joshu says *Mu!* That is, he said nothing (but said it immediately!). This is the main point about *koans*—they have no intellectual answers. They appear to be problems only upon the assumption of certain bases and conceptions which are to be left behind. Once a monk asked the master, "What happens to our thought systems when being and non-being are not distinguished?" The master laughed heartily and drank tea. And of course this was the only answer! No answer to the question would have done, for it would have required accepting the distinctions making possible the question, in this case the distinction between being and non-being.

The enlightenment (*satori*) at which Zen aims requires going beyond all distinctions, including the distinction between *is* and *is not*, upon which all thought systems rest. Consequently, no statement is possible of what enlightenment is, except negatively, by way of pointing out what it is not. But even this presupposes *is* and *is not*, and fails to provide much understanding of this important aspect of Zen. Short of practicing Zen and achieving some measure of enlightenment, perhaps the only way to get a feeling for the experience of *satori* is to talk with or read the biographies of people who have achieved *satori*. What impresses one when this is done is the almost unanimous reference to the over-coming of distinctions, and the beauty and perfection of the world just as it is—without any distinctions. This, of course, fits in with Nagar-juna's observation that between *nirvana* and *samsara* there is no difference at all.

Turning to the teachings of Zen, it must be pointed out that the actual teachings of Zen are primarily teachings connected with the practice of *zazen*, *koan*, and question-and-answer sessions. That is, they are practical teachings, directed to fostering the way of life that Zen is. Nevertheless, these questions, as well as the practices to which they are essentially connected, have certain philosophical presuppositions. These presuppositions can be seen in the Mahayana philosophies of the Yogacara and Madhyamika schools.

As the Yogacara philosophy developed it came to regard the empirical world—the world of intellectual consciousness—as the world of *Mind-only*, since what was known thereby was only consciousness. But a reality beyond this was presupposed. It was, of course, beyond reason, but could—by practicing the Noble Eightfold Way—be experienced. Most importantly, to experience this reality would be to put an end to suffering. This ultimate reality is referred to variously as the "pure mind," and "undivided being," and the "Buddha-nature." Buddha-nature, or the pure mind, as the ultimate reality is a basic teaching of Mahayana Buddhism, and underlies the practical aim of becoming one with the all-illumining Buddha-consciousness. To achieve enlightenment is to go beyond seeing everything as mental phenomenon, or of the nature of consciousness, to seeing reality as whole, undivided and without distinction.

This teaching is important for Zen, but the texts containing the teachings about this point are quite confusing, because the expression "mind" is used in different ways. The word is used in two quite different senses, sometimes even in the same passage. We need to ask, "What is meant by mind?" The one sense of mind found in Mahayana is the ordinary view of mind as consciousness engaged in differentiating things. The other Mahayana notion of mind is something else. It is called variously *Buddha-nature, the Enlightened mind, Emptiness, No-mind, Mind-only*, and *Suchness*. These expressions all refer to the same reality, which is the very basis of human reality. The discriminating consciousness is just one expression of this reality. Feelings, emotions, and volitions are other aspects. One could go on indefinitely enumerating aspects of this reality. But the important thing to note is that this enumeration, and every assumption of a perspective which makes possible an aspect is just another activity of discrimination. In other words, all aspects and characteristics exist only as the result of discriminatory activity.

So far there is no problem. But the damage is done when this discriminatory activity, usually called intellectual or rational activity, presents itself as the ultimate judge of truth—the God's eye point of view which contains all perspectives and all truths. The result is that the perspectives of intellect are taken to be ultimate and absolute when they are only partial and dependent. The chief activity of intellect is to divide reality and to isolate the divided aspects, representing these aspects as objects or activities existing independently of each other. Furthermore, when intellect is taken as ultimate the division between subject and object—between *I* and the *that*—is taken as absolute. The result is that the individual is set apart from the reality in which he lives.

Now when the world consisting of the objects of our knowledge is described by saying "all this is mind only," the reference is clearly to the world differentiated by intellect, which means it is indeed the product of consciousness only. But this does not mean that there is nothing other than this consciousness. It means only that the world of which we are intellectually conscious is a world represented from merely one perspective: the perspective of lower discriminatory consciousness, and it should be recognized for what it is—the result of intellectual differentiation. I think it can be seen now that, at least in part, the thrust of the mind–only teaching is to call attention to the fact that we are ignoring the deeper basis of human existence by mistaking one aspect or expression of that basis for the whole reality.

The limitations of the rational consciousness are well illustrated in reason's eldest and most highly honored child, philosophy. It is well known that in any attempt to understand the world intellectually there must be a seeing of the relations between the parts that make up the whole. And these parts must themselves be understood. But to understand the parts or things that make up the world it is necessary to come to see them as they are in themselves. In order to get at things as they are in themselves there is an attempt to leave aside the personal and subjective elements in experience. This is greatly emphasized in scientific laboratory procedures where objective measurements, relying primarily on counting devices, are regarded as the key to objectivity. But what is overlooked is that the whole question of objective versus subjective is itself subjective. It is the subject's awareness of the object that must be considered. Nothing can be considered by reason except in conscious awareness. But are the objects represented in the subject's consciousness at all the same as the reality that exists outside of human consciousness? In science this question is ignored, basically because of the great confidence we have in intersubjective agreement as a guarantee of objectivity. But as soon as this attitude is stated its inadequacy is obvious.

Philosophers, in their preoccupation with this problem, have resorted to the notion of a noumenal reality, a thing-in-itself. The noumenal reality cannot itself be an object of knowledge, but it is what makes

possible whatever becomes an object of knowledge, for it is the basis of
the object's existence in consciousness. What is known is supposedly
the noumenon only as affected by the mind. But since things are known
only in consciousness, there is no way of telling whether what is present
in consciousness is in any way similar to the noumenal reality. And if
this is the case, then the noumenal reality postulated to explain the
relation of knowledge to reality is itself totally mysterious and entirely
without explanatory power. According to the Yogacara analysis, this
result is not at all surprising. The whole concept of noumenal reality,
which is the final result of the intellectual search for the underlying
principles of ultimate reality, is simply an abstraction arrived at to
solve a problem arising out of the ignorance of the limitations of the
viewpoint assumed by reason.

The emphasis in Yogacara Buddhism on the mental nature of the world
known in consciousness served to de-emphasize reason as the vehicle for
attaining absolute truth and wisdom. When reason was assigned a
secondary role the "thatness" of things achievable by reason also became
secondary. Primary now was the "suchness" of things, and the immediate
seeing into things just as they are. As a result, the development of techniques for experiencing the suchness of reality assumed greater importance than attempts to define and state what reality is. This resulted in
the emphasis on practice so characteristic of Zen, and which precludes
defining it as a philosophy. But Zen carries with it a mistrust of reason
which suggests that the Yogacara philosophy is taken seriously.

Despite the importance of the Yogacara analysis of consciousness for
Zen, it is the Madhyamika philosophy that provides the most adequate
foundation for this way of life. This philosophy emphasized the inability
of reason to solve the basic problems it sets for itself with respect to
subject and object and existence and non-existence. But rather than
regarding this as a cause for despair, it was taken as evidence for a higher
way of truth. This higher way, the way of wisdom, is the seeking by the
complete person for the ultimate reality. This way consisted in going
beyond all clingings by seeing the relativity of all things and rising above
limited perspectives. It was especially the development of relativism in
the Madhyamika philosophy that made it suitable as a basis for Zen,
for as shown in the previous chapter, this philosophy left no room for
theoretical absolutes, and made way for the development of practical
techniques related to the circumstances of each person.[1]

[1] See pp. 166–179.

But there are serious difficulties in attempting to provide a philosophical basis for Zen. Such difficulties can be seen clearly in Nagarjuna's attempts to point the bankruptcy of reason and the importance of a more basic encounter with reality. His middle-way philosophy claims that all philosophical views are untenable because they are ultimately self-contradictory. Furthermore, the negation of all views opens up the way for a direct apprehension that transcends mere thought and unites man with the real.

The difficulty with this argument is that the rejection of all views as self-contradictory presupposes the classification of all views, and this presupposes the validity of the principle of excluded middle in exhaustively classifying all systems. It also presupposes the principle of non-contradiction for purposes of rejecting views. But these two principles themselves belong to the thought systems of reason. So the Madhyamika philosopher is in a bind. If he wishes to reject philosophical systems he must embrace the very principles upon which they rest. This position, however, gives him a view subject to his own criticisms. The alternative is to give up the principles of excluded middle and non-contradiction. But then he is without the means for rejecting any views as inadequate.

Aware of this dilemma, the Madhyamika philosophers maintain that they have no view at all; the self-conscious awareness of all points of view, or of reason itself, is not another view. It is the transcending of all systems of thought. The Madhyamika position is that the direct apprehension of reality emerges when the obstacles of reason have been overcome. This seems a difficult position to maintain, however. How can it be known that what is directly apprehended is the real, and that it is being apprehended as it really is? Just because reason does not enter into this activity does not mean that the activity warrants itself. Nor does the fact that Madhyamika does not question the ontological status of this directly apprehended reality prove that it is not being distorted in being apprehended. After all, many philosophers have been without doubts that the reality they outlined in their theories was the true reality, but no Madhyamika philosopher would allow their confidence to serve as a guarantee of the truth of their views. But on what grounds can the Madhyamika philosopher disallow these claims? He cannot make any reply without contradicting his own position.

From a philosophical point of view then, we are left with the claim that since reason leads us into blind alleys, producing antinomies, there must be a means for getting in touch with reality higher than reason.

But this disjunction itself is the work of reason, so should not be allowed. Furthermore, even if the disjunction is allowed, the claim could be maintained only if it were shown that reality is, in its essence, understandable somehow—if not by reason, then by something higher than reason. And if this is not allowed, then we can challenge the second assumption of the Madhyamika, which maintains that there is a reality other than the ordinarily experienced reality. Obviously, reason cannot demonstrate this claim. But if this claim is not maintained then there is no basis for maintaining the distinction between the ultimate reality and the experienced reality. And without that distinction the Madhyamika philosopher has no basis from which to criticize the world of reason.

It would seem that there is nothing more for the Madhyamika philosopher to say. He cannot even say, as he did say historically, that all this just proves his point that reason is an inadequate means for investigating reality. However, just because there is nothing more for the philosopher to say it does not follow that there is nothing more for the Buddhist to do. Faced with these antinomies, he can resolve to practice Zen. The silence forced on the philosopher can be the beginning of a seeing into reality that goes beyond thoughts and words, and that does not leave behind any aspects of the person.

But to practice Zen is not to do philosophy, and success in Zen practice, no matter how much it improves or appears to improve the quality of life, does not constitute an argument for the correctness of any philosophical point of view. It would seem, therefore, that rather than trying to say what kind of philosophy Zen is we should conclude that it is a way of approaching reality that constitutes an alternative to the intellectual way. The rational and philosophical approach, so well known to the West, is one approach. The existential meditative way of Zen is another. The two do not exclude each other unless such exclusion is founded within a point of view assumed by one or both of these ways.

CHAPTER 14

BASIC CHARACTERISTICS
OF BUDDHIST CULTURE

THE religious-philosophical teachings of Buddhism outlined in the preceding pages have left their mark on much of Asian civilization. Buddhism, much more so than most religions, has permeated the cultures with which it has been associated. Consequently, in Ceylon, Burma, Cambodia, Thailand, and Laos, where Thervada Buddhism has held sway, and in Tibet, China, Korea, Japan, and Vietnam, where Mahayana Buddhism has been influential, we find rather distinctive Buddhist cultural traits. Prominent among these cultural characteristics are the following: (1) emphasis on the dignity of man, (2) an attitude of non-attachment, (3) tolerance, (4) a spirit of compassion and non-violence, (5) an inclination to meditation, and (6) a practical orientation.

THE DIGNITY OF MAN: In Buddhist cultures man has not been subordinated to things and machines. Man is regarded as self-creative, as the determiner of his fate by his own efforts. What greater dignity can be bestowed upon man than to recognize that he is the master of his own life and destiny? In theistic religions man is usually subordinated to his God, and is regarded as a thing fashioned by this God to suit His own aims. In a materialistic culture man is often subordinated to things in the world external to himself, and sometimes subordinated even to his own artifacts. But according to the teachings of Buddhism these alternatives represent the projection of, and ensnarement by, man's own ignorance. It is entirely up to man whether he will or will not subordinate himself to God or nature.

NON-ATTACHMENT: As a result of his conviction that there are no enduring selves or things in the world, the Buddhist does not attach himself either to his ego or to things in the world. Recognizing that impermanence is the mark of this world of suffering existence, he refuses to cling to absurd conceptions of permanence. As a result, he is unruffled by change, and faces the future with equanimity, and does not lament over what has gone by. Thus, a spirit of ready acceptance of life marks the Buddhist as a result of his non-attachment to permanence.

TOLERANCE: Buddhism is a way of practical realization of the truth of non-suffering attainable by self-discipline and mental purification. It is not based on the commands of jealous gods and is not affected by claims to exclusiveness that grow out of such jealousy. Consequently, it is tolerant both of other religions, and of differing individual inter-pretations of Buddhist teachings. Despite the many differences found among the Buddhists of the different countries of the world, they all recognize each other as Buddhists. Furthermore, they do not look upon non-Buddhists as inferior, without a hope of happiness, and for whom salvation is impossible because they live outside the fold of Buddhism. The sickness and suffering that dogs man accrues to the individual person, and it is the individual person who must make the Way from suffering to peace and happiness. This recognition lies at the bottom of the respect for individual differences in all spheres of life that is so characteristic of Buddhist cultures.

NON-VIOLENCE: In the twenty-five hundred years since its beginnings, Buddhism has spread throughout Asia and has made its way even to the other continents, claiming over four hundred million followers at the present time. During this time no wars have been fought and no blood shed in the propagation of the teaching. Violence is absolutely contrary to the teachings and practice of Buddhism. It is a common conviction of Buddhists everywhere that anger and violence only provoke more of the same, and that anger and violence are only appeased and removed by kindness and compassion. The compassion demonstrated by Gau-tama as he travelled around the countryside teaching the causes and cessation of suffering has permeated all of Buddhism, and in Mahayana occupies the central place in the religion, in the form of the *Bodisattva* ideal. It is a relatively easy thing to say, "Love thine enemies," but a much more difficult thing to do in the face of the enemies' anger, hatred, and violence. Nevertheless, the Buddhist record on this score is excellent, as is seen by the relative lack of war, revolution, or violence of any kind in predominantly Buddhist cultures.

MEDITATION: As a result of the Buddhist emphasis on self-discipline and self-purification, it is common practice for Buddhists everywhere to concentrate on emptying themselves of everything impure and conducive to suffering. The meditative techniques involved in these practices, despite the great variety of forms or degrees, are all essentially a matter of self-cultivation and self-discipline. Their aim is to enable a person to participate directly in reality without the intermediaries of false selves, desires, and ambitions estranging him from reality. The mark of these meditative practices in Buddhist lands is a calm peacefulness that characterizes the majority of the people.

PRACTICAL ORIENTATION: Practice in meditation produces an attitude that strikes an observer as very practical and down-to-earth. No doubt, this is due, at least in part, to the Buddhists' ability to immerse themselves in the activity of the present moment. When one is at peace with himself and not pulled by a thousand desires and nagged by ten thousand doubts he can freely and completely engage in the activities at hand. For example, a Buddhist does not ordinarily regard eating, working, and playing as simply activities to be gotten over with in order to get on to the "real business of life." Rather, these are counted as among the activities of which life is constituted. Consequently, these things are regarded as important, and participation is whole-hearted, occupying the total attention of the person. Yet they do not cling to these things and become long-faced and heavy-hearted when there is not quite enough to eat, or the work is hard.

Learning from the past and planning for the future are, of course, essential for improving the quality of life in all spheres. But learning from the past and planning for the future are themselves activities of the present moment, and should not be confused with living in the past or the future. There can be no real happiness in brooding over the future which has not yet come. Nor can happiness be found in lamenting the past. The Buddhists' recognition of this fact and, in consequence, their relatively complete engagement and immersion in the activities of the immediate present results in an attitude that strikes an "outsider" as extremely practical.

PART THREE

Chinese Philosophies

Portrait of Confucius. *Courtesy of the Field Museum of Natural History*

CHAPTER 15

BASIC CHARACTERISTICS
OF CHINESE PHILOSOPHIES

CHINESE civilization and culture rest upon a philosophical basis shaped primarily by the principles of Confucianism, Taoism, and Neo-Confucianism. These three philosophies have guided and shaped the lives and institutions of the Chinese people for more than twenty-five hundred years. Stressing the importance of preserving, cultivating, and making great human life, Chinese philosophy has been closely connected with politics and morality and has assumed most of the functions of religion. Consequently, the study of Chinese philosophy is valuable not only because of its intrinsic merit, but also because of the insights into the Chinese mind that it makes possible.

The basic aim of Chinese philosophy has not been primarily that of understanding the world, but primarily that of making man great. Although the various Chinese philosophies share this common aim, they differ considerably as a result of different insights into the source of man's greatness. Thus, in Taoism, the emphasis is upon becoming great by becoming one with the inner way of the universe. On the other hand, in Confucianism, the emphasis has been upon developing man's humanity by cultivating human-heartedness and the social virtues. Neo-Confucianism combines these emphases.

Being great has a double aspect in Chinese thought. First of all, it involves *inner greatness*, which is a magnitude of spirit reflected in the peace and contentment of the individual in his completeness. Secondly, it involves *outer greatness*, which is manifested in the ability to live well practically, dignifying the social context of one's ordinary day-to-day existence.

This twofold greatness is basic to both Confucianism and Taoism, the philosophies which provide the foundations and inspiration for the later Neo-Confucian philosophy. Lao Tzu says that unless one knows and lives according to the inner laws of the universe, which he calls the "invariables," he ends up in disaster. According to this mystic sage:

> To know the invariables is called enlightenment. He who knows the invariable is liberal. Being liberal, he is without prejudice. Being without prejudice, he is comprehensive. Being comprehensive, he is vast. Being vast, he is with the Truth. Being with the Truth, he will last forever, and will not fail throughout his lifetime. Not to know the invariable and to act blindly is to go to disaster.[1]

For Confucius the most basic thing was to cultivate one's human-ness and to regulate all activities in accord with this developed human-ness. According to one of the chief texts of Confucianism,

> The ancients who wished to manifest their clear character to the world would first bring order to their states. Those who wished to bring order to their states would first regulate their families. Those who wished to regulate their families would first cultivate their personal lives. Those who wished to cultivate their personal lives would first rectify their minds. Those who wished to rectify their minds would first make their wills sincere. Those who wished to make their wills sincere would first extend their knowledge. The extension of knowledge consists in the investigation of things. When things are investigated, knowledge is extended; when knowledge is extended, the will becomes sincere; when the will is sincere, the mind is rectified; when the mind is rectified, the personal life is cultivated; when the personal life is cultivated, the family will be regulated; when the family is regulated, the state will be in order; and when the state is in order, there will be peace throughout the world.[2]

This pervasive aim of becoming great internally and manifesting this greatness externally has tended to make Chinese philosophy inclusive of all aspects of human activity. Philosophy is not divorced from life, and practice is considered inseparable from theory. There have been very few professional philosophers in China. Nearly all of China's great philosophers have held administrative positions in government or

[1] *Tao Te Ching*, Ch. 16. All references to, and quotations from, this work are taken from *The Way of Lao Tzu*, trans. by Wing-Tsit Chan (Indianapolis: Bobbs-Merrill, 1963).

[2] *The Great Learning (Ta-Hsüeh)*, in *A Source Book in Chinese Philosophy*, trans. and compiled by Wing-Tsit Chan (Princeton: Princeton University Press, 1963). pp. 86–87.

have been artists. And the assessment of philosophers in China depends, in the last analysis, upon their moral character. It is not conceivable that a bad man could be a good philosopher, or that a good philosopher could be a bad man. The real test of a philosophy is its ability to transform its advocates into greater persons.

Since greatness of persons is the basic concern, considerations for people come first in China. The world of man is primary; the world of things is of secondary importance. In Confucianism this characteristic is manifested in the emphasis on social humanism. In Taoism it is evident in the mystical ontological unity of man and the universe.

Emphasis on man's greatness leads naturally to emphasis on ethics and the spiritual life. The spirit of man rather than the body, is the most important aspect of being human. This spirit must be nourished and cultivated in order that it might develop according to its capacities. And for this development the moral life is a first prerequisite. This is a very obvious characteristic of Confucianism, where there is really no distinction between the moral and the spiritual, and where man is defined as a moral animal. But it is also a characteristic of Taoism, which stresses the quality of life and aims at a higher level of human existence.

Putting greatness into practice led to emphasis on the familial virtues, especially the concept of filial love, which provides the very cornerstone of Chinese morality. The immediate environment surrounding infants in a civilized society is a social structure constituted by the family. Here the child's moral and spiritual character is shaped and molded. Here the beginnings of smallness or greatness are established. Only through great love and respect within the family can greatness be cultivated in persons.

Turning to methodology, it can be seen that the emphasis on inclusiveness of views has been a primary consideration. Rather than seeking truth by excluding various alternative views as false, Chinese thought has tended to look for truth in the combination of partially true views. This leads to a spirit of synthesis and harmony which results in tolerance and sympathy. Persons, practices, and views that are different are to be tolerated and considered sympathetically in order to appreciate their value. It is characteristic of Chinese philosophy that it emphasizes complementariness rather than contrariness. Often views and principles can be seen to be not only different, but also opposed. But, of course, if they are opposed it is necessary that they have a common basis. In Chinese thought it is this common basis that is emphasized, and the differences are regarded as complementary rather than contrary.

The differences are viewed as completing each other, thereby constituting a whole. Instead of thinking, "A and B are opposed, therefore one must take either A or B," one thinks, "A and B are opposed, therefore both are needed for the whole." For example, one does not choose between practice and theory, but chooses *both* theory *and* practice.

This emphasis on complementariness in Chinese philosophy is reflected in a synthetic attitude which sees harmony in apparently conflicting theories and modes of life and fuses them together into a new whole. For example, there are basic differences between Taoism and Confucianism, and Buddhism does not appear to have a great deal in common with either of these philosophies. Yet Buddhism found a welcome home in China, and more than a thousand years ago these three philosophies contributed the materials required for the imposing edifice of Neo-Confucianism. In addition, this synthetic attitude leads to tolerance for the thoughts and actions of others, and promotes sympathy and appreciation for what is different.

This summary of basic characteristics of Chinese philosophy indicates a rich and complex philosophical heritage. The emphasis on the greatness of man and the preference for methodological inclusiveness suggest that this tradition should be considered in its own context and in terms of its own merit, for it does not fit neatly into European intellectual categories, which have resulted from an emphasis on the greatness of the external world, and a preference for methodological exclusiveness.

CHAPTER 16

HISTORICAL PERSPECTIVES

CHINESE philosophy as a critical investigation of man and his environment has its beginnings in the sayings of Confucius and Lao Tzu. Although this means that Chinese thought prior to around the middle of the sixth century B.C. is pre-philosophical, it does not mean that the philosophies of Confucius and Lao Tzu can be understood without investigating China's pre-philosophical tradition. On the contrary, since both Confucianism and Taoism are critical reactions to earlier theories and practices, it is imperative to have a picture of pre-philosophical China in mind in order to give these philosophies the context requisite to their understanding.

Although there is evidence of advanced civilization in China in very ancient times, actual recorded history begins in relatively recent times, with the Shang dynasty, in the fourteenth century B.C. Available evidence indicates that this was an advanced civilization. For example, art from this period is quite sophisticated, even according to modern standards. This dynasty ended with the invasion by the more primitive Chou people, who according to tradition established the Chou dynasty in 1122 B.C. Although more primitive artistically and culturally, the Chou were a powerful and determined people. They conquered huge portions of China by sheer force and might. Not having the means to administer all of the conquered territory as one central state, the Chou delegated administrative power to friendly chiefs and nobles, providing parcels of land in exchange for the friendship and cooperation of these newly endowed landholders. Apparently this feudal system worked quite well during the early Chou period, as each vassal had considerable freedom and power within his own territory, and this seemed well worth the taxes and military conscription owed the king in return for these privileges. Although there is nothing to indicate that the first half of the Chou period was anywhere nearly as advanced as the earlier Shang period, it was a time of relative peace and security within the structure of the new feudal system. And because of this peace it came to be regarded later on as a "golden period" in China's early history.

This peace was relatively short-lived, however. It was only the might of the Chou kings that prevented the vassals and the oppressed serfs from rebelling. As time went on, it was recognized that the kings did not really have the strength to control all of the conquered land, even through the device of feudalism. There came to be greater and greater unrest in the country. Feudal lord turned against feudal lord, and serfs rebelled when they thought the lords sufficiently weak and ineffectual. As neighboring states became weakened by war and strife they were attacked by larger and more remote lords. By 770 B.C. things had degenerated to the point where a coalition of feudal lords were able to launch a successful attack on the Chou capital in the west. They killed the king and usurped his power. From this date on the Chou kings were puppets controlled by the coalition of feudal lords who happened to be in power at the time. Power was constantly shifting hands, and war and strife were the order of the day during the two centuries immediately prior to Confucius' birth. Violence and intrigue characterized the political scene and expediency took the place of morality. Cheating and trickery provided the basis for the intrigues that functioned in lieu of political government. The costs of these intrigues and the resulting wars in terms of poverty, suffering, and death is almost unimaginable.

It is in the context of this severe crisis crippling China in the centuries immediately preceding the birth of Confucius and Lao Tzu that these philosophers must be viewed. And granted this context, it is not at all surprising that they should both be reformers. For Confucius, born in 551 B.C., it was obvious that the problems of the people stemmed from sovereign power exerted without moral principle and solely for the benefit of sovereign luxury. Small wonder, then, that he urged social reforms that would allow government to be administered for the benefit of all the people. This could be done, he urged, if the people in government were of the highest personal integrity, understood the needs of the people, and cared as much for the welfare and happiness of the people as they did for themselves. "Do unto others as you would have done unto you," represents a brilliant and daring principle of reform in the context of the pre-Confucian China just outlined. It is a principle resulting from reflections on the conditions required for an ideal society. The attitude underlying these reflections regards knowing man as more important than knowing nature. If man cannot know and regulate man, how can he hope to know and control all of nature? Furthermore, Confucius did not look for the basis of human goodness and morality outside of man. Within man himself was to be found the source and structure of human goodness and happiness. It is this attitude that makes Confucianism a humanism rather than a naturalism.

Confucius lived from 541 to 479 B.C., but some of the ideas of Confucianism are derived from earlier times, and other ideas are not developed until later. According to tradition, Confucius drew inspiration from the Five Classics, and the expression of his thought is contained in the Four Books. The Five Classics are as follows: (1) *Book of Poetry* (*Shih Ching*), a collection of verses from the Chou period; (2) *Book of History* (*Shu Ching*), a collection of records, speeches, and state documents from 2000 to 700 B.C.); (3) *Book of Changes* (*I-Ching*), a set of formulae for explaining nature, widely used for purposes of divination (this work is traditionally attributed to Wen Wang, 1100 B.C.); (4) *Book of Rites* (*Li Chi*), a collection of rules regulating social behavior. This was compiled long after Confucius, but may well represent rules and customs from much earlier times; (5) *Spring and Autumn Annals* (*Ch'un Ch'iu*), a chronicle of events from 722 to 464 B.C.

The Four Books are: (1) *Analects of Confucius* (*Lun Yu*), which are sayings of Confucius to his disciples, collected and edited by them; (2) *The Great Learning* (*Ta Hsueh*), teachings of Confucius containing his suggestions for governing. This work reflects Hsun Tzu's development of Confucius thought; (3) *Doctrine of the Mean* (*Chung Yung*), teaching attributed to Confucius concerning the regulation of life; (4) *Book of Mencius* (*Meng Tzu*), an elaboration of some Confucian principles by Mencius, an early commentator of Confucius.

The essence of the Confucian teachings contained in this literature is expressed in the teaching that by developing the humanity within him, man can become great both in his personal conduct and private life, and in his relations with others. When all individuals do this, goodness will abound and happiness will be achieved.

In addition to the development of Confucianism by Mencius (ca.

371–289 B.C.), further elaborations on the teachings of Confucius are found in the *Hsun Tzu*, attributed to Hsun Tzu (ca. 320–238 B.C.). Hsun Tzu emphasized the need for the Confucian virtues by pointing to the inherent badness of human nature. Thus, whereas Mencius emphasized the need to practice the virtues of humanity, righteousness, and filial piety in order to preserve man's goodness, Hsun Tzu claimed that they must be practiced to root out the evil in man and replace it with goodness.

The desperate conditions of the times also provide an explanatory context for the rise of Taoism, which emphasized the need to look beyond the promises and treaties of man for a source of peace and contentment. Lao Tzu, born late in the sixth century B.C., urges a simple and harmonius life, a life in which the profit motive is abandoned, cleverness discarded, selfishness eliminated, and desires reduced. In the context of a China in which greed and desire were bringing about nearly unimaginable hardship and suffering, a philosophy emphasizing the need to return to nature's way to avoid the viciousness of man's way would understandably find a ready following. Yang Chu's (ca. 440–ca. 366 B.C.) claim that he would not exchange even a single hair for the profits of the entire world makes sense against the background of graft and corruption that resulted from preoccupation with profit. Lao Tzu, who is earlier than Yang Chu, felt that so long as human actions were motivated by greed and avarice there was no hope for peace and contentment, and so he advocated the principle that only those actions which were in accord with Nature should be undertaken.

Taoism, the philosophy of the natural and the simple way initiated by Lao Tzu, received a foundation of metaphysical monism from Chuang Tzu (fourth century B.C.). This philosopher also sharpened the emphasis on the natural way as opposed to the artificial and contrived way of persons. In fact, it was a revival of Chuang Tzu's development of metaphysical doctrines of naturalism that provided the common meeting ground for Taoism and the Buddhism that developed in China during the fourth and fifth centuries A.D.

Although Confucianism and Taoism were to become the most influential of the early philosophies of China, they were by no means the only philosophies of the day. Mohism, which received its main direction from Mo Tzu (468–376 B.C.), shared the Confucian interest in advocating the increased welfare of man, and also agreed that the measure of man's welfare was man himself rather than Nature or the Spirits. But Mo Tzu felt that the Confucian emphasis on cultivating humanity was too vague and general for actually bringing about an improved human condition. He argued that the way to improve man's condition was to tend to the immediate welfare of the people. The slogan of the school became "promote general welfare and remove evil." The criterion advocated for measuring human happiness was utility. Ultimately, according to Mohism, value was to be measured in terms of benefits to the people. Benefits, in turn, could be measured in terms of increased wealth, population, and contentment.

Although Mo Tzu saw himself in opposition to Confucius, probably thinking of himself as a practical reformer and Confucius as an idealistic dreamer, the long-run effect of his philosophy was to strengthen Confucianism by adding external sanctions and criteria to the internal sanctions and criteria advocated by Confucius. The result was a humanism with a utilitarian flavor and a greater practical emphasis. The special strength of this combination was due to the moralistic emphasis of Confucianism which served as a corrective to utilitarianism, while utilitarianism added a practicalness to the moralism.

The School of Names had its early development in the work of Hui Shih (380–305? B.C.) and Kung-sun Lung (b. ca. 380 B.C.). The main interest of philosophers of this school was in the relationship between language and reality. Their motivation appears to have been primarily theoretical, as these logicians were interested in knowledge for its own sake rather than for its utility. This interest in knowledge for its own sake makes the school unique, and caused it to be the source of ridicule for members of the other schools. But despite the opposition between the logicians and the other philosophers of China at this time, the investigation of the relations between words and things, and the concern with knowledge for its own sake served an important antidote to the excessive practicalness of the other philosophers. It served to keep alive an interest in theory, and the studies in the relations between words and things became useful later in both Taoism and Confucianism as they sought a metaphysical basis for their social philosophies.

The Yin-Yang school, concerned with cosmogony and cosmology, also was influential in the time of early Confucianism and Taoism. Since no individual philosophers connected with this school are known it is not possible to provide specific dates. But most likely this school goes back to late Shang or early Chou times in its beginnings, and continues to be important until long after Confucius.

The beginnings of the *yin-yang* speculation apparently are contained in a natural curiosity of the people about the workings of nature on all sides of them. For an agrarian people living very close to nature and feeling the rhythms of her workings, nothing could be more natural than to speculate about the principles, or "inner workings," of nature's functions. There were two questions implicit in this early curiosity about nature. On the one hand, there was the question about the structure of the universe, What is the organization or plan of the universe? On the other hand, there was the question about the origin of the universe, Where did the universe come from, and how did it originate?

The theory of the Five Elements is essentially an answer to the question about the structure of the universe. The *yin-yang* theory is essentially an answer to the question of the origin of the universe. According to early versions of the Five Elements, or Agents, theory, the five powers of the universe that control the functioning of nature are symbolically represented by Wood, Fire, Metal, Water, and Earth. The combinations of these powers determine the workings of the universe. For example, when the power represented by Wood is dominant it is spring. When the power of Fire dominates it is summer. Autumn represents the ascendancy of Metal, and winter results when Water is dominant. In late summer Earth is dominant. The important thing about the Five Elements theory is that it was an attempt to explain the functions of nature by appeal to inner principles, or powers, which are really the forces responsible for the manifestations of nature.

According to the *yin-yang* theory, the universe came to be as a result of the interactions between the two opposing universal forces of *yin* and *yang*. The existence of the universe is seen to reside in the tensions resulting from the universal force of non-being, or *yin*, and the universal force of being, or *yang*. Whatever is experienced simultaneously has being and lacks being; it comes into being and passes out of being. But this is just to say that it is being pulled between the forces of *yin* and *yang*. The changing world that is experienced—that is characterized as nature—can exist only when there is both being and non-being, for without being there is no coming-into-being, and without non-being there is no passing-out-of-being. Hence *yin*, the negative, and *yang*, the positive, are required as a source of nature.

Both the Five Elements theory and the *yin-yang* theory were influential in the rise of Neo-Confucianism. In the formulations of various later thinkers these theories underwent metaphysical interpretation and found their place in a general theory of existence.

The other early school of considerable importance is that of Legalism. The most important philosopher of this school is Han Fei Tzu (d. 233

B.C.), though the school itself is several hundred years older. The basic presupposition of this school is that man is basically evil, and consequently the authority of laws and the state are required for human welfare. Although this school is opposed to the Confucian inasmuch as Confucius emphasized morality and goodness over laws and punishment as a means for promoting human happiness, and the Legalists advocated law and authority, the long-term effect of the Legalist emphasis was to add to morality a dimension of legality, making the law a vehicle for morality. In this way the Legalist school added a considerable measure of strength to Confucianism.

In early medieval times, Hui-nan Tzu (d. 122 B.C.) a relatively late Taoist, developed a cosmology according to which the unfolding of *Tao* produced successively space, the world, the material forces, *yin* and *yang*, and all the things. According to this theory *yin* and *yang* become the principles of production and change among all the things in the world. Tung Chung-shu (176–104 B.C.), a late Confucianist, also referred to the *yin* and *yang* as the principles of things. According to him, all activities are due to the forces of *yin* and *yang*, which manifest themselves through the five elements.

That the Taoist Hui-nan, and the Confucianist Tung Chung-shu, should both make use of the *yin-yang* and Five Elements theories shows that these philosophies were coming closer together at this time and finding a common ground of explanation. The revitalization of both of these philosophies as a result of their meeting and the resulting cross-fertilization had to wait for many centuries, however, until the catalyst of Buddhism had been introduced. In fact, it was not until around 900 A.D., with the rise of Neo-Confucianism, that the meeting of Confucianism and Taoism prepared by Hui-nan Tzu and Tung Chung-shu bore fruit in the form of a vigorous new philosophy.

Part of the reason for the long delay is due to the fact that Tung Chun-shu was successful in getting Confucianism adopted as the state ideology. This of course meant that Taoism was out of official favor, and removed most of the critical challenges required for a vigorous and healthy philosophy. For nearly the next thousand years after being adopted as the state ideology, the philosophy of Confucianism was to see little development, as most of the emphasis was upon putting the philosophy that had already been developed into practice, rather than on developing further the philosophy itself.

Although Buddhism was introduced into China from India prior to the end of the first century A.D., it remained almost entirely without influence until after the fifth century. All of the different Buddhist schools of philosophy were introduced into China, but only those which could be reconciled with the principles of either Taoism or Confucianism became forces in shaping the future development of the Chinese mind. The realistic philosophies of Vaibhashika and Sautrantika which supported Theravada Buddhism failed to take hold in China because of their insistence on the momentary and fleeting character of reality. The idealism of the Yogacara philosophy did not suit the practical emphasis of the Chinese temperament, and the skepticism of the Madhyamika proved too radical for a pragmatic people.

The Buddhism which was accepted by the Chinese and which has been influential right up to our own times was a modified version, adapted to the inclusive and synthetic tendencies of the Chinese mind.

The Buddhist school of uncompromising idealism, emphasizing the reality of "Consciousness-only" and the causality of ideas only, found its counterpart in the Hua-yen school of Chinese Buddhism. But here ideational causation became a universal or total causation, according to which all the elements of reality are perfectly real and reflect each other, being at the same time simple and complex, pure and impure, subtle and gross, conscious and unconscious. In this way, far from distinguishing between conscious and unconscious reality and denying reality to the latter, this school of Buddhism held that the universe is a grand harmony of conscious and unconscious, pure and impure, simple and complex. The Indian disjunction, "either conscious or unconscious," had become the conjunction, "both conscious and unconscious." The Grand Harmony was the harmony of all opposites in the universe and the harmony was possible because each of the ultimate elements of which the universe is composed contained within itself all of the differing aspects and tendencies in the world.

The T'ient-t'ai school of Buddhism, which has its beginnings around the beginning of the seventh century A.D., evolved what it called the "Round Doctrine." The school began with the teaching of the non-being of all reality. From this doctrine of the Void, wherein things are held to be unreal, they moved to the position that things have temporary existence. From the temporary existence of things, they moved to the position that things in their temporary existence represent the true state of Being. The "roundness" of the doctrine consists in the fact that these three—the void, the temporary, and the true—constitute the fullness of existence, and they are all three identical.

The other two schools of Chinese Buddhism that flourished are the Pure Land school, which is mainly religious, and the Ch'an (Zen) school. The Ch'an school is really a method of meditation rather than a philosophy, but it is underwritten by the philosophical attitude that through the negation of being, being is affirmed in its true nature. The meditation involves negating both production and extinction; arising and ceasing; annihilation and permanence; and unity and plurality. But this negation is simply an aspect of affirming the presence of the Buddha-nature in all things. The enlightenment marked by coming to see the presence of the Buddha-nature in all things is the aim of the Ch'an meditation.

The tendency to synthesize opposing features of metaphysical views so clearly evident in Chinese Buddhism was the most significant factor in the rise of Neo-Confucianism. Chinese philosophers had tended to be highly critical of Buddhist philosophies ever since their introduction to China. They objected to the emphasis on overcoming suffering and death, which to them seemed little more than selfish escapism. The monastic aspect of Buddhism which involved the renunciation of the family and society seemed wrong-headed, since it was clearly impossible that man, a social being, could ever escape society so long as he lived, even though he desert family and friends. They were also critical of the Buddhist emphasis on metaphysics which led to the denial of being, on the grounds that to regard all things, including food and clothes, as unreal and yet to depend on them was contradictory. But perhaps the deepest difference between the Chinese philosophers and the Buddhist schools that were introduced to China was due to the emphasis on society as the primary metaphysical reality by the Chinese, as opposed to the emphasis on the non-social by the Buddhists.

Granted these differences and the critical attitude of the Chinese philosophers toward Buddhism, the rise of Neo-Confucianism is not hard to understand. It represents the attempt of the philosophers from the tenth century A.D. on to counteract Buddhism with a more comprehensive and superior philosophy. And granted the synthetic tendency of the Chinese philosophers, it is not difficult to predict that the new philosophy would incorporate features of Buddhism along with features of Taoism and Confucianism. Furthermore, granting the preoccupation with social reality that characterized earlier Chinese philosophy, it is not surprising that Confucianism should have the primary role in this reconstruction.

Although the beginnings of Neo-Confucianism can be traced to Han Yu (768–824), it was not until Sung times that a comprehensive and definitive formulation was achieved. It was during the Sung period (960–1279) that the school of Reason of the Ch'eng brothers (Ch'eng Hao, 1032–1085, and Ch'eng Yi, 1033–1108) arose, and the great synthesis of Chu Hsi (1130–1200) was achieved. The school of Mind, which leaned in the direction of idealism, also originated during this period. The two most illustrious philosophers connected with this school are Lu Chiu-yuan (1139–1193) and Wang Yang-ming (1473–1529). The third phase of the development of Neo-Confucianism is represented by the Empirical school of the Ching period (1644–1911).

The key concept in the Reason school of Neo-Confucianism is that of the Great Ultimate (*T'ai-chi*). This Great Ultimate is the ultimate reality and underlies all existence. It is the reason or principle inherent in all activity and existence. Through activity it generates *yang*. Upon reaching its limit, activity becomes tranquil, and through tranquillity the Great Ultimate generates *yin*. When tranquillity reaches its limit, activity begins, the one producing the other as its opposite. This reversal of opposites is a notion of Taoism, where it is held that reversal is the way of the Great Way, the Tao of the universe. Through the interaction between *yin* and *yang* the five elements are produced, the ten thousand things in the universe are produced, and the seasons run their course. The Great Ultimate, which produces all things and determines their functions, is a combination of matter (*ch'i*) and principle (*li*). The nature of things is the result of what they are and how they function. The stuff of which they are made is their matter, or *ch'i*, and their function is their principle, or *li*. When *ch'i* and *li* are in harmony, things are in order and there is a grand harmony. Since the Great Ultimate represents a harmony of *ch'i* and *li*, order is the law of the universe. It remained for Chu Hsi to observe that the Great Ultimate is nothing but the principle of ultimate goodness, to transform this pervasive metaphysics into a groundwork for a social philosophy.

The Reason school was dualistic in positing matter (*ch'i*) and reason (*li*) as the ultimate realities. Wang Yang-ming (1472–1529) was monistic in his emphasis, holding that mind alone was ultimately real. He did not deny the reality of things external to the mind, but emphasized that it is only through consciousness, or mind, that a person becomes aware of things. Thus mind is the primary reality. The essential character of mind, according to this philosopher is its capacity for love. In its pristine goodness the mind of man forms a unity with heaven and earth and consequently the ideal man views all things as one and extends a universal love to all things. This universal love becomes the basis for all existence and all relationships. In the Ch'ing period (1644–1911), Wang Yang-ming's idealism came to be tempered with the empiricism of the Empirical school of Neo-Confucianism. Chu Hsi had emphasized the superiority of principle, or reason, over matter. Tai Chen (1723–1777) objected to this emphasis on the grounds that neither matter nor principle could be considered superior to the other, since reality could not be cut up in this way. In reality, there is no distinction between principle and matter. In the transformations of matter, principle is manifested, and the orderliness of transformations is due to principle. But there is no transformation without order, and there is no order without transformation. At best these two—matter and principle—are just two different ways of looking at reality, the basis of which is *jen*.

In the Empirical school, there is a return to the empirical and the particular, a greater concern with the position of the individual in society, and less interest in speculative metaphysics. In this respect, the third phase of Neo-Confucianism is closer to earlier Confucianism.

The development of philosophy in China in contemporary times is a subject which is not susceptible to analysis for a variety of reasons, chief of which is the lack of communication between the Chinese and the Western world.

In summing up the development of philosophy in China it could be said that Confucianism represents the *yang* of Chinese philosophy whereas Taoism represents its *yin*. Philosophy, as everything else, has its *yin* and *yang*, and finds perfection in the Grand Harmony of these two opposing principles. In China it was Neo-Confucianism that sought the harmony of all principles, drawing upon the various earlier philosophies.

CHAPTER 17

CONFUCIANISM

CONFUCIUS

IT has already been noted that the times of Confucius were marked by political and social disintegration and a widespread breakdown of morality. Granted these conditions, it was natural that Confucius should turn his attention to the reform of society. Having been introduced to hard work, suffering, and responsibility at an early age, he knew from personal experience the poverty, political abuse, and hardship that affected the lives of the ordinary people. No doubt his background aided his understanding of both government and the problems of the ordinary people.

At an early age Confucius found himself with a position in the government of his native state of Lu. There he could not only observe the inadequate administration of the kingdom of Lu, but could also, in a small way, do something about this administration by properly carrying out his own duties. He thus got a taste of practical politics, and this probably was a factor in his decision to turn his attention to the problems of government. From a background where he could see the misery of the people and the bad administration of the rulers, a person of Confucius' humanistic bent would naturally set himself to thinking about the correction of society.

Recognizing that his times were not all they should be, what was Confucius to do about it? How could a new order (or, what comes to the same thing, an old order) in society be established? In short, how is the well-being of society to be achieved? Confucius' answer to this question is his philosophy, a humanistic social philosophy. It is obvious that if Confucius' philosophy is a social philosophy it is about man and his society rather than about nature and man's knowledge of nature. But what does it mean to say that this is a *humanistic* social philosophy?

The most significant feature of humanism is the conviction that man is ultimate. To say that man is ultimate has a special meaning, as can be seen by contrasting humanism with naturalism and supernaturalism. According to naturalism it is nature—the non-human world—that is taken as ultimate. Here the principles for human action and life are taken from nature. Man should act in certain ways because the world is what it is. Discovering how human beings should act is a matter of discovering how nature acts, so that man's actions can be in accord with those of nature.

According to supernaturalism, a force or power other than man or nature is taken to be ultimate. This supernatural force is seen as regulating both nature and man, making them subordinate to this supernatural and superhuman power. The supernatural may be regarded as creating both nature and man and determining their behavior. According to this view, discovering how humans should act is a matter of discovering how this supernatural power intended them to act. In a theistic religion this might be seen as a matter of knowing and doing God's will.

Humanism becomes possible when man rather than nature or supernature is taken as ultimate. When man is taken as ultimate there is nothing superior to man as a source of human principles. Man does not look to either nature or supernature for norms of life and action; rather, he looks to himself to find the principles that provide for goodness and happiness. Thus, to call Confucianism a humanism is to note that it is a philosophy that answers the question "How can goodness and happiness be achieved?" by pointing to the principles of action found within man himself. The source of these principles is what makes human beings human. In Confucianism, that which gives human beings their humanity is called *jen*, and it is the source of all human actions and principles. Consequently, the first principle of Confucianism is to act according to *jen*. When all human relations are properly ordered according to *jen*, happiness will be achieved. *Jen* is the source of human actions and human relation, but *li* (order) is needed for their regulation and control. These twin concepts of order (*li*) and humanity (*jen*) constitute the basis of Confucianism.

It is recorded that one day, after a ceremony, Confucius heaved a great sigh, and upon being asked why he was sighing, replied, "Oh, I was thinking of the Golden Age and regretting that I was not able to have been born in it and to associate with the wise rulers and ministers of the three Dynasties."[1] As Confucius went on to explain how and why this was such a golden age, he remarked that the founders of the Great Dynasties

> were deeply concerned over the principle of *Li*, through which Justice was maintained, general confidence was tested, and errors of malpractice were exposed. An ideal of true manhood, *Jen*, was set up and good manners or courtesy was cultivated, as solid principles for the common people to follow. . . .[2]

The importance Confucius attached to *li* is also seen by his remark that "*Li* is the principle by which the ancient kings embodied the laws of heaven and regulated the expression of human nature. Therefore he who has attained *Li* lives, and he who has lost it, dies."[3]

What is this principle of *li*, to which Confucius attaches so much importance, and how is it related to good conduct and good government? No brief answer to this question can be satisfactory, because *li* is all pervasive, being the very basis, the *sine-qua-non*, of government for Confucius. *Li* represents an entire social and moral philosophy, which rests upon the principle of harmony in essential human relationships.

The word "*li*" means many things. It means religion; it means the general principle of the social order; it means the entire body of social, moral, and religious practices taught and rationalized by Confucius. It also means ritual and ceremony. It means a system of well-defined social relationships with definite attitudes toward one another, love in the parents, filial piety in the children, respect in the younger brothers, friendliness in the elder brothers, loyalty among friends, respect for authority among subjects and benevolence in rulers. It means moral discipline in man's personal conduct. It means propriety in everything.

Thus, the concept of *li* is seen to include many notions, more or less closely related, and while it is true that the concept of *li* is basic to Confucian philosophy it must be realized that in the sense that *li* provides the basis for Confucius' philosophy it is general, being constituted by several rather more specific concepts, such as *jen* (human-heartedness), *yi* (righteousness), and *hsiao* (filial piety). Consequently, an understand-

---

[1] *Li Chi*, Ch. IX, trans. by Lin Yutang, in *The Wisdom of Confucius* (New York: The Modern Library, 1938) p. 227.
[2] *Li Chi*, in *The Wisdom of Confucius*, p. 229.   [3] *Ibid.*

ing of *li* in the broad sense is to be achieved by first understanding the rather more specific virtues that make up *li*.

Since *li* is of such importance in Confucian philosophy it is appropriate that it be explored both from the point of view of its history and from the point of view of its content.

The earliest notion of *li* is of religious character, where *li* is concerned with rites regarding religious performances. It soon came to denote other rites, such as marriage, military, festival, government, etc.

This sense of *li* coincides with a more or less elaborate set of rules and convention which demand strict observation in carrying out various activities, mainly religious or social in character.

The second notion of *li* refers to a customary code of social behavior. In this sense *li* is the customary law, or common morality. *Li*, in this sense, takes the place of written law, although it differs from written law in that it is positive rather than negative ("do this," rather than "don't do this"), it does not bring with it automatic punishment, and it generally is assumed to refer to the behavior of the aristocracy rather than ordinary persons.

The third, and extended, meaning of *li* is anything which is reasonable, anything which has a rational basis. It is this third sense of *li* that is of most importance for understanding Confucius, although Confucius uses the term "*li*" in all of its meanings. This is not surprising, since the meanings of "*li*" are all related. This third sense of *li* is more basic and more nebulous in character than the first two, and it will be easier to make clear the character of *li* in the third sense by analyzing the concepts contained within it, rather than attempting a summary statement.

The most important virtues comprising *li* are *hsiao*, *yi*, and *jen*. It has been said that *yi* is the essence of *li*. It has also been said that *hsiao* is the foundation of all the virtues, and it is commonly said that *jen* is the key to Confucian philosophy. What are the concepts embodied in each of these virtues?

Hsiao, usually translated "filial piety," is the virtue of reverence. First of all, the parents are revered because life itself is generated from them. In showing reverence for parents it is important to protect the body from harm, since the body is from the parents. Therefore, to protect the body is to honor the parents. But even more, reverence should be shown for parents by doing well and making their name known and respected. If it is not possible to bring honor to the name of one's parents, at least they should not be disgraced. Thus, *hsiao* does not consist merely in giving one's parents physical care, but also in bringing them emotional and spiritual richness. And, equally important, after parents are dead, their unfulfilled aims and purposes should be the aims and purposes of the children. This is even more important than offering sacrifices to the departed spirits of deceased parents.

But *hsiao* is not merely a family virtue. Originating in the family, this virtue influences actions outside the family circle. It becomes, by extension, a moral and social virtue. When children learn respect and reverence for their parents they can have respect and love for their brothers and sisters. And when they have accomplished this, they can respect and love all mankind. And when all actions are directed by love of mankind they are acting according to their humanity, or *jen*. Thus the beginnings of *jen* are found in *hsiao*.

Yi, often translated "righteousness," refers to a moral disposition to do good. It is the recognition of what is right and proper, and also refers to something like a moral sense, an ability to recognize what is right and good. What is according to *yi* is unconditional and absolute. Some actions must be performed for the sole reason that they are right. A person ought to respect and obey his parents because it is morally right and obligatory to do so, and for no other reason. Other actions ought to be performed for the sake of something valuable they bring about. Such actions, done for the sake of attaining something else, are performed for the sake of profit. They are to be contrasted with actions performed according to *yi*, for these actions are performed only because they are right, and not because of what they produce. When a person does all actions for the sake of *yi*, or because they are the right things to do, he is not far from *jen*. To practice *jen* is to act out of a love and respect for humanity for no other reason than that it is the right, or human, way to act.

Jen, translated "benevolence," "human-heartedness," "true manhood," etc., is remarked by both Confucius and Mencius to be *love of man*. It represents the relation that should exist between two men, a relation of love and harmony. To practice *jen* is to love man as man. It includes the universalization that whatever is undesirable is undesirable for everyone, and whatever is desirable is desirable for everyone. *Jen* refers to the seed of humanity present in all persons. The cultivation of *jen* refers to the development of this seed until it becomes the sole principle of action in man. Only when all actions issue from a person's humanity and are for the sake of humanity has one achieved *jen*.

It is the concept of *jen* that supports and makes possible the famous Golden Rule of Confucius, which expresses the notion that man is the measure of man. When a person has developed his humanity he will be able to use himself as a "measuring square," and do to others what he wants done to him, and avoid doing to others what he does not wish done to him.

Hsiao, jen, and *yi* are the characteristics of the superior man, the man who has developed his humanity and who is morally cultivated and aware. This superior man is opposed by the small, or inferior, man who is morally uncultivated, who acts on instinct and for profit.

It is the conviction of Confucius that the cultivation of *jen* through *hsiao* and *yi* will lead to a personal embodiment of virtue which will result in a well-ordered society, because the well-ordered society is based on virtue, which is rooted in *jen.* There is no sharp distinction here between ethics and politics. If man is true to himself, having good faith or sincerity, then he will embody the various virtues. And if every man does this, good government and a happy social order will be assured.

The idea of government by virtue, or goodness, rather than by law may sound rather strange to Western ears, but government by virtue is exactly what Confucius was hoping to achieve. Before questioning this utopia, the various relations between the virtues embodied in *li,* especially those aspects of *li* known as *jen* and *hsiao,* need to be examined.

The most comprehensive statement of the Confucian philosophy is contained in the *Great Learning.* There, after observing that true greatness consists in manifesting the great virtues, loving the people, and achieving the highest good, eight ethical-political items are enunciated as means of achieving greatness. The text reads as follows:

> The ancients who wished to preserve the fresh or clear character of the people of the world would first set about ordering their national life. Those who wished to order their national life, would first set about regulating their family life. Those who wished to regulate their family life would set about cultivating their personal life. Those who wished to cultivate their personal lives would first set about setting their hearts right. Those who wished to set their hearts right would first set about making their wills sincere. Those who wished to make their wills sincere would first set about achieving true knowledge. The achieving of true knowledge depended upon the investigation of things. When things are investigated, then true knowledge is achieved; when true knowledge is achieved then the will becomes sincere; when the will is sincere, then the heart is set right; when the heart is set right, then the personal life is cultivated; when the personal life is cultivated, then the family life is regulated; when the family life is regulated, then the national life is orderly, and when the national life is orderly, then there is peace in this world.[4]

---

[4] *The Great Learning (Ta Hsueh),* trans. by Lin Yutang, *The Wisdom of Confucius,* p. 139.

The last statement in this quotation—"When the national life is orderly, then there is peace in the world"—is an expression, maybe utopian, of what most people would expect from government. Peace within a particular social entity and peace among neighboring social entities depends upon a great many factors, such as enough to eat, a place to sleep, security against disease, self-expression etc., all of which may be reduced to the factors of material and spiritual sufficiency. Sufficient material wealth and ample means and opportunity for spiritual development and expression (art, education, religion, etc.) are necessary (though they may not be sufficient) conditions of peace. A pervasive morality may also be needed to regulate competition and to prevent strife and conflict.

It is to be seen therefore, that the task given to government by Confucius is gigantic, because so utopian. According to him, it is the business of government to insure that material and spiritual sufficiency exist and that people act morally in order that peace be achieved. Granted that this is very nice and very idealistic, but isn't it terribly impractical? After all, how can the government take care of all the material needs, to say nothing of the spiritual needs, of every individual? Is not morality a matter for individuals rather than the province of government? Besides pointing to the fact that the goal of government for Confucius was very high, such questions point to the way in which Confucius regarded government. One way of regarding government is to take the attitude that the obvious means to material and spiritual plenty, if provision of these is to be regarded as the function of government, are the passing of laws, the raising of taxes, the building of schools, churches, museums, etc., and the regulation of production and labor so that enough will be produced and each person will get his share of the production. Putting this into action would, of course, require great bureaus with much paper shuffling, and hordes of government workers.

However, in the Confucian ideal state the main functions of government are carried out at a local rather than national level, in the communities and the families. The national governor is something of an overseer. The actual government is effected not really by government workers, but by each citizen observing his proper relations to other individuals. When proper relations exist between all persons in society the aim of government will have been achieved.

Obviously, the Confucian concept of government is that of a moral system. When all individuals act morally in all of their relations with other persons there will be no social problems. This is why Confucius can say that to achieve world peace it is necessary and sufficient to set right one's heart, cultivate his personal life, and regulate family life properly. When these three things are done *jen* will be cultivated and morality and goodness will prevail.

The above quotation, concerning the way to world peace, reflects not only the idea that education (investigation of things) is a basic element of Confucian social philosophy, but suggests also a certain philosophy of education, in the sense that it is most important to come to know man. For man's good it is necessary to know both what man is and what things are, so that man's life may be ordered in a way conducive to his welfare, making the best use of things in the world. Confucius says, "The principles of the higher education consist in preserving man's clear character, in giving new life to the people and in dwelling (or resting) in perfection, or the ultimate good."[5] Only through education will man know himself and the world. Without this knowledge it is very difficult to order life so that it will be in harmony with things of the world; only when life is in harmony with the world is there peace and happiness.

According to Confucius, "true knowledge" ensues when the root, or basis, of things is known. An example of what it is to have true knowledge is afforded by Confucius when he says, "In presiding over lawsuits I am as good as anyone. The thing is we should make it our aim that there not be any lawsuits at all, . . ."[6] In other words, one should remove the evil by removing the causes of the evil. Knowing the basic causes is primary in the rectification of malfunctions. So, if one has true knowledge, i.e. knowledge of the basic causes, of crime, then it may be possible to do away with crime itself, thereby eliminating lawsuits.

Man's most important knowledge, however, is self-knowledge rather than knowledge about external things such as social conditions and institutions. "Having knowledge" is above all knowing who and what one is, and this means knowing the principles upon which he acts. Accordingly, true knowledge is had only when there is self-knowledge, for in Confucianism it is always the moral and social self that is taken as ultimate.

When it is said that the will becomes sincere when there is knowledge, the reference is to self-knowledge, and the point is that one who has self-knowledge will not deceive himself about the motives and principles of his actions. Thus it is said, "What is meant by making the will

[5] *The Great Learning (Ta Hsueh), op. cit.*, p. 139.   [6] *Ibid.*, p. 143.

sincere is that one should not deceive himself."[7] A person should not try to deceive himself that if he does something in private no one will know and therefore it is all right. The wrong action will be known to himself immediately, and soon the effects will be known not only to himself but to others as well. Corruptness of private character does not remain purely private—a person does not live in isolation—but affects, and is affected by, the whole community of men.

When a person is upset by worries and cares, or is overcome with joy or passion, then his heart is not right. Then he is hardly in position to make fair and just decisions concerning any matters, personal or public. If his decisions are unjust, those persons affected by his decisions may be adversely affected. When on the other hand "the heart is set right," one avoids the excesses and defects that affect one's ability to make good decisions, or according to the Confucian statement, "The cultivation of the personal life depends on setting one's heart right." If one has the proper attitude toward the things of life he will remain calm even in joy and sorrow and will be able to live a good personal life.

If the parents are morally upright there can be a family in which the proper relationships exist. If the father, himself a good man, is respected and obeyed, and the mother, a good woman, is loved and cherished, harmony can exist in a home. And if there is harmony in every home, then there is harmony in the whole country.

This emphasis on proper familial relationships is one of the most important ideas of Confucius and is worthy of some elaboration. Suppose children are born into a family where love and goodness abound. These children will grow up seeing parents loving and respecting each other and will have a model on which to develop their own sense of respect and love. Here the children see their parents respecting other adults, the various offices and officials of government, morality and law. Not only is it possible for the father to rule properly in this family, but respect and obedience are natural to the children.

Psychologists, with good evidence in support of their remarks, report that the first five years of human life are the most important for establishing basic attitudes and behavior patterns. This being so, what better way of insuring respect for law, government, and people than by good education of the child in his early years? Since, except in unfortunate cases, the first five years or so are spent in the home, the education

---

[7] *Ibid.*, p. 144.

must take place in the home. There is no question here of educating or not educating a child from birth to say, five years. Education will take place, based mainly on imitation of a model, and the question is whether the education will be good or bad, which reduces to the question of whether the parents provide the proper model for their children or not.

Suppose that children, maybe unwanted in the first place, are born into a family where little love or respect is shown one parent by the other and where fighting is part of the daily fare. If also the parents show no respect for anyone or anything else, what will the situation in the home be like? Where will the children learn to respect themselves and other men and the institutions of men? Statistics offered by sociologists suggest that this latter kind of family situation produces criminals, or at best, maladjusted persons.

It is hard to think of anything more important for good government and peace than proper family relationships, where this means the kind of familial relationships that enable children to grow up with respect for authority, love for their fellow men, and a sense of the propriety of things. A nation is only a collection of individuals which have joined together for their common good, agreeing to the rule of the few for the good of the many. The good of the many is the good of many individuals. Since government is for the sake of the individual, and it is the individual who benefits or suffers from government, it would seem only natural to study means and ways of government from the point of view of the individuals concerned. Put in other words, the study of government ought to start with man, not institutions. This is precisely what Confucius is doing. He begins with man in his fundamental relationships with other men. And where is the best place to begin with man? Begin with the beginning of man! A man begins in a family where he is born. If education is the key to good society education must begin when man does, and this is in the family when the man is born. The family is the basic stable unit of society, and traditionally the most influential unit socially. Larger units of government can easily be imagined as "merely larger families."

With the individual and the family viewed in this way it is easy to understand why Confucius stressed the virtue of *hsiao*, and regarded it as basic to all the virtues. Nothing can be more important than that a child should develop the proper attitudes to the rest of the family. If he doesn't come to have respect and love for his parents and brothers and sisters, and from them learn respect for other men and institutions of men, and if within the familial situation he does not learn respect for himself, it is hardly to be expected that upon becoming an adult he will become a model citizen.

It is now easy to see that certain aspects of Confucius' analysis of social structure might illuminate problems of our own times. What is uncommon is the role that goodness is expected to play in government. Goodness, for many people today, is something for philosophers to talk about, or a subject for religion. Government based on goodness or virtue is almost unthinkable; yet this is what Confucius was suggesting, and is what Mencius, a follower of Confucius, taught even more clearly. It is important to see how Confucius, in all seriousness, could suggest as a basis for government that which today seems, at first glance at least, completely impractical and impossible.

It is not so much that Confucius had a different view of the basic nature of man than that commonly held today, but rather that Confucius had quite a different idea concerning the aims of education and government than we have today. While Confucius nowhere explicitly affirms that man's nature is basically good, still, it is implicit in his view of government and education, and it is explicitly stated by Mencius that man is basically good. Now it is not uncommon for people today also to hold that man is basically good, and needs only to develop this goodness. But it is also commonly held today that at bottom man is the kind of being Hobbes saw, selfish and demanding, using other people to serve his own end. It makes little difference which of these views is held—in either case goodness will be claimed as an impossible basis for government. The need to develop laws and to punish infractions will always be one of the necessary conditions of government, and one of its most basic tasks. If people are good it will be easier to carry out the laws, in the sense of enforcing them, but it will never make law unnecessary.

There is an important reason for this attitude in our own times. Today, in the Western world, whether man is regarded as basically good or basically evil, the purpose of his education is regarded as the mastery of a skill or trade that may enable him to obtain sufficient material goods. Young people are urged to go to college so they can get a good job; once enrolled at a university or college they are advised how best to prepare themselves for the professional labor market. If this observation is slightly exaggerated, it nonetheless points toward a fundamental difference between our contemporary philosophy of education and the Confucian purpose of education as the development of man's moral character. Confucius tells us that "the only way for the superior man to civilize the people and establish good social customs is through education. A piece of jade cannot become an object of art without chiselling, and a man cannot come to know the moral law without education."[8]

One cause, perhaps, for this difference in aims of education is that for Confucius the final good, or happiness, of man (in this life at least, if another be assumed) is thought to be spiritual in nature, not material.

If, without enforced positive law (in the relevant sense), there is to be peace and well-being, it is necessary that everyone act appropriately, or practice the virtue of *li*. To act appropriately one must respect and care for others, or practice the virtue of *jen*, and this respect for men is learned early through respect for the parents, or by practicing the virtue of *hsiao*. This will produce a true moral self, a "real man." So it is that if the true moral self is to be realized there must be education at all levels. Each individual must take seriously his responsibility for guiding those whom he influences. When the true moral self is achieved then the person is in harmony with all things and there is peace and fulfillment.

The character of and means to good government should now be clear. Here is how a modern student of Confucianism sums it up:

> To be kept stable, society must have leaders who can be trusted; that the only leaders to be trusted are men of character; that character is to be developed through education acquired both from others and through self-discipline; that no man is a safe leader who goes to extremes; that the right cultivation of his own character must be the chief concern of every leader; that no parent, teacher, or public officer has the right to take lightly his responsibilities for guiding, through percept, rules and example, the conduct of those who are under him.[9]

This is the conviction of Confucius, a conviction that by cultivating his human-ness (*jen*) man can perfect this society and achieve happiness.

The main question of Confucius is, What should our conduct be with respect to other human beings? The one and only answer given by Confucius, though taking many forms and assuming many details, is that actions should proceed from *jen* and be regulated by *li*.

The Confucian philosophy outlined so far probably represents primarily the thought of Confucius, though it is extremely difficult to keep separate and distinct the various streams of thought contributing to Confucianism. There is no doubt that the realism of Hsun Tzu and

---

[8] *Book of Rites (Li Chi)*, trans. by Lin Yutang, *The Wisdom of Confucius*, p. 241.
[9] D. Willard Lyons, as quoted by Clarence Burton Day, in *The Philosophers of China* (New York: The Citadel Press, 1962), p. 43.

the idealism of Mencius were influential in the development of Confucius' thought into Confucianism. While Confucius emphasized *li* and
regarded *jen*, *yi*, and *hsiao* as necessary for a well-developed and regulated
individual and for a well-ordered society, he did not attend to the question of *why* man should practice these virtues. He simply assumed that
if man wanted to be happy he *should* act this way. Mencius and Hsun
Tzu, on the other hand, were very much concerned with the question of
why man should live in accord with *jen*, practicing *yi* and *hsiao*. Mencius
held that it was because of the original goodness of human nature that
man should practice the virtues stressed by Confucius. Hsun Tzu,
on the other hand, took the view that it was because of the original
evilness of human nature that man should practice these virtues. The
direction given to the development of Confucianism by these two philosophers was determined by their answers to the question of *why* man
should practice *jen*.

MENCIUS

Mencius agreed with Confucius that *jen* is basic, that it is the source
and foundation of all goodness and virtue. And he also agreed with
Confucius that *li*, or rules for proper behavior, was required for the
development and manifestation of *jen*. In addition, *hsiao* was recognized
to be the beginning point for goodness. But Mencius gave a more important role to *yi* than did Confucius. It is *yi*, or righteousness, that above
all else contains they key to the development and cultivation of *jen*
according to Mencius.

The reason for the emphasis on *yi* is due to a recognition by Mencius
of the distinction between goodness and rightness. *Jen* refers to the
goodness that is basic to man's nature. But *yi* refers to the rightness of
human actions. The need for the distinction is due to the fact that although
all men possess *jen*, or humanity, not all men act in the right way.
For Mencius, who claimed that *jen* was an actual beginning of goodness
present in each person, the problem was to explain how the evil that
everyone recognizes could be present in the world. Explaining as he did,
that evil was due to wrong actions, it was necessary to distinguish between the rightness of actions and the goodness of human nature, or the
presence of *jen*. Despite the presence of goodness in man it is possible
that man should occasionally act in a wrong way and thus bring about
evil in the world. Because this is so, it is necessary to emphasize *yi*, or
the correctness of action, in order to rid the world of evil. But, of course,

Mencius did not hold that a distinction between *yi* and *jen* was equivalent to claiming that they are totally different and do not meet. Rather, he held that if *jen* is completely developed, *yi* will naturally follow. And if all actions are in accord with *yi*, *jen* will come to be developed. But it is easier and more successful to begin with the correction of the actions of persons than with developing the natures of persons. Hence *yi* comes first.

The two most significant points of difference between Confucius and Mencius are their views about the nature of man, and the relation between goodness and rightness. Confucius claimed that man has a *potential* for goodness, and Mencius claimed that man possesses an *actual goodness* as part of his nature. Confucius regarded goodness and rightness as the same, but Mencius distinguished between them.

Mencius did not simply state that man possesses an innate goodness, but presented arguments for this view. The first argument runs as follows: (1) All men are alike by nature; (2) the sage, who is good by nature, is a man; (3) therefore all men are good by nature. According to the second argument, the goodness of man is evident in the virtues of *jen*, *yi*, *li*, and *chih* (moral wisdom). All men possess the beginnings of these virtues as can be seen by the universality of the basic feelings that constitute the beginning for them. Compassion is the beginning of *jen*. Any person would have compassion for a child who had fallen in a well, and would attempt to save the child. Shamefulness is the root of *yi*. Any person who robs another person and thereby causes the death of that person will feel shame and try to make retribution. Reverence is the beginning of *li*. The universality of this beginning can be seen in the fact that all children have a natural reverence for their parents, and in the presence of superiors all people feel their own shortcomings and are modest and reverent. If one were to simply throw the body of a parent in a ditch instead of burying it, and later were to come and see the birds and beasts preying on it, a natural reverence would cause one to hurry and bury the body. The knowledge of right and wrong is the root of the virtue *chih*. Since every person draws his or her ideas about the rightness and wrongness of actions from reflections in his or her own mind, it follows that these innate ideas of right and wrong must be found in every person.

The conclusion of these arguments is that man is a moral animal, for because of his innate goodness he knows right and wrong, has compassion, reverence, and modesty, and knows shame, and consequently can distinguish between right and wrong.

But if this innate goodness of man be granted, how is one to account for the presence of evil in the world? According to Mencius, evil in the world has three sources. First, evil is due to external circumstances. Although man is by nature good, still his nature is distorted by the externals of life. Society and culture are responsible for the presence of wrong actions and evil in the world. Secondly, evil is due to the abandonment of self. Man abandons his innate goodness. Rather than allowing his nature to manifest itself in goodness he forsakes this goodness and determines to do evil. Thirdly, evil is due to the failure to nourish the feelings and the senses. That is, though the intentions are good, one is incapable of doing the right things because of a lack of knowledge on which to make the correct decision.

Upon accepting Mencius' arguments for the innate goodness of man and agreeing with his explanation of the source of evil in the world, it follows that the reason why man should live according to *jen*, *yi*, and *li* is that through acting correctly one's humanity is developed, and thereby human behavior will become well regulated. Furthermore, to regulate one's actions by *li* is to live according to the innate goodness that is man's basic nature. In brief, man should live the way Confucius said he should because it is his nature to do so.

HSUN TZU

The views of Hsun Tzu on this point are diametrically opposed to those of Mencius. According to Hsun Tzu, human nature is originally evil. It is through social institutions and culture that man becomes good. Although man is said not only to lack the beginnings of the four virtues claimed by Mencius, but to actually possess the beginnings of evil in that he has an inherent desire for profit and pleasures, it is held to be possible for every man to become a Sage, for what every man does possess is intelligence, and through the employment of intelligence goodness is brought about. Mencius said that man is born good; Hsun Tzu says that man is born evil. Mencius said that society and culture bring about evil; Hsun Tzu says that society and culture bring about goodness. Whereas Mencius says that anyone can become a Sage because of his innate goodness, Hsun Tzu says that anyone can become a Sage because of his innate intelligence and educability.

The problem for Hsun Tzu is to show how it is that if man is born evil he can become good. He argues that goodness comes about as the result of social organization and culture. Social organization and culture come as the result of (1) the drive to live better, and (2) the need to overcome other creatures. The arguments are (1) man cannot provide the goods needed to live, let alone to live well, except through the cooperation of other persons, and (2) man cannot make himself secure from the various creatures and forces of nature without mutual cooperation. And without security, the structures of society required to improve the quality of life are not possible.

Since it is clear, for these two reasons, that man requires social organization, the question is that of how social organization brings about goodness. Hsun Tzu's answer is that social organization requires rules of conduct, which bring about goodness. His theory is that man is born with desires, some of which are ordinarily unsatisfied. When desires remain unsatisfied man strives for their satisfaction. When many persons are striving for the satisfaction of their conflicting desires without rules or limits there is contention and strife which brings about disorder. This is harmful to everyone. Accordingly the early kings established rules of conduct regulating the activities involved in attempting to satisfy desires: in this way the various rules required for social living came about. Within this line of reasoning, goodness is brought about as a result of the regulation of human conduct required for social living.

Hsun Tzu also argues for the creation of goodness through the employment of intelligence. He observes that it is not the absence of hair or feathers on this two-legged creature that distinguishes man from other animals, but it is the ability to make distinctions. Man's intelligence is displayed in his making of social distinctions. Since it is the making of social distinctions and the resulting social relationships regulated by li that distinguish man from the birds and the beasts, man ought to act according to li in order to preserve and manifest his nature.

Both lines of argument given by Hsun Tzu emphasize that goodness is the result of human creation through the employment of intelligence and the making of distinctions in the social sphere. He differs from Confucius in distinguishing between goodness and intelligence and in stressing the actual evil present in the nature of man. Through their attempts to support the social philosophy of Confucius by providing an answer to the question, Why regulate life by li, and, why develop jen by practicing yi? Hsun Tzu and Mencius strengthened the philosophy considerably. What happened historically was that neither of these philosophers was rejected in the favor of the other, but rather, both the idealism of Mencius and the realism of Hsun Tzu were added to the philosophy of Confucius, thus rounding out the philosophy of Confucianism. From

Mencius was taken the emphasis on determining the correctness of action as a means to the development of man's humanity, and from Hsun Tzu, was taken the emphasis on following rules of behavior for developing man's nature. By adopting both views, Confucianism favored equally respect for internal sanctions, using the internal feelings as guides to behavior, and the external sanctions, using social rules as guides to behavior. This is roughly equivalent to employing both the internal criteria of conscience and the external criterion of law to determine how one should live.

Through his emphasis on the utility of rules, or *li*, for guiding conduct Hsun Tzu was able to add to Confucianism the insights of the Utilitarians (Mohists) and through his emphasis on social rules and external sanctions he was able to add the insights of the Legalists, or positivists, to Confucianism.

MO TZU

The Utilitarian school of Mo Tzu was a strong and popular school in ancient times. Mo Tzu was critical of the Confucian emphasis on goodness as the key to successful social organization on the grounds that it was not sufficiently practical. He was also critical of the traditional institutions, charging that they were not sufficiently useful for achieving the well-being and happiness of the people. The key principle of this school is that the correctness of actions can be determined by reference to their usefulness in producing benefits for man. This principle derives from a theory of the origin of society according to which the social institutions of man were established to obtain benefits for the people and eliminate their hardships, to enrich the poor and increase the population, to replace danger with security, and confusion with order.

Since Hsun Tzu had a similar view of the origin of society, it was possible for him to adopt Mo Tzu's utility principle as a criterion for determining both the goodness of government and the correctness of actions without denying that *jen* and *li* were the foundations of happiness and goodness.

HAN FEI TZU

The Legalist school, which is best represented by Han Fei Tzu, a student of Hsun Tzu, advocated the establishment of infallible laws designed to meet the needs of the time. Prior to Han Fei Tzu it was common to regard history as something essentially static, with the same things happening over and over again. In this context it was natural enough to expect that traditions, institutions, and customs that had served earlier generations would be adequate for the present generation. Han Fei Tzu, however, regarded history as essentially a matter of change. Consequently, he argued that as times changed the institutions and practices of the past became inadequate for solving present problems. This view, though commonplace today, was quite revolutionary, and by no means widely accepted at the time. Consequently, his proposal that laws be created to deal with current problems, and that authority be established to administer these laws, was viewed with considerable skepticism at first.

The key principle of the Legalist school was that rewards and punishments could be used to regulate and make good the actions of people. It was not necessary to wait until the people became good to have good behavior; good behavior could be produced through a system of law to which were attached rewards and punishments as sanctions. Although this principle is opposed to the Confucian principle that goodness and order in society can be produced only by cultivating the moral nature of man, the philosophy of Hsun Tzu made it possible to combine these two views by the twin processes of legalizing morality and moralizing legality. Thus through the philosophy of Hsun Tzu, the significant dimension of law came to be added to Confucianism.

On the other hand, Mencius' emphasis on *yi* led to greater emphasis on *hsiao*, or filial piety, and provided greater support for the attitude that regarded the family as the basic social structure. It thus directly led to increased moral training in terms of example and guidance at a very early age in the family. This insured a secure basis for *li* in later life, for it tended to encourage respect for laws and superiors. Consequently, people were inclined to act morally both because they felt it was the right thing to do and because various rules of society required such action.

Even though Confucianism, as a result of the influence of various other schools and the contributions of Mencius and Hsun Tzu, had various external criteria available for determining the correctness of actions, it continued to be the case that the primary stress was on the humanity that each person possessed within himself. A person knows what to do here and now because all men have within them a measure for determining whether or not to do something, because everyone possesses *jen*, or humanity. All that is required is that the Golden Rule be applied. If it is not something you would like done to you, then do not do it to anyone else. It is probably this humanistic measure of goodness that constitutes the timeless essence of Confucianism. Confucianism as a thoroughgoing humanism with respect to the conduct of life and society is something not merely of historical, antiquarian interest. Rather, it is a permanent social spirit that will exist as long as men have respect for themselves and their fellow men—as long as men are truly men.

CHAPTER 18

TAOISM: THE METAPHYSICS OF NATURE

Taoism, is contrast to Confucianism, seeks its principles and rules for human life not within man himself, but within nature. Consequently, instead of emphasizing man and society, this philosophy emphasizes the metaphysical foundations of nature.

The story of Taoism can be told in two installments. The first part of the story deals with the philosophy developed in the classical work known as *The Treatise on the Way and its Power (Tao Te Ching)*. This is traditionally regarded as the philosophy of Lao Tzu. The second part of the story is concerned with the Taoism of Chuang Tzu, who drew out the epistemological and mystical implications of this philosophy.

LAO TZU

Taoism, just as Confucianism, has its beginnings in a philosophical protest against the conditions of the times. The times of Lao Tzu were approximately the times of Confucius, and Lao Tzu's charges that poverty and starvation were caused by bad rulers, that greed and avarice resulted in wars and killings, and that desires for wealth, power, and glory were bringing about the destruction of society, reveal that his philosophy is inspired by a concern with the deplorable social conditions of the times. However, despite having this inspiration in common, the two philosophies developed in quite different and even opposing ways.

Whereas Confucianism stressed the moral goodness of man as the key to happiness, the Taoists stressed the harmony and perfection of nature. The Taoist attitude is that the contrivances and artifacts of man lead to evil and unhappiness. To find peace and contentment man must follow the Way, or *Tao*, of the universe, and achieve a oneness with this *Tao*.

In Confucianism the complex and well-developed life is taken to be the ideal. Lao Tzu, however, considered the ideal life to be simple and harmonious. A simple life is one which is plain, wherein profit is ignored, cleverness abandoned, selfishness minimized, and desires reduced. This last feature of the simple life serves well to contrast Lao Tzu and Confucius. Confucius advocated rites and music so that the desires and emotions might be developed and regulated, for therein lay the development of *jen*, or humanity. To Lao Tzu, efforts to develop and regulate the desires and emotions seemed artificial and tended to interfere with the harmony of nature. Rather than organize and regulate things to achieve perfection, Lao Tzu would let things work to their perfection naturally. This means supporting all things in their natural state, allowing them to transform spontaneously. In this way no action is needed, no regulations required, and yet everything is done and all things are regulated. It is not the case that the contrast between Confucius and Lao Tzu is that between action and inaction, or doing and non-doing. Rather, it is between holding that man is the measure and source of all things, and holding that nature is the measure and source of all things.

In Confucianism man and nature are differentiated, and goodness and well-being are considered to proceed from what belongs to man rather than nature. Taoism sees man and nature as a unity and does not differentiate between the two. According to this philosophy, the basis of man's being is not of his own making, but is contained in the being and the function of the totality of the universe. Consequently, in its critical and negative aspects, Taoism analyzes the deficiencies and evils confronting man and concludes that they stem primarily from a wrong view of man and the universe. The Confucian views on the nature of man and the universe are criticized as inadequate and incapable of providing for a solution. Constructively, Taoism is concerned to provide more adequate views of man and the world. Here Taoism offers a picture of the universe and man as a unity. Man's knowledge transcends the limits of percepts and concepts. It is direct and immediate, not being dependent upon a false duality between the knowing subject and the known object. The principles that are to guide life and regulate the actions of man are the principles that regulate nature. Life is lived well only when man is completely in tune with the whole universe and his action is the action of the universe flowing through him. The institutions of society are regulated by allowing them to be what they are naturally; society, too, must be in tune with the universe. The task of philosophy is to lead man to a unity with the universe by illuminating its *Tao*, or Way. The word "*Tao*" refers to a path or a way, and in Taoism means the source and principle of functioning of whatever exists. When the *Tao* of man and the *Tao* of the universe are one, man will have realized his infinite nature.

The ethical and social teachings of Taoism represent a constructive attempt to preserve and make great human life. To preserve life is to protect it from threats to its very existence. Making life great assumes the preservation of life and consists in improving the quality of life. It is above all else the attempt to provide a *Tao*, or Way, to a completely satisfying and fulfilled life that motivates the Taoist philosopher. Lao Tzu's teachings concerning the *Tao* of human life in society can be summed up in the following nine principles:

(1) People generally act to fulfill their desires.

(2) The result of many individuals attempting to satisfy their desires is competition and conflict.

(3) In order to provide peace and harmony among individuals struggling to satisfy their desires, standards of human rightness and morality are devised.

(4) Obviously the erection of moral standards does not solve the problem, for competition and conflict remain. Rules are broken and new rules are devised to protect the old rules. But new rules and old rules are broken and desires remain unsatisfied while wrongdoing and evil are fostered.

(5) Since devising moral standards does not solve the problem, the solution lies in giving up moral standards.

(6) However, standards can be abandoned only when desires as sources of action are given up.

(7) Actions arising out of desires can be given up only when people adopt the "easy way" of action.

(8) The "easy way" of action presupposes being in tune with the universe and acting in accord with the universal *Tao*.

(9) Regulation of society and government of the people should be according to the easy and natural way and should foster the natural way in the people.

In attempting to rectify the social evils present in his society Lao Tzu recognized the necessity of understanding the basic causes of these evils. For this it is important to know the sources and guides of human actions. As he turned his attention to these matters it appeared obvious to Lao Tzu that the choices and actions of most people proceed from their desires, and are guided by the satisfaction of these desires. Accordingly, the most basic regulatory principle of action is the ful-fillment of desires.

Now if people act in order to fulfill their desires, and if different per-sons desire the same things, and if there aren't enough goods to go around, there will be competing and conflicting actions. It is, of course, notoriously the case that people are never able to satisfy all of their desires and that they often desire the same things. Consequently, they compete with each other and conflicts arise. When competition is unregulated and conflicts are settled through the use of power and force the whole fabric of society is threatened. Therefore, to regulate competition and reduce conflicts moral rules are introduced as guides to human behavior.

The primary function of moral rules and social institutions is to regulate the .ctions of the people in order to provide for a maximum satisfaction of desires for everyone. Lao Tzu has no quarrel with the aims of morality; rather, he questions the possibility of achieving this aim through the regulation of competition and conflict. Observing that when the great *Tao* prevailed there was no strife and competition, he remarks, "When the Great *Tao* declined, the doctrines of humanity and righteousness arose."[1] The doctrines of humanity (*jen*) and righteousness (*yi*) are the basis of the Confucian morality, and have as their object the satisfactory ordering of all human actions and social institutions. Lao Tzu's remark, however, reveals that he considers morality an inadequate solution, for it comes about only as a result of the decline of the great Way of nature.

Undoubtedly, Lao Tzu saw the failure of Confucian morality to achieve ideal social conditions as a sign of the inadequacy of the moral approach. Morality does not attack the problem at its root. By allowing desires

[1] *Tao Te Ching*, Ch. 18, trans. by Wing-tsit Chan, *The Way of Lao Tzu* (Indianapolis: Bobbs-Merrill, Inc., 1963).

to function as legitimate sources of human action, morality could not remove competition and strife. The best it could do was to regulate the competition and reduce the strife. But this simply complicates the matter of satisfying desires in accord with the moral rules, and leads to rule breaking, thereby bringing about immorality. It does not remove the competition and does not provide for the complete satisfaction of all desires. Hence Lao Tzu said, "Therefore when *Tao* is lost, only then does the doctrine of virtue arise. When virtue is lost, only then does the doctrine of humanity arise."[2]

Since morality is incapable of providing for peace and happiness, it should be regarded as an unsuccessful solution to the problem of achieving the ideal society and abandoned in favor of a different solution. But morality cannot be abandoned without changing the conditions which inevitably lead to the regulation of action by moral rules. These conditions, a world of competition and strife where the powerful subdue the weak at their pleasure, are the result of acting for the sake of satisfying desires. Since acting to satisfy desires brings about the conditions requiring morality, morality cannot be abandoned until desires as source of actions are abandoned. The reason why acting out of desires leads to evil is that it is contrary to the Way, for the great *Tao* is always without desires. The good is accomplished not by action driven by desire, but by inaction inspired by the simplicity of *Tao*, according to Lao Tzu. He says, "Simplicity, which has no name, is free of desires. Being free of desires it is tranquil. And the world will be at peace of its own accord."[3]

Advocating giving up desires as sources of action, the important question for Lao Tzu is, How then should people act? His answer, in brief, is that people should adopt the "easy way" of *Tao*, not inflicting their desires upon nature, but following her. With regard to society, he advocates a government of the people which is in accord with the easy and natural way of *Tao*, and which fosters the natural way in the lives of the people.

To understand this answer of Lao Tzu, it is necessary to turn to his conception of *Tao* and its manifestations, *te*. Prior to Lao Tzu the principles of *yin* and *yang* were known. They were regarded as opposites, and all of the things in the world were considered to be the production of the interaction between *yin* and *yang*. But *yin* and *yang*, opposed as light and dark, cold and warm, being and non-being, etc., being opposite,

---

[2] *Tao Te Ching*, Ch. 38.   [3] *Ibid.*, Ch. 37.

could not of their own nature either produce themselves or interact with each other. A third something providing a basis and a context for the interaction of *yin* and *yang* was required. The great contribution of Lao Tzu was his recognition of *Tao* as the source of both being and non-being—of *yin* and *yang*—and the function of *Tao* as the basis for the interaction of *yin* and *yang*.

As the absolutely first principle of existence, *Tao* is completely without characteristics. It is itself uncharacterized, being the very source and condition of all characteristics. In this sense it is non-being. But it is not simply nothing, for it is the source of everything. It is prior to all the existing things, giving them life and function, constituting the oneness underlying all the diversity and multiplicity of the world. Lao Tzu says, "The *Tao* that can be told of is not the eternal *Tao*; the name that can be named is not the eternal name. The Nameless is the origin of Heaven and Earth; the named is the mother of all things."[4]

The reason *Tao* cannot be named is that it is without divisions, distinctions, or characteristics. It is unified, like an uncarved block, being without change, knowing neither beginning nor end. But if *Tao* cannot be named, what is named by "Tao"? Lao Tzu's point in saying that the *Tao* is beyond all names is that the fundamental source and principle cannot be named, for it is the very source of names and descriptions. Consequently, "Tao" is a non-name; it does not refer to any one thing. Rather it points to that which enables things to be what they are; it is that which gives them existence and allows them to pass into non-existence. When it is said that *Tao* is the source of all being, and non-being, the word "*Tao*" functions very much like the word "that" when it is said "the 'that' from which being and non-being proceed."

The importance of *Tao* lies in the recognition that there is something which is prior and anterior to the various particular things that exist in the world, something which gives unity to all the existing things and which determines the very existence and function of everything that exists. What that something is cannot, of course, be said, for whatever can be talked about is limited and determined, whereas it cannot be said that the source is limited and determined, for it is the very condition of limits and determinations.

Although what *Tao* is cannot be said, but can only be pointed to, a feeling for what *Tao* is can be achieved by considering the functioning of *Tao*. Strictly speaking the function (*te*) of *Tao* cannot be stated or

---

[4] *Tao Te Ching*, Ch. 1.

observed, but since it is the function of *Tao* that supports all things in their natural state something of the function of *Tao* can be seen, at least partially, by looking to nature. The function of *Tao* is manifested in the workings of nature, for what individual things possess of *Tao* is the *te*, or function, of *Tao*. *Tao*, as a source, provides for the very existence of things, but the function of *Tao* provides for their distinctness. Examining the working of things in their natural conditions, Lao Tzu observes that no-action (*wu-wei*) is what they inherit from *Tao* as their function. He says, "*Tao* invariably takes no action, and yet there is nothing left undone."[5] What he means by "taking no action" is not straining and contriving to accomplish, but letting things be accomplished in a natural and spontaneous way. Thus, immediately after the remark quoted above he says, "If kings and barons can keep it, all things will transform spontaneously."[6] The reference here is to *Tao*. If the ruler will keep to the way of *Tao*, government will proceed in a natural and spontaneous way. There will be no need for harsh laws, conscriptions, punishment, and wars.

Lao Tzu's advice to the rulers is that they should govern as little as possible, keeping to the natural way, letting people go their own way. He suggests that the people are difficult to rule because the ruler does too many things. What the ruler should keep in mind is that "ruling a big country is like cooking a small fish." In cooking a small fish one must take care not to handle it too roughly for too much handling will spoil it. In ruling a country care must be taken not to push the people around, forcing them to rebel. When the people are satisfied there will be no rebellion or wars. Therefore the easy way of governing is to give the people what they want and make government conform to the will of the people rather than trying to force the people to conform to the will of the government.

When Lao Tzu suggests that the ruler should know the mystic *Tao*, and in his ruling emulate the function of *Tao*, he has in mind that the perfection of all things lies in expressing the *Tao* they possess. The job of the ruler is to let the *Tao* operate freely, rather than trying to resist and change its function. What *Tao* is, and how it functions, is revealed in the fourth chapter of the *Tao Te Ching*, where Lao Tzu says:

> *Tao* is empty (like a bowl).
> It may be used but its capacity is never exhausted.
> It is bottomless, perhaps the ancestor of all things.
> It blunts its sharpness.

[5] *Tao Te Ching*, Ch. 37.   [6] *Ibid.*

> It unties its tangles.
> It softens its light.
> It becomes one with the dusty world.
> Deep and still, it appears to exist forever.

To say *Tao* is empty is to note that it is without characteristics; it is empty of all particularity, for it is the possibility and source of all particularity. Even though it is empty of particular things it is the most useful of all things. Just as the most useful thing about a house is its emptiness—its space—so the most useful thing about *Tao* is its emptiness of characteristics, for this means it has infinite capacity. Thus the emptiness of *Tao* is synonymous with its being the infinite source of all things. The functioning of *Tao* is eternal and recurrent, producing all things and directing their activities. Comparing the functioning of *Tao* to blunting sharpness, untying tangles, and softening light draws attention to reversal as the movement of the *Tao*. The lesson the Taoists drew from nature is that when a thing reaches one extreme, it reverses and returns to the other extreme. Thus, the advice is given that if one would assist the ruler with *Tao* he does not use force and violence, for this would bring about a reversal.[7] When it gets very cold, reversal sets in and it begins to get warm. When it gets very warm, reversal again sets in and it begins to get cold. This is the way of nature as seen in the passing of the seasons. In similar fashion, when a person becomes extremely proud and conceited, disgrace and humility will follow. To know the reversals that constitute the functioning of *Tao* and to adapt oneself to these movements is the way to peace and contentment. Just as one does not dress lightly in winter and suffer in the cold, and does not dress warmly in the summer and suffer in the heat, but dresses warmly in the winter and enjoys the cold, and dresses lightly in the summer and enjoys the warm weather, so one should not resist the natural way, but should act in accord with the Way of the Great *Tao* in all things.

To recognize that *Tao* becomes one with the dusty world is to understand that *Tao* is not transcendental, but immanent. That is, *Tao* does not remain aloof from the world, directing it from afar, but functions through the world, and is indistinguishable from the functioning of the world. *Tao* is not to be found aside from life, but within life in the world.

When the ruler knows the *Tao* and its *te* he knows how to stay out of the way of the people and serve them without intruding. Thus, Lao

---

[7] *Tao Te Ching*, Ch. 30.

Tzu says that the people "are difficult to rule because the ruler does too many things."[8] In accord with the function of *Tao*, Lao Tzu says, "Administer the empire by engaging in no activity." Supporting this advice, he notes that "the more taboos and prohibitions there are in the world, the poorer the people will be," and, "the more laws and orders are made prominent, the more thieves and robbers there will be."[9]

By giving up desires and letting the *Tao* enter and pervade oneself, life will rise above the distinctions of good and evil. All activity will proceed from *Tao*, the very source of existence, and man will be one with the world. This is the solution Lao Tzu brought to the problem of evil and unhappiness in man's life. It is a solution that depends ultimately upon achieving a unity with the great inner principle of reality, and is therefore, basically mystical.

CHUANG TZU

Although the positive foundations of Taoism are mystical, there are good reasons for seriously considering this way of life, as Chuang Tzu points out. Chuang Tzu (ca. 369–286 B.C.) developed a philosophy not basically different from Lao Tzu's, though he does develop further the concepts of the total spontaneity of nature, the incessant activity of things, and the underlying unity of all existence. He emphasized that man's ultimate freedom lay in identifying with the *Tao* of reality, where this means transcending ordinary reality. The most valuable contribution of Chuang Tzu, however, lies in the *arguments* he provided for rejecting other ways of life and accepting the Taoist Way.

The philosophy of Chuang Tzu is based on the conviction that true happiness is dependent upon transcending the world of ordinary experience and cognition and identifying oneself with the infinity of the universe. This conviction appears quite clearly in his description of the man who has achieved complete happiness. Of the happy man, the true sage, the perfect man, Chuang Tzu says, "Suppose there is one who chariots upon the normality of the universe, rides upon the transformation of the six elements, and thus makes excursions into the infinite, what has he to depend upon? Therefore it is said that the Perfect Man has no self; the Spiritual Man has no achievement; the Sage has no name."[10]

[8] *Tao Te Ching*, Ch. 25.   [9] *Tao Te Ching*, Ch. 57.
[10] As quoted in Fung Yu-Lan, *History of Chinese Philosophy*, trans. Derk Bodde (Princeton: Princeton University Press, 1952), vol. 1, p. 243.

This remark is intended to suggest that the ordinary cognitive scheme wherein one distinguishes between self and other, between doing and not doing, and between names (words) and realities (things) is inadequate. It is claimed to be inadequate because of its limitations; its finiteness. Consequently, in the *Book of Chuang Tzu* it is suggested that the finite point of view (the ordinary cognitive point of view, which is dependent upon perception and conception) should be exchanged for an "infinite," or "transcendent," point of view. This infinite point of view is regarded as becoming one with *Tao*, the essence (normality) of the universe.

Not infrequently the aspects of his philosophy just referred to are regarded as evidence that Chuang Tzu was a Chinese mystic. Being so labeled, Chuang Tzu could be dismissed from further philosophical consideration. But such dismissal is unfortunate, for Chuang Tzu does not merely suggest that the finite point of view should be exchanged for the infinite. He argues, quite ingeniously, for the acceptance of the infinite point of view by trying to show that the finite point of view (the ordinary cognitive scheme) is inadequate.

The arguments against accepting the ordinary cognitive scheme, which constitute Chuang Tzu's arguments for an infinite point of view, can be classified as (1) the argument from the relativity of distinctions, (2) the argument from the complementariness of opposites, (3) the argument from perspectives, and (4) the argument from general skepticism.

1. The first argument, the argument from the relativity of distinctions, would have it that judgments about values and matters of taste are subjective and therefore relative. A particular sauce may be sour to A's taste, but sweet to B's taste. Thinking about the relativity of distinctions may be good for X, and bad for Y. This relativity is taken to hold for all distinctions. Chuang Tzu says, "Let us take, for instance, a large beam and a small beam, or an ugly woman and Hsi-shih [famous beauty of ancient China], or generosity, strangeness, deceit, and abnormality. The Tao identifies them all as one."[11] He also says "There is nothing in the world greater than the tip of a hair that grows in autumn, while Mount T'ai is small. No one lives a longer life than a child who dies in infancy, but P'eng-tsu (who lived many hundred years) died prematurely. The universe and I exist together, and all things and I are one."[12]

[11] In Wing-tsit Chan, trans. and compiler, *A Source Book in Chinese Philosophy* (Princeton: Princeton University Press, 1963), p. 184.
[12] *Ibid.*, p. 186.

The basic reason for regarding all distinctions as relative is that it is held that the characteristics attributed to things or events in the making of distinctions are generated by the mind, which is regarded as independent of the so-called characteristics of things generated by it. Chuang Tzu says, "A road becomes so when people walk on it, and things become so-and-so [to people] because people call them so-and-so. How have they become so? They have become so because people say they are so. How have they become not so? They have become not so because [people say] they are not so."[13] The argument from the relativity of distinctions is intended to prove the triviality of knowledge. If the possibility of knowing what is good, or big, or sweet is claimed, and it can be shown that the concepts of good, big, and sweet are relative, it follows that the knowledge claimed is relative, and therefore can be regarded as trivial or unreal.

This argument is directed primarily against the Confucianists and Mohists, both of whom claimed they had genuine knowledge of right and wrong, but who disagreed on nearly every point. Chuang Tzu says, "There have arisen the controversies between the Confucianists and the Mohists, each school regarding as right what the other regards as wrong. . . ."[14] The Mohists were pragmatists, accepting practice as the criterion of knowledge. Their view was that knowledge is possible, for in the main, man lives in such a way as to avoid a lot of unpleasantness. Now, since on pragmatic or utilitarian grounds the rightness and wrongness of actions is determined by the amounts of pleasantness and unpleasantness respectively, right and wrong can be known simply by looking to the pleasantness and unpleasantness brought about by actions. The Confucianists, on the other hand, maintained that knowledge of right and wrong proceeded immediately and intuitively from an internal moral sense.

Chuang Tzu uses the argument from relativity to show that pleasantness and unpleasantness are relative concepts, and though people appear to get on well in this life, this may be a mere appearance and not the case at all. Furthermore, it is not clear how practice can serve as a criterion of knowledge, and it may be possible that there is no way of knowing whether or not practice is an adequate criterion of knowledge, for practice itself is relative. For the Confucianist, the problem lies in showing that the moral sense, which is supposed to provide knowledge of right and wrong, is any less relative than any of the other senses.

[13] *Ibid.*, pp. 183–184. (Brackets are Chan's.)   [14] *Ibid.*, p. 182.

Both the Confucianist and the Mohist would agree, though for different reasons, that we can have genuine knowledge of the fact that it is wrong to kill. Employing the relativity argument of Chuang Tzu, however, it can be seen that this is not absolute knowledge, but only relative knowledge. From another perspective it might turn out to be mistaken opinion. Suppose it is claimed that it is wrong to kill. Now if a man is starving and the only way to escape death is to kill a hare, all would agree that it is right to kill the hare. But someone might suggest that though in need it is right to kill animals, it is always wrong to kill a man. If, however, the only way to prevent the death of his wife and family is for a man to kill the attacker, it would again be conceded that in this special case it would be right for a man to kill, but only because of the special circumstances. Somewhere along the line it could be suggested, by someone using Chuang Tzu's argument, that there can never be any real knowledge of the wrongness of an action such as killing, because right and wrong are purely relative. Everything depends on who is doing the killing, who the considering, and what the circumstances are. There can be no absolute right and wrong because rightness and wrongness are relative to the circumstances of the actions in question. And if this is the case there is no real knowledge of rightness and wrongness, for one might always be mistaken in thinking he knew that a particular action was right or wrong.

Of course, it might be argued against Chuang Tzu that if all knowledge is purely relative, then so is this knowledge; namely, the knowledge that all knowledge is relative and trivial. But Chuang's suggestion is that because of the relativity of knowledge you could never really know that that bit of knowledge is trivial. It will not do to return the compliment by claiming that he can never really know either that that, or any knowledge, either is or is not trivial, because the point of Chuang Tzu's argument from skepticism is precisely this: to maintain the impossibility of certain, indubitable knowledge.

Chuang Tzu's position is clear. If it is certitude of knowledge that is doubted, indubitable knowledge is impossible without begging the question. And there seems no way, other than by knowing, of ascertaining that there is indubitable knowledge. Thus, Chuang Tzu's argument, on these grounds at least, is unanswerable.

2. The second argument, from the complementariness of opposites, suggests that any concept logically implies its negation, and that without its negation, or opposite, a concept could not exist. The argument is intended to show that affirmation and negation are simply different

ways of looking at the same thing. If *A* is *A*, then *A* is not *not-A*. Or, the negation of *A* is the affirmation of *not-A*. In a similar way, right and wrong are the same thing looked at differently. If *A* is right, then *A* is not-wrong. If there were no right, there would be no wrong (and vice versa). For if *A* is right, then *A* is not wrong, implying a wrong that *A* is not, and in virtue of which *A* is, or can be, right. In other words, *what is* involves *what is not*, and opposites, from this point of view, turn out to be complementary. Chuang Tzu says, "Nevertheless, when there is life there is death, and when there is death there is life. When there is possibility, there is impossibility, and when there is impossibility there is possibility. Because of the right, there is the wrong, and because of the wrong there is the right."[15] He also says, "There is nothing that is not the "that" and there is nothing that is not the "this." Therefore I say that the "that" is produced by the "this" and the "this" is also caused by the "that."[16]

Chuang Tzu appears to be thinking in terms of pairs of correlative terms. For example, if there were no concept of up, there could be none of down, and the same holds true for left and right, right and wrong, self and other, etc. For such pairs of concepts, the existence of one presupposes the other and the removal of one is the removal of the other. It might be objected that it is by no means clear that all concepts can function only as correlatives. In fact, if one avoids adjectival concepts and concentrates on substantive concepts, it is by no means clear that a concept is possible only if it is opposed by another concept. By what concepts need the concepts *man*, *house*, *dog*, etc. be opposed in order that they can function as concepts?

According to Chuang Tzu's argument, however, even a concept such as *dog* involves, at least implicitly, the concept of *not-dog*, for if there were no concept of *not-dog*, the concept of *dog* could not be used discriminately. That is, it would be impossible to decide what to call and what not to call a dog. And if a person could never properly use a concept in a discriminatory fashion this would be sufficient evidence for claiming that he did not have the concept at all. But a necessary condition of using a concept properly is being able to discriminate between what the concept refers to and what it does not. Thus, in terms of the present example, having the concept *dog* involves knowing what is not-dog, or of having the concept of *not-dog*. The same line of reasoning can be used with any substantive concept, for having a concept of anything

[15] *Ibid.*, p. 183.   [16] *Ibid.*, p. 182.

presupposes an ability to discriminate between that to which the concept refers and that to which it does not, and this involves knowing what the concept is not. In this way it is seen that a concept of something is always relative to what that something is not. Thus, Chuang Tzu says, "the 'this' is also the 'that'," and, "when 'this' and 'that' have no opposites, there is the very axis of *Tao*."[17]

The question could be asked, Which is the essential feature of knowledge, the not-dog or the dog? According to Chuang Tzu, the answer is neither, since both are necessary. Coupled with the argument from skepticism, this argument implies neither that there is no real knowledge nor that real knowledge is impossible, but that we can never know (i.e. be certain) either what this or that knowledge really consists in, or whether or not we really have knowledge.

3. The third argument, the argument from perspectives, presupposes the previous two arguments. It is obvious that the same thing appears differently to different people if their perspectives are different. Or, the same thing appears different to me if I change my perspective. If my organs of sensing were different, no doubt I would perceive things differently. The point of this is that the same thing has many appearances, depending upon the perceiver. Which of the appearances is the correct or true appearance? Is what the worm or the cat perceives the same as what a person perceives? Is what is perceived now the same as what was perceived a minute ago?

Chuang Tzu's point is that these questions cannot be answered. Each thing is just what it is and not another and it is what it is independent of how it appears to anything or anyone. It is contained in itself, in its own perspective, and the only way to get at the way it is, is to transcend our own perspective and view the other as a totality, from its own perspective. The claim is that everything in the world is a self-sufficient unit with a perspective of its own. Everything has a view of itself and has a function. From its own point of view everything is a totality. But if everything is a totality from its own point of view and no other, then it appears that morality and knowledge are purely relative. And if everything is looked at from its own point of view, right and wrong disappear. This is exactly what Chuang Tzu recommends: obtain the transcendent point of view from which everything is seen in its proper perspective, from its own point of view. Then there will be unity with the universe; there will be enlightenment; the *Tao* will be found in every-

[17] *Ibid.*, p. 183.

thing. According to Chuang Tzu, "Things do not know that they are the 'that' of other things; they only know what they themselves know."[18] And, "Only the intelligent knows how to identify all things as one."[19] The point is illustrated with the butterfly story:

> Once I, Chuang Chou, dreamed that I was a butterfly and was happy as a butterfly. I was conscious that I was quite pleased with myself, but I did not know that I was Chou. Suddenly I awoke, and there I was, visibly Chou. I do not know whether it was Chou dreaming that he was a butterfly or the butterfly dreaming it was Chou.[20]

Going further, Chuang Tzu advises giving up a particular perspective and adopting a universal perspective:

> We say this is right or wrong, and is so or is not so. If the right is really right, then the fact that it is different from the wrong leaves no room for argument. Forget the passage of time (life and death) and forget the distinction of right and wrong. Relax in the realm of the infinite and thus abide in the realm of the infinite.[21]

Here the point of the argument is that we can never really know what a thing is in itself. To make this point, the argument *assumes* a transcendent point of view, for by its own premises, ordinary experience could never show anything about things as they are in themselves, as totalities with their own perspectives. Only by assuming a transcendent point of view can it be known that there are things in themselves, locked within their own perspectives and not accessible to ordinary means of knowledge. To assume a point of view is not the same thing as to argue for a point of view. The argument for a transcendent point of view depends on showing that the ordinary cognitive point of view leads to skepticism, and because of this the argument from skepticism is relevant at this point.

4. Chuang Tzu's fourth argument, the argument from skepticism, advances the claim that the question, Is that really so? can never be answered. Suppose, for example, that it is claimed that X is red. The retort is, "But how can it be shown to be *really* red?" The difficulty in proving that the claim is true is that the claim cannot be compared with what is actually the case, because any claim about what is actually the case would be subject to the same doubts as the original claim. What is needed is a standard to judge the first standard, a standard to judge the second standard, etc., *ad infinitum*. But it appears that choosing

18 *Ibid.*, p. 182.   19 *Ibid.*, p. 184.   20 *Ibid.*, p. 190.   21 *Ibid.*

even a third standard is impossible, for if *A* and *B* have opposite views, a standard acceptable to *A* would be unacceptable to *B*, and a standard acceptable to *B* would be unacceptable to *A*. And if the standard is acceptable to no one, it is of no use. Therefore is would seem impossible to defend the claim that *X* is really red.

On one occasion Chuang Tzu presented the skeptical argument in the form of the following question: "How can it be known that what I call knowing is not really not knowing and what I call not knowing is not really knowing?"[22] On another occasion he presented the argument in the form of a different question: "For knowledge depends on something to be correct, but what it depends on is uncertain and changeable. How do we know that what I call nature is not really man and what I call man is not really nature?"[23]

This skepticism is pushed even further in the following statement:

> Suppose we make a statement. We don't know whether it belongs to one category or another. Whether one or the other, if we put them in one, then one is not different from the other. However, let me explain. There was a beginning. There was a time before that beginning. And there was a time before the time which was before that beginning. There was being. There was non-being. There was a time that was before that non-being, and there was a time before the time that was before that non-being. Suddenly there is being and non-being, but I don't know which of being and non-being is really being or really non-being. I have just said something, but I don't know if what I have said really says something or says nothing.[24]

Chuang Tzu, in suggesting that it is impossible to know whether what is called man is really man or whether it is really nature, or that it is impossible to tell whether it is Chuang Tzu dreaming he is a butterfly or a butterfly dreaming it is Chuang Tzu, is obviously assuming the skeptic's role. Taking the butterfly example, it can be seen that Chuang Tzu's problem is that of ascertaining whether he was dreaming or being dreamed. Chuang Tzu can find no indubitable criteria that can be used to distinguish between being awake and dreaming, and no indubitable criteria to distinguish being dreamed from dreaming. Hence he cannot be sure that he does not exist merely as a character in a butterfly's dream.

The obvious answer to this kind of skepticism is that the doubts expressed make sense only within a certain cognitive scheme, in this case a cognitive scheme wherein individuals such as Chuang Tzu and

---

[22] *Ibid.*, p. 187.   [23] *Ibid.*, p. 191.   [24] *Ibid.*, pp. 185–186.

Sage in Meditation. *The Metropolitan Museum of Art, Rogers Fund, 1923*

butterflies can be identified and differentiated. When Chuang Tzu goes on to use this cognitive scheme to reject this identification and differentiation he is rejecting the very conditions in terms of which it makes sense to question such identification and differentiation. In this way he rejects the grounds which make possible the first doubt and which are needed to make sense of his skepticism. For unless Chuang Tzu could accept "Once I, Chuang Tzu, dreamed I was a butterfly" he could not go on to doubt whether he dreamed or was dreamed.

Though the above answer may be sufficient to refute skepticism generally, it will not refute Chuang Tzu's general position. To see this, recall that Chuang Tzu is arguing for a transcendent point of view. His arguments are negative, in the sense that they are aimed at refuting a finite point of view. Suppose for a moment that Chuang Tzu's only argument is the skeptical one, and that the above argument adequately refutes the skeptical argument.

Has Chuang Tzu been refuted by the above argument? Not at all. In fact, his position has been strengthened. The reason for this is that Chuang Tzu is arguing that the ordinary cognitive framework is inadequate, and that a new cognitive framework, a universal cognitive framework, must be adopted in order to escape the limitations of the limited cognitive scheme ordinarily employed. It is for this reason that the fact that though thorough-going skepticism is self-contradictory in terms of a conceptual framework which is limited in the relevant ways (e.g. a conceptual framework that is essentially spatial-temporal), this is not an argument for the rejection of thorough-going skepticism, but is an argument for rejecting the limited cognitive scheme.

Does recognition of the limitations of ordinary cognitive schemes and adoption of a transcendent perspective mean rejecting the ordinary and mundane world? The answer is no, for to interpret Lao Tzu and Chuang Tzu in this way is to ignore their concern with social rectification, the concern inspiring their philosophies. Kuo Hsiang, a later commentator on Chuang Tzu, puts the matter as follows:

> To cry as people cry is a manifestation of the mundane world. To identify life and death, forget joy and sorrow, and be able to sing in the presence of the corpse is the perfection of the transcendental world . . .

He then goes on to point out that the true sage, the person who is fully able to transcend the mundane world, finds his happiness in the mundane world. He says,

> There has never been a person who has roamed over the transcendental world to the utmost and yet was not silently in harmony with the mundane world, nor has there been anyone who was silently in harmony with the mundane world and yet did not roam over the transcendental world. Therefore the sage always roams in the transcendental world in order to enlarge the mundane world. By having no deliberate mind of his own, he is in accord with things.[25]

In the sage the transcendental and the mundane meet, for here the *tao*, or way of man, is identical with the *Tao* of the universe. Man's will is in accord with nature and his actions are spontaneously produced by *te*.

[25] *Ibid.*, p. 330.

CHAPTER 19

NEO-CONFUCIANISM:
THE GRAND HARMONY

THE third major indigenous philosophical movement in China is that of Neo-Confucianism. This philosophy represents a harmonizing of the underlying principles of Confucianism and Taoism, in an effort to reduce the influence of Buddhism in China. The introduction and development of Buddhism in China provided a strong catalyst in the philosophical milieu during China's middle ages. But Neo-Confucianism also is indebted to developments in Neo-Taoism, the School of Names, and the metaphysical developments in the *Yin-Yang* interactionist school. Without all of these elements it is unlikely that the Ch'eng brothers and Chu Hsi could have reinterpreted the principles and concepts of Confucianism in such a way as to include and coordinate the apparently conflicting principles of the other schools of philosophy in China.

In 221 B.C. the state of Ch'in succeeded in subduing all of the states of China: for the first time China was a unified country. But despite the Confucian teachings that government should proceed according to moral principles, and the Taoist teachings that government should leave the people alone as much as possible, not interfering in the lives of the people except when necessary for their own well-being, the unification of China came about as the result of military power and economic control. However, this event, though brought about by means contrary to both philosophies, did not refute either Taoism or Confucianism. In fact, in the long term it tended to confirm them both, for the excessive regulation of the people coupled with the harshness of the rule and lack of concern for moral qualities led to rebellion against the Ch'in dynasty, and by 206 B.C., just fifteen years later, the Han dynasty controlled the country. The Han dynasty lasted for more than four hundred years, its longevity being due, at least in part, to its attempts to provide for political unity and to construct a new social order along the lines of the Confucian philosophy.

From the point of view of Neo-Confucianism, the most significant feature of the unification of China was the adoption of Confucianism as the state philosophy. It was primarily the work of Tung Chung-Shu that was responsible for making Confucianism the national philosophy of China, to the exclusion of other philosophies. This was possible because of the close relation between politics and philosophy in China which permitted the foundation of a civil service examination system designed by Tung Chung-Shu to be based on the Confucian texts. In addition to this, Tung Chung-Shu helped found the Imperial University, where the Confucian texts were the basis of all education. Although these programs secured the continuation of Confucianism it did not preserve the Confucianism of Confucius and Mencius in its purity, for Tung Chung-Shu had interpreted the Confucian texts in the light of his systematization and amplification of the *yin-yang* and the Five Elements, or Five Agents, theories, into which he had incorporated certain aspects of Taoism.

From an objective philosophical point of view, the most serious effect of adopting Confucianism as the state philosophy and excluding the philosophies of Taoism, Mohism, Legalism, and the School of Names was that without the challenges of different philosophical perspectives and positions there was really very little philosophical development. Instead of undergoing further philosophical development, Confucianism was allowed to remain essentially static, since the main effort of Confucian scholars was to put into practice this philosophy rather than develop it further philosophically. But, of course, a system of philosophy cannot remain static. If it is not subjected to criticism and analysis it not only fails to develop further, but it becomes empty and hollow, being little more than a concatenation of names and formulas. Consequently, since the other schools of philosophy had been officially silenced and therefore never became sufficiently influential to attract the kind of intellectual attention they needed for fuller development, and since Confucianism was relatively lifeless and static, there was little indigenous philosophical development in China from around the beginning of the Christian era until the beginnings of Neo-Confucianism.

During this same period, however, Buddhism was introduced into China, and underwent considerable development and became quite influential. In fact, all of the Neo-Confucian philosophers took considerable pains to discuss the weaknesses of Buddhism in an attempt to decrease the influence of Buddhism and increase the importance and influence of Confucianism. Part of the reason for the growth and development of Buddhism in China was due to the fact that all of the different schools of Buddhism were brought to China and there was, therefore, the stimulation of mutual criticism right from the beginning. In addition, Buddhism represented a systematic explanation of the world and man in which practical living was defined by reference to theoretical principles, such as the nature of causality, the nature of Buddhahood, and the nature of consciousness or the mind. Indigenous philosophies of China had not managed to combine systematic completeness with detailed prescriptions for living. In Taoism the base was sufficiently broad, but the philosophy remained too abstract to be practical. In Confucianism there was a wealth of detailed rules for the guidance of life, but no theoretical and systematic foundation for these prescriptions. By contrast, therefore, Buddhism immediately appeared attractive, and won sufficient attention from Chinese scholars and intellectuals to ensure translation not only into the Chinese language, but also into Chinese philosophical concepts and practice. As it turned out historically, many of the Buddhist schools were too theoretical in their emphasis to catch on in China, and the Buddhist philosophies that did take hold underwent modifications that increased their concern with morality and politics and gave them a more practical bent. But despite the extent to which schools such as the Hua-yen, Chen-yen, T'ien-t'ai, Ch'an, and Ching't'u became modified by the Chinese scholars responsible for their development, they continued to be regarded as foreign and extraneous philosophies, and among the Confucian scholars there was an increasing concern to replace these foreign philosophies with something having roots in China's ancient past. Since Confucianism was still officially the state philosophy and the civil service and university systems were based on this philosophy, it is natural that it should be regarded as the basis from which a philosophy could be derived which would prove superior to the Buddhist philosophies. In this way Buddhism proved the critical catalyst in Confucian studies that produced Neo-Confucianism.

Neo-Confucianism begins with an attempt to find a metaphysical explanation of the universe that is as comprehensive as the Buddhist, but which is completely affirmative, being built upon the supremacy of the individual person and the particular thing, and which emphasizes the moral features of the universe and provides for the achievement of moral goodness among the people. Granting this metaphysical accomplishment, the ethical and social philosophies of Confucianism could be recast, putting them upon this new basis. In effect, this new basis would allow for a synthesis of Taoist, Buddhist, and Confucian principles and tendencies, and give expression to the practical philosophies of Taoism and Confucianism. Buddhism was very influential in China from around 800 A.D. to 1200 A.D. After that period, however, from about the beginning of the thirteenth century, when Neo-Confucianism came into its own, Buddhism was on the decline, and the next eight hundred years of Chinese philosophical history are clearly Neo-Confucianist.

CHOU TUN-I

It was Chou Tun-i who was directly responsible for laying the foundations of Neo-Confucianism. He was born at a time when the ascendancy of Buddhist philosophies in China was viewed by government officials as a threat to the social organization of the country. These officials feared that the negative attitude of the Buddhists toward life in the world and their preference for retreating from active social life into monasteries would undermine the ancient forms of Chinese social organization.[1] Ou-yang Hsiu (1007–1072 A.D.) tried to cast this concern into a program by suggesting that Buddhism could be opposed by displaying the indigenous philosophies of China, showing them to be superior to Buddhist philosophies. The difficulty of achieving what Ou-yang Hsiu proposed was due largely to the fact that the various Buddhist philosophies could boast a complete philosophy of life wherein practical considerations rested upon solid metaphysical principles. The Chinese philosophies, on the other hand, were not systematically complete. Chinese philosophers had tended to be concerned only with things at hand and did not concern themselves with the elegance of complete systems. Consequently, though they had maxims and rules for living, they were not in a position to justify these rules and maxims by appeal to a comprehensive philosophy.

The problem, therefore, in opposing Buddhism was that of having to

---

[1] The point here is not that the Buddhist philosophies are life-negating and unconcerned with practical social matters, but that they were so regarded by the Chinese officials in question.

construct a systematic philosophy of man and the world which would show the relations between man and nature and between man and man, and which would, of course, be completely life-affirming, emphasizing the importance of particular things and individual persons.

Han Yü was expressing a prevalent criticism of his day when he said, "But now the followers of Lao-tzu and the Buddha who talk about rectification of the mind ignore this world and their native land and reduce the normal duties required by heaven to nothingness. Following the ideas of Lao-tzu, a son does not have to consider his father as a father, nor does a man have to regard the king as a king. He does not even have to discharge his duties as a subject."[2] He went beyond mere criticism, however, and urged a return to Confucius. As he saw it, this meant a return to an all pervasive love as the common basis for all human activity. This universal love proceeds from the basic nature of man, for it represents the humanity (jen) of man. In addition to jen, human nature is constituted by propriety, sincerity, righteousness, and wisdom. Three grades of persons can be distinguished on the basis of how these five virtues constituting human nature are practiced. If one of these—jen—is the ruling virtue and if the other four are also practiced the person is superior. If no one of these is perfected and they are practiced only sometimes and in impure form the person belongs to the medium grade. When jen is rejected and actions are not in accord with the other four the person is inferior. This system of three grades, usually acknowledged to be an original contribution of Han Yü, emphasizes the priority he gave to the moral principles of Confucianism.

It would appear that Han Yü's objections were primarily due to the excessive interest in metaphysical things in Taoism and Buddhism at the expense of practical things. Therefore he argued that the Tao (Way) of life consists in loving the people and observing the proper human relationships. This concern for practical things and the belief that Confucianism was fully the equal of Buddhism and Taoism is also clearly evident in Li Ao, a pupil of Han Yü. Li Ao says, "Everybody has joined the schools of Lao-tzu, the Buddha, Chuang-tzu and Lieh-tzu. They all believe that the Confucianist scholars were not learned enough to know about nature and the heavenly order, but that they themselves are. Before those who raise this hue and cry I do my best to demonstrate the opposite."[3]

In his attempt to demonstrate the adequacy of Confucianism, Li Ao

---

[2] Carsun Chang, The Development of Neo-Confucian Thought (New Haven: College and University Press, 1963), p. 96.
[3] Carsun Chang, op. cit., p. 109.

argued that human nature is originally good, but failure to control and quiet the feelings, or emotions, leads to corruption. The Confucian virtues are required to regulate the feelings. But apparently he did not distinguish clearly between the Confucian virtues and the Buddhist (*ch'an*) way of overcoming desires and cravings, for when he was asked how man can return to the original goodness of his nature, he replied, "As long as there is no deliberating and no thinking, one's emotions are not in action. When emotions are checked one has the right way of thinking. Right thinking means no deliberating and thinking. In the *I-Ching* it is said: 'Where evil thoughts are cleared, truth will be kept.'"[4]

Although Han Yü and Li Ao did not succeed in their attempts to revive Confucianism as a powerful rival of Buddhism, they did pave the way for the first attempt to provide a theoretical basis for Confucianism by Chou Tun-i.

By bringing together and reinterpreting concepts from a variety of philosophies, Chou Tun-i managed to construct a metaphysical basis broad enough for all existence. The notions of *yin* and *yang*, as negative and positive concepts of reality respectively, were familiar to Chou Tun-i. The idea that these two principles were not absolutely first was also familiar to him, for the Taoists had argued that *Tao* was prior to all things, and was the source of being and non-being, or *yang* and *yin*. The difficulty with the Taoist notion, however, was that *Tao* itself was regarded as non-being, and therefore the whole philosophy tended to have a negative character. But if the source of the principles of *yin* and *yang* were positive instead of negative there would be a basis for a philosophical explanation which could emphasize the ultimacy of the particular, while at the same time having a principle for explaining the particular. This is precisely what Chou Tun-i achieved by regarding the Great Ultimate (*T'ai-chi*) as the source of all things. He regarded the Great Ultimate as productive of *yin* and *yang*. In turn, the interactions between *yin* and *yang* produce the Five Elements of Water, Fire, Wood, Metal, and Earth. By further interaction, all of the rest of reality is produced.

Describing the production of *yin* and *yang* from the Great Ultimate, Chou Tun-i says, "The Great Ultimate through movement generates *yang*. When its activity reaches its limit, it becomes tranquil. Through tranquillity the Great Ultimate generates *yin*."[5] His explanation of how

---

[4] *Ibid.*, p. 110.
[5] As translated by Wing-tsit Chan in *A Source Book in Chinese Philosophy* (Princeton: Princeton University Press, 1963), p. 463.

the *yin* and the *yang* are produced from the Great Ultimate leans heavily on the Taoist notion of "reversal as the movement of the *Tao*." According to the Taoists, reality is the manifestation of the reversing of *Tao*, as it goes from one extreme back to the other. Thus, he goes on to say, "When tranquillity reaches its limit, activity begins. So movement and tranquillity alternate and become the root of each other, giving rise to the distinction of *yin* and *yang*, and the two modes are thus established."[6]

Having thus provided a basis for the principles of *yin* and *yang* in the Great Ultimate, Chou Tun-i explains that through the interaction of these two principles and their resulting mutual transformation the powers or principles of particular things came to be produced. He says, "By the transformation of *yang* and its union with *yin*, the Five Agents of Water, Fire, Wood, Metal, and Earth arise."[7] These Five Agents, or Elements, are taken to be the material principles of things. They are not themselves regarded as things, but as *principles* of things. For example, as principle of direction, Wood is east, as principle of the seasons, Wood is spring, as principle of the body, it is liver, and as principle of color, it is blue. Because these Five Agents are not conceived of as things, but as principles, they can be considered to be the common basis of all things.

Given the Great Ultimate and the two principles of *yin* and *yang* along with the principles of the material forces of the universe, it remains to explain how these can act on the unproduced and non-existent and bring it into existence. Chou Tun-i explains this as follows:

> When the reality of the non-ultimate [non-existent] and the essence of *yin*, *yang*, and the Five Agents come into mysterious union, integration ensues. *Ch'ien* (heaven) constitutes the male element, and *K'un* (earth) constitutes the female element. The interaction of these two material forces engenders and transforms the myriad things. The myriad things produce and reproduce, resulting in unending transformation.[8]

The model for production is the symbolic male and the symbolic female, for male and female are readily understood as principles which by their union bring into existence what was previously non-existent. The union between the non-existent and the principles of *yin* and *yang* and the Five Agents is said to be mysterious, for it is not clear how what exists can be related to what does not exist. Yet if some relation were not possible how could the non-existent be brought into existence? The particular things that are brought into existence through this

---

[6] *Ibid.*   [7] *Ibid.*   [8] *Ibid.*

mysterious union possess their own modes for reproduction, and consequently there is the ceaseless productive activity of things.

In this part of his explanation of the Great Ultimate, Chou Tun-i has managed to give a metaphysical picture of the origin of things, tracing them to the Great Ultimate. To complete his explanation he needs to show how man and the practical affairs of man fit into this picture. This he does in the following words:

> It is man alone who receives (the material forces) in their highest excellence, and therefore he is most intelligent. His physical form appears, and his spirit develops consciousness. The five moral principles of his nature (humanity or *jen*, righteousness, propriety, wisdom and faithfulness) are aroused by, and react to, the external world and engage in activity; good and evil are distinguished; and human affairs take place.[9]

The point of this description of man's place in the total order of the universe is that the principle of the sage, or perfect man, is one with the principle of the Great Ultimate, and therefore man, in his perfection, forms a harmony with the universe. The beginnings of sagehood are received from the Great Ultimate, just as are the beginning of everything else that exists. In man these beginnings are the moral principles of his nature, which are listed as humanity (*jen*), righteousness, propriety, wisdom, and faithfulness. To become a sage and be in harmony with the universe man must be true to these moral principles. This is what Chou Tun-i means when he says that *Ch'eng* is the foundation of the sage, for *Ch'eng* (faithfulness, or sincerity) means being true to one's nature.

In this way the moral principles advocated by Confucius come to be put on a metaphysical foundation by Chou Tun-i. The reason man must act in accord with the fundamental moral principles is that these constitute man's fundamental nature as produced by the Great Ultimate.

PHILOSOPHY OF PRINCIPLE

Although it may be said that Neo-Confucianism received its foundation from Chou Tun-i, it was the brothers Ch'eng Hao (1032–1085) and Ch'eng I (1033–1107) who gave Neo-Confucianism its enduring structure. This they accomplished by making principle (*li*) the basis for their philosophy. Building upon the work of Chou Tun-i, who had been their teacher for one year, the Ch'eng brothers replaced the concept of the Great Ultimate—which impressed them as being too abstract and excessively Taoistic—with principle. The main philosophical reason for the

9 *Ibid.*

substitution was to put the perfection of human nature on a secure basis. Chou Tun-i was concerned primarily with a metaphysics of reality, and found in the concept of the Great Ultimate the key to the overarching unity of things. The Great Ultimate was entirely too vague and abstract, however, to provide a foundation for a practical philosophy of morality, which was the chief concern of Ch'eng Hao and Ch'eng I.

The Ch'eng brothers could concentrate almost exclusively upon the philosophy of human action because Chou Tun-i had already provided an explanation for the metaphysical unity of reality and had laid the basis for a complete philosophical explanation of man and reality. Concentrating on explaining how human nature could be perfected so that every person could become a sage, and all persons could live harmoniously together, the Ch'eng brothers realized the need to have a first principle that is operative in every thing, person, and action. It must be more than simply a source from which all proceeds, for otherwise the connection of the particular person and the particular action with the ultimate source of everything would not rest on a secure basis. Consequently, they substituted principle for the Great Ultimate, regarding principle not only as a source of things, but also as the law of being inherent in every being, giving it existence and directing its function. Because they regarded the principle from which all things proceed to be the same as the principles inherent in particular things, the difference being only one of manifestation or embodiment, they conceived of all things as forming a unity with respect to principle. When principle is realized and exhibited in all actions, the perfect harmony will be achieved.

Ch'eng I says, "That which is inherent in things is principle," and:

> Principle in the world is one. Although there are many roads in the world, the destination is the same, and although there are a hundred deliberations, the result is one. Although things involve many manifestations and events go through infinite variation, when they are united by the one, there cannot be any contradiction.[10]

Ch'eng Hao, discussing principle as the unifying factor in reality, says, "The reason why it is said that all things form one body is that all have this principle, simply because they all have come from it."[11] He also says, "There is only one principle in the world."[12]

These remarks by the Ch'eng brothers reveal that they regarded principle both as a source of things and as the directive force within

---

[10] *Ibid.*, p. 571.   [11] *Ibid.*, p. 533.   [12] *Ibid.*, p. 534.

things. That is, although principle was regarded as one, the source of all, it is also regarded as many, for it is inherent in all of the many things that have proceeded from the source. How can principle be both one and many? To answer this question it is necessary to understand both the concept of principle generally, and the specific concept of principle that the Ch'eng brothers used.

From the fact that the Ch'eng brothers considered the production of things to be dependent upon material force (ch'i) and principle, plus the fact that principle was regarded as the determination and manifestation of specific things out of material force, it appears that they considered principle to be the inner working of nature through things. It is obvious that different things are different; apples are not trees and trees are not men. To what is the difference due? The Ch'engs' answer is that it is due to form and function. Apples do not function or behave the way trees or men do. They do not give off the same colors, odors, sounds, flavors, etc. The reason they appear different in color, odor, sound, taste, shape, etc., is because of their different principles. If this is the case it is clear that the general concept of principle is that of *the reason why something is just what it is rather than something else*. Since there are differences between things, and since these differences can be explained, it follows that there are reasons for the differences, and reasons are possible because things are distinguished according to their principles. That is, in the last analysis, the reasons for distinguishing between any two things consist in identifying the principles of those things; the reasons reveal the principles.

The Ch'eng brothers extended this notion of principle to the totality of what exists. Everything that exists—heaven and earth and "the ten thousand things"—exists due to principle. That is, there is a reason for the existence of things. Furthermore, this principle of the universe is not really different from the principle in any particular thing, for the particular thing exists only as a manifestation of the supreme principle. Things are distinguished according to the *embodiment* of principle, not according to principle as such. What makes a particular thing what it is, is the principle embodied and manifested in a certain way in material force.

It would appear, therefore, that principle in the philosophy of the Ch'eng brothers referred to the reason, or law, operating within things which gives the universe its order. The importance, therefore, of making principle the basis of their philosophy is that it provided them with an ordered universe. Thus, the order in society that issues from the ordering and rectification of the individual was held to have a foundation in the very structure of the universe. This concept gave to Neo-Confucianism the metaphysical basis for its social philosophy it had been lacking.

With this general idea in mind of the kind of concept principle is, and the function it served in the philosophy of the Ch'eng brothers, it is possible to turn to the writing of Ch'eng Hao and Ch'eng I for a more detailed analysis of principle, and the application of principle to the practical affairs of man.

Once someone asked Ch'eng I if in investigating things in order to gain understanding that would allow one to become a sage, a person should be concerned with internal things, such as feelings and thoughts, or with external things, such as natural happenings. His reply was "It does not matter. All that is before our eyes is nothing but things, and all things have their principles. For example, from that by which fire is hot or water is cold to the relations between ruler and minister, and father and son, are all principle."[13] This answer makes clear that the principle of a thing is regarded as the source of that thing's essential activity, for the essential activity of fire is to produce heat, and it is said that that from which fire is hot is principle. But it is also clear that it is not the multiplicity of detail that is to be investigated, but only the principles operating through the detailed manifestations of things. Thus, in answer to the question, "If one investigates only one thing, does he understand only one thing or does he understand the various principles?" the answer is, "We must seek to understand all. However, even Yen Tzu [a wise man referred to in the *Analects* of Confucius] could only understand ten points when he heard one. When one finally understands principle, even millions of things can be understood."[14] Obviously, millions of things in their details could not be understood, so the meaning is that millions of things could be understood in terms of their basic principle. For example, when the correct relation between father and son is understood the relations between fathers and sons in millions of particular cases are understood. When once the love a mother has for a newborn child is understood, then the love of millions of mothers for their newborn is understood even without investigating the particular cases. The reason is that one knows the principle involved. This is why Ch'eng I says, "All things under heaven can be understood in the light of their principle. As there are things, there must be specific principles."[15]

[13] *Ibid.*, p. 568.   [14] *Ibid.*, pp. 568–569.   [15] *Ibid.*, p. 563.

On another occasion he said, "A thing is an event. If the principles underlying the event are investigated to the utmost, then all principles will be understood."[16] It would appear, therefore, that the principles of specific things, or specific kinds of things—*qua* principle—are the same, although with respect to their embodiment and manifestation in material force they differ. For example, the principle of a dog is different than the principle of a man. If this were not the case one could not distinguish between the two. But this difference is due to the embodiment of principle in the particularizing material force, and does not proceed from the nature of principle as such. By analogy, in comparing pieces of china one might notice that cups differ from saucers. It might be suggested that this is due to their different principles. But both cup and saucer are the same insofar as they are constituted by the kind of stuff called bone. It must be admitted that the bone embodied in the cup and the saucer is not different in the two cases. Likewise, it could be said that the great principle participating in the ten thousand things is not different in each case, though the embodiment is different.

The questions that arise from this analysis are: (1) What is the nature of the principle that is responsible for the substance and the function of the universe? (2) How is the principle of the universe related to man? and (3) Is man's mind different from this principle, or one with it? The answers to these questions are revealed in the practical philosophy advocated by the Ch'engs.

According to Ch'eng Hao, "The student must first of all understand the nature of *jen*. The man of *jen* forms one body with all things without any differentiation. Rightness, propriety, wisdom, and faithfulness are all (expressions) of *jen*."[17] The reason why the student must first understand *jen* is that *jen* is principle. In other words, the nature of principle in man is *jen*. But since principle is the same in nature as it is in man, the cultivation of *jen* is at the same time the establishing of a unity with all things. As Ch'eng Hao points out, "There is no difference between Nature and man."[18] Thus, to know *jen* is to know principle, and to know principle is to know (in a way) all things and to be in harmony ("form one body") with all things.

Ch'eng I points out that knowing *jen* is not a matter of having information about it, but is a matter of having experienced this principle. He explained this point as follows:

> True knowledge and ordinary knowledge are different. I once saw a farmer who had been wounded by a tiger. When someone said that the tiger was

16 *Ibid.*, p. 552.   17 *Ibid.*, p. 523.   18 *Ibid.*, p. 538.

hurting people, everyone was startled. But in his facial expression the farmer reacted differently from the rest. Even a young boy knows that tigers can hurt people, but his is not true knowledge. It is true knowledge only when it is like the farmer's. Therefore when men know evil and still do it, this also is not true knowledge. If it were, they would surely not do it.[19]

So, when Ch'eng Hao says that the student must first of all understand *jen*, he is really saying that he must first of all cultivate his own humanity, living according to the principle of *jen*. This, of course, is the most important and most difficult of all tasks, for it is the task of becoming a Sage.

Ch'eng I notes that in the school of Confucius there were three thousand pupils, but only one—Yen Tzu—was praised as loving to learn. The reason Yen Tzu was singled out is that he alone concentrated wholeheartedly on learning the way of becoming a Sage. Becoming a Sage is the highest goal, for the Sage represents the perfect person, and in a philosophy where the reality of the person is regarded as the highest reality, the perfection of a person represents perfection of the ultimate reality.

But is it possible for man to learn to become a Sage? Ch'eng I answers this question in the affirmative.

> From the essence of life accumulated in Heaven and Earth, man receives the Five Agents (Water, Fire, Wood, Metal, and Earth) in their highest excellence. His original nature is pure and tranquil. Before it is aroused, the five moral principles of his nature called humanity, righteousness, propriety, wisdom, and faithfulness, are complete. As his physical form appears, it comes into contact with external things and is aroused from within. As it is aroused from within, the seven feelings, called pleasure, anger, sorrow, joy, love, hate, and desire, ensue. As feeling becomes strong and increasingly reckless, his nature becomes damaged.[20]

Having thus postulated the original goodness and purity of man and having attributed the evil in man to a disturbance of this original goodness due to uncontrolled feelings, it is possible to suggest that one can learn to become a Sage by learning to control the feelings and thereby return to the original principle in its purity. Accordingly, Ch'eng I said, "The way to learn is none other than rectifying one's mind and nourishing one's nature. When one abides by the mean and correctness and becomes sincere, he is a Sage."[21]

These statements reveal that for the Ch'eng brothers principle is the inner law of a thing's nature which is received from the inner law of the universe. Man also receives the law of his being from the inner

[19] *Ibid.*, p. 551.   [20] *Ibid.*, p. 548.   [21] *Ibid.*, p. 548.

law of the universe, and therefore is in union with the universe with respect to principle. Since mind refers to the original essence of man, it turns out that mind is identical with principle. Man's nature—his principle—is that of a moral being, and since morality issues from *jen*, it follows that man's nature is *jen*. Since this is the original principle of man's being, to realize his perfection he must be true to this principle (practice *ch'eng*, or sincerity) and cultivate it. For this the virtues of propriety, wisdom, and righteousness are also needed.

CHU HSI

The problem of how *jen* (humanity) can be cultivated and perfected is the central problem for all Neo-Confucianists. The chief obstacle to be overcome in solving this problem is that of the relation between good and evil. Chu Hsi's importance in the Chinese mind (he is considered to be in the same league with Confucius and Mencius) is due primarily to his ability to reinterpret and synthesize the philosophies of earlier Neo-Confucian thinkers in such a way that he was able to construct a complete and systematic philosophy in which he reconciled the presence of evil with the basic goodness of human nature. This he was able to do along the lines suggested by Confucius and Mencius by incorporating the metaphysical philosophies of earlier Neo-Confucian philosophers. This enabled him to achieve a systematic completeness that Confucius and Mencius had lacked, while providing a more detailed practical philosophy than his Neo-Confucian predecessors had managed. In Chu Hsi's philosophy the problem of the relation between good and evil is considered in terms of the relation between man and nature and in terms of the relation between man's basic nature and his feelings.

For both Confucianists and Neo-Confucianists the central concern of philosophy was the cultivation of *jen*, rectification of the basic human relationships, and development of the constant virtues. The five basic relations between persons are those between ruler and subject, between father and son, between husband and wife, between elder and younger children, and between friends. The constant virtues are righteousness, propriety, sincerity, and wisdom. The three activities of philosophy, cultivation, rectification, and development, are all the same essentially, for when the relations are rectified and the virtues developed, *jen* will be cultivated. And when *jen* is cultivated, the virtues will be developed and the relations will be rectified. And when these three are accomplished, evil will have been removed and peace and goodness will reign supreme in the world.

The difficulty encountered in advocating and supporting this philosophy stemmed from the problems encountered in trying to explain the sources of good and evil and the relations between them. The difficulty was felt already prior to Mencius, who attempted to resolve the problem by claiming that man's nature is essentially good, but is corrupted by society and culture. Hsun Tzu, on the other hand, tried to resolve the problem by arguing that man's nature is essentially evil, but through education and culture this evil can be rooted out and replaced with goodness. Neither of these theories proved satisfactory, however, for if man's nature is essentially good, as Mencius would have it, then how can society and culture, which proceed from man, be evil and corrupting? On the other hand, if man's nature is essentially evil, as Hsun Tzu would have it, how can what proceeds from man's nature— in the form of culture and education—be good, and opposed to man's evil nature?

During the centuries following the Mencius–Hsun Tzu controversy it was generally agreed by Confucianists that man is basically good, but no satisfactory theoretical support for this position was worked out. Han Yu, a pioneering figure in the Neo-Confucian movement, suggested that man's nature was of three kinds, good, bad, and good and bad mixed. But there was no satisfactory explanation of how human nature could be all three simultaneously. Consequently, the need for a philosophical theory of the nature of good and evil continued to be keenly felt by the Neo-Confucianists, for without it their emphasis on the removal of evil by the cultivation of *jen* would be unsupported.

Chang Tsai made a significant step forward when he distinguished between the essential nature of man and the physical nature. But since he failed to establish a satisfactory relationship between the two his theory was deficient. The Ch'eng brothers also made an important contribution to the problem with their theory that principle and human nature were identical. But it was left for Chu Hsi to show how the basic nature of man was identical with the supreme principle of the universe, and therefore of the nature of pure goodness, while the secondary nature of man, created by the association of principle with material stuff (*ch'i*) was impure and the source of evil. According to this explanation the source of goodness was man's basic nature. But man is also a concrete being with body, and feelings, as well as mind; man's embodied nature gives rise to evil, for from the feelings come those passions that obscure the original goodness, that deviate from *jen*, the supreme principle of man.

Distinguishing between principle in itself and principle as embodied in concrete things, Chu Hsi says: "What exists before physical form is the one principle harmonious and undifferentiated, and is invariably good. What exists after physical form, however, is confused and mixed, and good and evil are thereby differentiated."[22] This statement is the key to Chu Hsi's solution to the problem of how the presence of evil can be reconciled with the goodness that is man's basic nature. The distinction he makes is between the goodness of principle and the evil-producing material stuff of which particular things are composed. In man, as in all things, principle combines with material stuff, and therefore goodness is mixed with evil. But man's fundamental, basic nature is identical with principle, which is of the nature of *jen*; the material stuff constitutes a secondary nature. Since *jen* is the basic nature of man and this is good, the removal of evil depends upon the cultivation and development of *jen*, or the basic nature, over the secondary nature.

This distinction between basic and secondary natures on the basis of the distinction between principle and material stuff requires a general theory of the nature and source of things as an explanatory context. According to Chu Hsi, all things are the result of a combination of material stuff (*ch'i*) and principle (*li*). He says, "Man and things are all endowed with the principle of the universe as their nature, and receive the material force of the universe as their physical form..."[23] That there is principle is obvious from the fact that things are what they are rather than something else. That man is different from dog is due to different principles. However, differences in principles are not merely differences in principles, but also involve differences in matter. Nothing whatsoever is found that does not involve both principle and material stuff, and the manifestation of principle is regulated by the material stuff while at the same time principle determines the material stuff. When Chu Hsi was asked for evidence that there is principle in material force he replied, "For example, there is order in the complicated interfusion of the *yin* and the *yang* and of the Five Agents. Principle is there. If material force does not consolidate and integrate, principle would have nothing to attach itself to."[24]

In explanation of what principle and material stuff are and how they are related Chu Hsi said:

---

[22] *Ibid.*, p. 597.   [23] *Ibid.*, p. 620.   [24] *Ibid.*, p. 635.

> Throughout the universe there are both principle and material force. Principle refers to the Way, which exists before physical form [and is without it] and is the course from which all things are produced. Material force refers to material objects, which exist after physical form [and is with it]; it is the instrument by which things are produced. Therefore in the production of man and things, they must be endowed with principle before they have their nature, and they must be endowed with material force before they have physical form.[25]

It would appear from this explanation that principle is prior to material stuff in two senses, for principle is the essential reason for the being of something, and principle is also the knowable characteristic of a thing. Thus principle is first in the order of being and in the order of knowledge. But despite this priority, it remains the case that nothing exists except through the combination of principle and material stuff.

Still, the things that exist have a source from which they receive their natures, and for Chu Hsi's explanation to be complete he must relate principle and material stuff—as the determinants of things—to their source. This he accomplishes by integrating Chou Tun-i's concept of the Great Ultimate into his system. His view is "The Great Ultimate is nothing other than principle."[26] In other words, principle is the ultimate source of all things. As such it gives a unity—a unity of principle—to the manifoldness of reality and serves to integrate all of reality into a harmonious whole. In Chu Hsi the Great Ultimate is regarded as "the principle of heaven and earth and the myriad things."

> With respect to the myriad things, there is the Great Ultimate in each and every one of them. Before heaven and earth existed, there was assuredly this principle. It is the principle that "through movement generates the *yang.*" It is also this principle that "through tranquillity generates the *yin*"[27]

And, of course, through the activity of *yin* and *yang* the Five Agents came about and by their power produced the ten thousand things that make up the concrete reality surrounding us. Thus, Chu Hsi has provided for a systematic explanation of the origination and nature of things through his discovery of principle and material stuff and the relation between them.

Applying this explanation to the problem of evil in human nature Chu Hsi said, "The Great Ultimate is simply the principle of the highest good. Each and every person has in him the Great Ultimate and each and every thing has in it the Great Ultimate."[28] The importance of this

[25] *Ibid.*, p. 636.   [26] *Ibid.*, p. 638.   [27] *Ibid.*, p. 638.   [28] *Ibid.*, p. 640.

view is connected with the priority of principle over material stuff. If principle is more fundamental than material stuff, and if there is the Great Ultimate in man as the principle of his mind, then this will be prior to the material stuff. On the strength of this it can be claimed that the basic nature of man is principle, though the secondary nature is the embodiment of principle in material stuff. Because man possesses the Great Ultimate it follows that *jen* is the basic nature of man. Chu Hsi shows this by pointing to the two essential relationships involved. First, after identifying mind with the basic nature of man, he says, "The principle of the mind is the Great Ultimate."[29] Secondly, he says, "*Jen* is man's mind."[30] These two statements together mean that the Great Ultimate is identical to *jen*. Chu Hsi supports this view in his treatise on *jen*:

> In the production of man and things, they receive the mind of Heaven and Earth as their mind. Therefore, with reference to the character of the mind, although it embraces and penetrates all and leaves nothing to be desired, nevertheless, one word will cover all of it, namely, *jen* (humanity).[31]

Granted that *jen* is man's basic nature—"the principle originally inherent in man's mind"[32]—the question of greatest importance is how to realize *jen*. According to Chu Hsi's philosophy, there are two equally important practices essential to the realization of *jen*. On the one hand, since *jen* is already there as the basic nature of man, one must concentrate on preserving one's true nature. On the other hand, the nature of man is learned and realized through its function: understanding of the function of anything depends upon empirical investigation to discover the nature of principle.

> The mind embraces all principles and all principles are complete in this single entity, the mind. If one is not able to preserve the mind, he will be unable to investigate principle to the utmost. If he is unable to investigate principle to the utmost, he will be unable to exert his mind to the utmost."[33]

The twin doctrines of preservation (of goodness) and investigation (of principle) rest upon the distinction between substance and function. Substance refers to what something is, and function refers to how something operates. The distinction itself goes back as far as Lao Tzu, who distinguished between *Tao* (the substance) and *te* (the function of *Tao*), but in Chu Hsi the distinction is applied to principle. Thus man's basic nature, or principle—the character of his mind—as substance is *jen*.

[29] *Ibid.*, p. 628.   [30] *Ibid.*, p. 594.   [31] *Ibid.*, pp. 593–594.   [32] *Ibid.*, p. 633.
[33] *Ibid.*, p. 606.

But the function of man's mind is love. In other words, the function of humanity is love. Love, as the function of *jen*, comprises the other virtues and is the basis for the proper human relations. Chu Hsi puts the matter as follows:

> The moral qualities of the mind of Heaven and Earth are four: origination, flourish, advantages, and firmness. . . . Therefore in the mind of man there are also four moral qualities—namely *jen*, righteousness, propriety, and wisdom—and *jen* embraces them all. In their emanation and function, they constitute the feeling of love, respect, being right, and discrimination between being right and wrong—and the feeling of commiseration pervades them all.[34]

The nature of something provides for its function, and its function expresses its nature. Therefore *jen* provides for the function of man, namely, acting in accord with the moral qualities, and functioning in accord with the moral qualities is the expression of *jen*.

> If we can truly practice love and preserve it, then we have in it the spring of all virtues and the root of all good deed. This is why in the teachings of the Confucian school, the student is always urged to exert anxious and unceasing effort in the pursuit of *jen*.[35]

This, then, is the foundation Chu Hsi provides for the practical philosophy of Neo-Confucianism which can be summed up in his own words as follows: "To be sincere, empty of self, courteous and calm is the foundation of the practice of love . . . To love others as we love ourselves, is to perfect love."[36]

WANG YANG-MING

The distinction between principle and material force enabled Chu Hsi to recognize both the reality of the mind and the reality of things external to the mind. In philosophical terminology, he was rationalistic to the extent he emphasized principle, but empiricistic to the extent he emphasized the investigation of things. He was idealistic to the extent that he emphasized that the Great Ultimate is both the basic nature of all things and the essence of mind, but he also insisted that without material force to embody principle there could be nothing.

After Chu Hsi, however, developments in the school of Principle through the work of Lu Hsiang-shan and his pupils led to the identification of principle with mind in the philosophy of Wang Yang-ming.

---

[34] *Ibid.*, p. 594.   [35] *Ibid.*, p. 594.
[36] As quoted by Clarence Burton Day in *The Philosophers of China* (New York: The Citadel Press, 1962) p. 209.

According to him "there are neither principles nor things outside the mind."[37] A philosophy built upon such a principle is quite sharply opposed to Chu Hsi's, for only when a distinction is made between what belongs to mind and what is outside of mind can the investigation of the things be emphasized as the key to the cultivation of *jen*, and investigation of things is one of the two pillars upon which Chu Hsi's philosophy rests. The other pillar—preservation of the original mind—was perfectly acceptable to Wang Yang-ming, but it was not emphasized by Chu Hsi's followers.

Among the reasons for the ascendancy of Wang Yang-ming's idealism during the Ming dynasty (1368–1644), two stand out. First, from 1313 on, Chu Hsi's interpretation of the Confucian classics enjoyed the status of being the official state philosophy in China. In addition to discouraging other philosophies, this meant that the civil service examinations were based on his interpretations.

As so often happens, the security attending such entrenchment led to the decline of Chu Hsi's philosophy. Without the need to establish itself against other strong systems of thought there came to be increasing attempts to consolidate and refine translations and definitions, and there was too little attention given to reexamination and rethinking of basic principles and arguments. Such a lack is, of course, fatal to a philosophy, for philosophy cannot be done once for all time. It it is rather like loving someone. Just because someone in the past established a happy relationship based on love does not mean that love has been established in the world. Love is something that must be experienced by every individual in every generation. When it is not it is lost. In a similar way, a philosophy is a kind of overview fitting together the various aspects and activities of life and providing a secure ground for the meaning and value of the activities of life. And this is something that each person in each generation must do for himself. If it is not done the person is shallow and life is hollow. Now, since Chu Hsi's interpretation of Confucianism had, as Wing-Tsit Chan points out, "degenerated into trifling with what Wang [Yang-ming] called 'fragmentary and isolated details and broken pieces'"[38] it did not provide an adequate basis for assisting the people in forming a satisfactory philosophy of life. Consequently, there was a ready reception for a fresh and vigorous philosophy such as Wang Yang-ming proposed.

Secondly, following Chu Hsi's emphasis upon investigation of things,

---

[37] See *Source Book in Chinese Philosophy*, p. 673.   [38] *Ibid.*, p. 654.

but slighting his emphasis on preserving the original mind of man, his followers got further and further away from the moral emphases that were the distinguishing characteristic of Confucian thought. When Wang Yang-ming turned his attention almost exclusively to moral matters it was greeted as a welcome return to the central concern of philosophy.

Wang Yang-ming's philosophy is characterized by its preoccupation with moral values. It rests upon the principles of the all-inclusive character of the mind and the unity of knowledge and action. These two principles give rise to the doctrine of the extension of the innate knowledge of the good (*chih liang-chih*). These features of his philosophy are all reflected in the following statement: "The learning of the great man consists entirely in getting rid of the obscuration of selfish desires in order by his own efforts to make manifest his clear character, so as to restore the condition of forming one body with Heaven, Earth, and the myriad things, a condition that is originally so, that is all. It is not that outside of the original substance something can be added."[39]

There is here no appeal to the investigation of things as an essential part of learning or cultivating *jen*. Knowledge is not distinguished from action, for true knowledge is action that proceeds from the love that constitutes the humanity of man. In Wang Yang-ming's words, "Knowledge is the beginning of action and action is the completion of knowledge. Learning to be a sage involves only one effort. Knowledge and action should not be separated."[40] The basis for the unification of knowledge and action is Wang Yang-ming's emphasis on will or choice rather than reason or knowledge. Intellectual or discursive knowledge of the kind characteristic of the sciences can, of course, be separated from choice and morality. But practical knowledge of the value of things has no significance apart from the activity of choosing and acting. When what a person does is regarded as more fundamental than what he knows or says, then the kind of knowledge required for making choices becomes more important than theoretical knowledge. Furthermore, a person's choices are revealed in the action taken and this shows the combination of knowledge and action. This is why Wang Yang-ming can claim that the learning of the great man consists in getting rid of selfishness and in manifesting his good character. The general point involved here is that action is more basic than knowledge and all knowledge is for the sake of action. In the language of classical philosophy, this means that Will is higher than Reason.

[39] *Ibid.*, p. 660.   [40] *Ibid.*, p. 674.

Wang Yang-ming's philosophy is most clearly revealed in his inter-pretation of the *Great Learning (Ta Hsueh)*, a classical Confucian text that served as an inspiration to many of the Neo-Confucian philosophers. The text of the *Great Learning* consists in a statement and explanation of "three major chords" and "eight minor wires." The three major chords are (1) manifestation of the clear character, (2) loving the people, and (3) abiding in the highest good. Asked about manifesting the clear character, Wang Yang-ming replied, "The great man regards Heaven and Earth and the myriad things as one body. He regards the world as one family and the country as one person. As to those who make a cleavage between objects and distinguish between the self and others, they are small men."[41] The thinking behind this claim is that all things really form integral parts of one whole, just as the children and the mother and the father really are one family. In the family it is the bond of familial love that proceeds from human-ness of the individual person that creates the unity of one family. In the world it is the bond of great love proceeding from the *jen* of the universe that creates a unity. In the great man the *jen* of the universe is identified with the *jen* of the individual and there is a unity of all things ("forming one body").

When he was asked why the learning of the great man consists in loving the people, Wang Yang-ming replied, "Manifesting the clear character consists in loving the people, and loving the people is the way to manifest the clear character. Therefore, only when I love my father, the fathers of others, and the fathers of all men can my humanity really form one body with my father, the fathers of others, and the fathers of all men."[42] The explanation behind this is that by "clear character" is meant the original purity and goodness of man's basic nature or mind. According to Wang Yang-ming, this original goodness consists in love —a pervasive and universal love which both forms and proceeds from the basic principles of all things. When things are in accord with this love they are perfected. When man is in accord with this love he too is perfected. This can be seen in the fact that when the clear character of love is manifested the constant virtues are perfected and the human relations are rectified. Thus, Wang Yang-ming goes on to say that when his humanity forms one body with the fathers of all men, then the clear character of filial piety will be manifested. And when his humanity forms one body with the brothers of all men, then the clear character of brotherly love will be manifested. And in sum,

[41] *Ibid.*, p. 659.   [42] *Ibid.*, p. 660.

> Everything from ruler, minister, husband, wife, and friends to mountains, rivers, spiritual beings, birds, animals, and plants should be truly loved in order to realize my humanity that forms one body with them, and then my clear character will be completely manifested, and I will really form one body with Heaven, Earth and the myriad things.

When he was asked why the learning of the great man consists in abiding in the highest good, Wang Yang-ming replied,

> The highest good is the ultimate principle of manifesting character and loving people. The nature endowed in us by Heaven is pure and perfect. The fact that it is intelligent, clear, and not beclouded is evidence of the emanation and revelation of the highest good. It is the original substance of the clear character which is called innate knowledge of the good.[43]

All things are present in *jen*, which is the basis of man's nature. Therefore to realize his perfection man must cultivate this basic nature. But nothing external is required for this task, since this nature is pure and perfect of itself. To know the good is to do the good, and knowledge of the good is already contained in man's basic nature as *jen*. Therefore, what is required is the extension of this innate knowledge of the good into all spheres of action. As Wang Yang-ming puts it, "This is what is meant by 'manifesting the clear character throughout the empire.' This is what is meant by 'regulation of the family,' 'ordering the state,' and 'bringing peace to the world.' This is what is meant by 'full development of one's nature.'"[44]

After Wang Yang-ming, Neo-Confucianism underwent a movement away from the emphasis on principle that characterized the philosophy of the Ch'engs and Chu Hsi, and away from the introspective idealism of Wang Yang-ming. The emphasis in this new movement was on things and feelings.

TAI CHEN

Neo-Confucian philosophy through Wang Yang-ming had emphasized the principles of things over their material constitution and elevated the "fundamental mind" over the feelings. In the seventeenth and eighteenth centuries there was a reaction against this rationalism and idealism, and the empirical came to be emphasized more and more, both in the studies of man and in the studies of things. An objective study of things characterized by detailed and analytical investigations

---

[43] *Ibid.*, p. 661.   [44] *Ibid.*, p. 661.

of things came to be regarded as the path to truth, and the feelings of persons exhibited in day-to-day living came to be regarded as the real source of man's actions. According to Tai Chen, generally accepted as the greatest of the empiricistic Neo-Confucian philosophers, "A thing is an affair or event. When we talk about an event, we do not go beyond daily affairs such as drinking and eating. To neglect these and talk about principle is not what the ancient sages and worthies meant by principle."[45]

This remark clearly indicates the empiricist's impatience with metaphysical speculation and idealistic introspection. Tai Chen was concerned with the principles that could be discovered empirically in things, feelings, and actions; abstractions were useless. It is not the case that Tai Chen rejected the concepts and principles of earlier philosophers of the Sung period, but rather that he reinterpreted them in such a way that the concrete and particular were not overlooked. This, of course, gave a balance to Neo-Confucianism, bringing the metaphysics down to an empirically verifiable level. This was, by the same token, a paving of the way for the empirical sciences of physics and psychology which were to come later. In fact, much of Tai Chen's work is often regarded as scientific rather than philosophical because of his minute investigation of particular things.

The emphasis during this later period of Neo-Confucianism continued to be on the nature of man, however, and the nature of man continued to be regarded as a source of morality. Consequently, the primary objects of investigation continued to be the actions of human beings, and the categories used in this investigation were primarily moral. This means that instead of classifying and investigating the relations between the components of external things, human actions and relations between persons were classified and investigated. When external things are investigated it is important, for example, to know what neutrons, protons, and electrons are, and how they are related to each other. But when the moral nature of man is being investigated the virtues of humanity, righteousness, sincerity, propriety, and wisdom must be known, and the relations between these virtues in terms of the principal relations between persons must be investigated.

Throughout the earlier Confucian tradition it was man as moral agent and society as moral institution that were regarded as the primary objects to be known. In the Neo-Confucian tradition there was an

45 *Ibid.*, p. 713.

attempt to provide metaphysical support for this view that held morality to be the subject of ultimate concern. To Tai Chen it appeared that some of the Neo-Confucianists had allowed the metaphysics of morality to become the subject of primary importance. This he was concerned to rectify, for clearly the moral relations between persons and the moral virtues are of primary concern, and the metaphysics of morality is secondary, being merely for the sake of a theoretical defense of morality.

CHAPTER 20

MAO TSE-TUNG

Even as the emphasis on investigating particular things that characterized Tai Chen's empiricistic philosophy began to become influential, there were signs of a revived interest in metaphysics and in the rationalism of the Ch'eng brothers and Chu Hsi. The movement back to a philosophy of principle was slow in developing, however, and as a result of the political and social upheaval in China during the nineteenth and twentieth centuries, never matured beyond infancy. After the British defeated China in the Opium war of 1840–42 the people found themselves not only poor, hungry, and oppressed, but forced to admit tremendous loss of face. It was now exceedingly difficult to maintain the two-thousand-year-old tradition of the world's superior and only civilized people. Of course, a people finding themselves in such circumstances are not likely to pay nearly as much attention to working out satisfactory philosophical explanations as they are to trying to remedy things at hand. It appeared that the political situation was beginning to improve with the establishment of the Chinese Republic in 1912. Within a decade, however, it became clear that this government was not the answer to China's problems. Before a new solution could be tried Imperial Japan controlled the country. Since the removal of Japan, China has been preoccupied with internal revolution, and only since the establishment of the People's Republic of China under the dominance of the Communist Party has there been any climate at all conducive to philosophy. And since the Central government has encouraged only

Marxist-Leninist philosophy, Mao Tse-tung is regarded as the most important philosopher in China today.

In the troubled years between Tai Chen and Mao Tse-tung are found the beginnings of a number of attempts to turn philosophy from the empiricistic preoccupation with concrete things to a consideration of the underlying principles of things. K'ang Yu-wei (1858–1927), who in 1914 attempted to get Confucianism adopted as the state religion in the new Republic, emphasized love as the basis of humanity. He held that the love which makes human beings human is also, in its cosmic aspect, what makes anything what it is. He advocated a return to the reforms of humanity that he considered Confucius to have initiated in order that a higher order of society might evolve. Chang Tung-sun (1886–1926) combined his understanding of the traditional Chinese philosophies with his understanding of classical Western philosophies—especially Kant and Dewey—in advocating a philosophy based on a critical pragmatic theory of knowledge which views philosophical concepts as historical social creations. Fung Yu-lan (1895–) has been greatly influenced by Taoism and Neo-Confucianism, and under the influence of Western rationalism reconstructed the various Taoist and Neo-Confucian ideas into a systematic rational philosophy. Hsiung Shih-li (1885–1968) revived Wang Yang-ming's idealistic philosophy, putting it on the basis of his reinterpretation of the Buddhist Consciousness-only philosophy, thereby providing a basis for both the unity and plurality of the world.

These philosophers, along with others less well known, have written extensively, and their philosophies are more carefully worked out in terms of analysis and arguments than the classical Chinese philosophies. In terms of their content these philosophies are deserving of careful and detailed study. But they have not had much influence on the people, being confined mostly to the circles of professional philosophy. They never came to direct and regulate the lives of the people the way Taoism, Confucianism, Buddhism, Neo-Confucianism, and Maoism did.

Mao Tse-tung's philosophy is influenced greatly by Marx and Lenin, but is not basically out of tune with the principles and attitudes of traditional Chinese philosophies. Probably his most important philosophical work is the lecture delivered in 1937 entitled "On Practice." In this lecture he explained the relation between theory and practice, showing how theory originates in practice and returns to practice for its justification and fulfillment. This approach to the relation between theory and practice grew out of Mao's practice in reconciling the differences among the people as leader of the revolutionary forces. It is not a theory worked out for its own sake, but for the practical purpose of establishing the Great Harmony—the age-old Chinese utopia.

To see the practical aims presupposed by Mao's theory of the relation between practice and theory it is helpful to consider the address commemorating the twenty-eighth anniversary of the Communist Party of China. In that address Mao outlined the aims of Communist practices in China as follows: "When classes disappear, all instruments of class struggle—parties and the state machinery—will lose their function, cease to be necessary, therefore will gradually wither away and end their historical mission; and humanity will move to a higher stage."[1] The concluding phrase—"human society will move to a higher stage"— reveals Mao's concern for the human condition. Of course, improving the human condition has always been the foremost consideration among Chinese philosophers. It was the hope of the Confucians and Neo-Confucians that when *jen* was made to prevail the Great Harmony would be achieved. That Mao sees the aim of Communist practice to be the achievement of the Great Harmony is clear from his remark that the Party's function is that of ". . . working hard to create the conditions in which classes, state power, and political parties will die out very naturally and mankind will enter the realm of the Great Harmony."[2]

To accomplish the task of achieving the Great Harmony, Mao considers it necessary to understand the conditions which regulate the growth and development of man and the world generally, so that the natural processes of growth and development can be assisted in arriving at their final goal. Probably the most important principle to be understood in this connection is that "all processes have a beginning and an end; all processes transform themselves into their opposites. The stability of all processes is relative, but the mutuality manifested in the transformation of one process into another is absolute."[3] No doubt, this principle is the central feature of the dialectic of Marxism, but it also restates the Taoist principle that "reversal is the way of Tao," and that "all things have their opposites." It is a restatement of the Neo-Confucian explanation of the source and structure of all things that has its initial expression in Chou Tun-i's concept of the Great Ultimate, which generates all things through the interaction of the opposites *yin* and *yang*. Mao is quite aware that he is here well within the mainstream of traditional Chinese thought, for he remarks in the same paragraph, "We

[1] *Mao Tse-tung: An Anthology of His Writings*, edited with an introduction by Ann Freemantle (New York: The New American Library, 1962) p. 184.
[2] *Ibid.*, p. 185.   [3] *Ibid.*, p. 237.

Chinese often say, 'Things opposed to each other complement each other.'"[4]

According to the dialectical relation between knowing and doing that Mao presents in his lecture "On Practice," knowing begins with practice, moves to the stage of theory, and is completed in doing. Theory represents the half-way house of knowing. Taking seriously the principle that the great dialectic of nature is "reversal of opposites," and holding that the dialectic of any particular thing is also according to this principle, Mao is concerned with the opposites of theory and practice. His concern, of course, is with the successful democratic socialization of the People's Republic. This process, like any other process, proceeds according to its inner dialectic, and for the sake of successful practice Mao is concerned to understand the dialectical relation between practice and theory, for these are the two primary opposites in the Communist program.

This problem—the relation between knowing and doing—has nearly always been of central concern to Chinese philosophers. Mao's solution to the problem is in agreement with traditional solutions, for he holds that knowing and doing form a unity. His theory of knowledge maintains that "human knowledge cannot be separated the least bit from practice, and repudiates all incorrect theories which deny the importance of practice or separate knowledge from practice. . . ."[5] Verification of knowledge is had only when the anticipated results are achieved in the process of social practice. The principle is that "if man wants to achieve success in his work, that is, to achieve the anticipated results, he must make his thoughts correspond to the laws of the objective world surrounding him; if they do not correspond, he will fail in practice."[6]

In attempting to show the plausibility of the claim that social practice is the only criterion of truth, Mao argues that all knowledge has its beginnings in practice, in the activity of changing the world. "If you want to know the taste of a pear you must change the pear by eating it yourself."[7] This is the first stage in acquiring knowledge, the stage of perception. The next step consists in "making a rearrangement or a reconstruction; this belongs to the stage of conception, judgment, and inference."[8] Conception, judgment, and inference constitute rational, as opposed to merely perceptual knowledge, and as such provide for theories about the things perceived. But the acquisition of knowledge does not stop here. Just as perceptual knowledge leads to rational knowledge and is incomplete without it, so rational knowledge

[4] *Ibid.*, p. 238.   [5] *Ibid.*, p. 203.   [6] *Ibid.*, pp. 201, 202.   [7] *Ibid.*, p. 205.
[8] *Ibid.*, p. 207.

remains incomplete until it is applied in practice. As Mao points out, "What Marxist philosophy regards as the most important problem does not lie in understanding the laws of the objective world, thereby becoming capable of explaining it, but in actively changing the world by applying the knowledge of its objective laws."[9]

Knowledge is nothing but meaningless words and empty ideas until it gets embodied in experience. Only in the changing of the person and the changing of the reality encountered in practical activity does knowledge become real. From practice comes theory, and from theory practice proceeds. But theory and practice are not two different things. They are simply the dialectical opposites of one process—living in the world. The advance of knowledge is dialectically coupled to the advance of practice. The development of democratic socialism in China can ignore neither theory nor practice, but must combine them if the cause is to advance. Mao urges that ". . . the development of things should be regarded as their internal and necessary self-movement, that a thing in its movement and the things around it should be regarded as interconnected and interacting upon each other. The basic cause of development of things does not lie outside but inside them, in their internal contradictions."[10]

This is remarkably similar to the Neo-Confucian theory that through the interaction of the opposed principles of *li* and *ch'i* individual things develop and grow, and the universe as a whole is a cosmic dynamic structure of *li* and *ch'i*. The universe as a whole—as the Great Ultimate—functions through the opposites of *yin* and *yang*. The universe is a unity of all things and man participates in this unity. This unity is regarded as dynamic rather than static, being of the nature of process. The process is constituted by the relative processes of particular things. This metaphysical conception of the universe is described by Mao as follows: ". . . In the absolute, total process of the development of the universe, the development of each concrete process is relative; hence in the great stream of absolute truth, man's knowledge of the concrete process at any given stage of development is only relatively true. The sum total of innumerable relative truths is the absolute truth."[11]

It would appear, therefore, that in his metaphysics and epistemology Mao carries forward the traditional attitude which sees a unity in particular things and which sees knowledge as inseparable from practice. Consequently, his philosophy also places the traditional emphasis on the unification of humanity through improved practical living.

9 *Ibid.*, p. 209.   10 *Ibid.*, p. 216.   11 *Ibid.*, p. 212.

Suggestions for Further Reading

Glossary of Oriental Words

Index

Suggestions for Further Reading

The following books have been chosen as being among those most likely to be of assistance to readers wishing to continue their exploration of Oriental philosophies. The brief description of each item is intended to furnish clues to the kind of subject matter and treatment found in the book. Many of the books listed contain quite excellent bibliographies, and the reader is encouraged to use these to supplement the list of titles provided here.

I. SOURCE MATERIAL

There are two excellent collections of primary philosophical texts from the Indian and Chinese traditions. *A Source Book in Chinese Philosophy*, translated and compiled by Wing-tsit Chan (Princeton: Princeton University Press, Princeton paperback edition, 1969), contains nearly eight hundred pages of the most important Chinese philosophical texts arranged in a chronological order. The readability of the translations, the choice of materials and the explanations of difficult passages provided by Professor Chan combine to make this an exceedingly useful aid for the study of Chinese philosophy. *A Source Book in Indian Philosophy*, compiled and edited by Charles A. Moore and Sarvepalli Radhakrishnan (Princeton: Princeton University Press, Princeton paperback edition, 1967), contains standard older translations of selections from the major philosophical texts of India. Hinduism, Buddhism, Cārvāka and Jainism are all represented in this anthology which contains the *Bhagavad Gītā* and *Dhammapada* in their entirety. The introductions to each section are very useful.

Buddhism, as it developed in different Asian countries, is well represented in its religious and practical aspects as well as its theoretical aspects by the basic texts collected in *Buddhist Texts Through the Ages*, edited by Edward Conze, I. B. Horner, David Snellgrove, and Arthur Waley (New York: Harper and Row, Torchbook edition, 1964). Japanese Buddhism is well represented in *Sources of Japanese Tradition*, compiled and edited by Wm. Theodore de Bary (New York: Columbia University Press, 1958). This anthology also contains source material from the non-Buddhist sources of Japanese culture. The other two anthologies edited and compiled by Wm. Theodore de Bary, *Sources of Indian Tradition* (New York: Columbia University Press, 1958) and *Sources of Chinese Tradition* (New York: Columbia University Press, 1960), are not as good on the strictly philosophical texts as the source books by Chan and by Radhakrishnan and Moore, but have the advantage of containing excellent selections from the literary traditions of these cultures.

Three Ways of Thought in Ancient China, by Arthur Waley (Garden City, N.Y: Doubleday & Company, Anchor edition, n.d.), contains excerpts from Mencius, Chuang Tzu and Han Fei Tzu arranged and introduced by Waley so that the reader feels himself taking part in a discussion. Although it also contains some of his political and military thought, *Mao Tse-tung: An Anthology of his Writings*, edited, with an Introduction, by Ann Freemantle (New York: The New American Library, Mentor edition, n.d.), contains Mao's most important philosophical thinking. The classic Vedāntic text, *Vedārthasaṁgraha* by Śri Rāmānujācārya, English translation by S. S. Raghavachar (Mysore: Sri Ramakrishna Ashrama, 1956) presents an excellent introduction to the problem of the relations between selves, things and the ultimate reality based on Rāmānuja's interpretation of the major Upaniṣads. (This little book is available through Ramakrishna or Vedānta centers in the U.S.A. and Canada.)

II. SECONDARY MATERIAL

An Introduction to Indian Philosophy by S. C. Chatterjee and D. M. Datta (Calcutta: Calcutta University Press, 1960) is an extremely well organized and lucid introduction to the philosophies of India which focuses on the central aspects and problems of the various systems. The reader who is interested in the historical development and continuity of Indian thought might well turn to *Outlines of Indian Philosophy* by M. Hiriyana (London: George Allen & Unwin, 1964). This book combines the historical approach with a sharp focus on philosophical concepts and arguments, but avoids becoming overly technical. For the reader who wishes to go beyond these two books there is the excellent detailed scholarly two-volume work by S. Radhakrishnan, *Indian Philosophy* (London: George Allen & Unwin, 1962). Karl Potter's recent book,

Presuppositions of India's Philosophies (Englewood: Prentice Hall, 1963), is helpful in showing how certain basic concepts determine the structure of the various philosophical systems. For the reader interested in getting a feel for Hinduism as a living philosophy, guiding and directing the lives of the majority of India's peoples, there is Radhakrishnan's *The Hindu View of Life* (New York: Macmillan, 1964).

One of the most helpful books available for understanding Buddhism as a complete way of life is *What the Buddha Taught*, by Walpola Rahula (New York: Grove Press, Evergreen edition, 1962). This is a simple but masterly introduction to the basic features of Buddhism by a practicing Buddhist Monk who is an excellent scholar. The emphasis is on Buddhism as a way of life rather than either a philosophy or a religion. A more technical account of the main features of Buddhism is found in *The Essentials of Buddhist Philosophy*, Junjiro Takakusu (Honolulu: University of Hawaii, 1947). *Buddhist Thought in India* by Edward Conze (Ann Arbor: The University of Michigan Press, paperback edition, 1967) is an excellent study in the basic concepts of Buddhism as they developed historically. *The Central Philosophy of Buddhism* by T. R. V. Murti (London: George Allen & Unwin, 1955) and *Nāgārjuna's Philosophy*, Venkata Ramanan (Rutland, Vermont: Charles E. Tuttle Company, 1966) focus on the Mādhyamika philosophy, and from the point of view of this central school of Buddhism give excellent accounts of Buddhist philosophy. Both are scholarly works, containing much critical analysis of concepts and arguments while remaining sympathetic to the Mādhyamika philosophy. Zen, which represents the practical rather than the theoretical aspects of Buddhism, is presented in an extremely fascinating and illuminating manner by Philip Kapleau in *The Three Pillars of Zen* (New York: Harper and Row, 1967). Instructions for practice and autobiographical statements describing the achievements of Zen adepts accompany the explanations of principles underlying this form of Buddhism, providing for a many-faceted look at Zen. *Zen Buddhism: Selected Writings of D. T. Suzuki*, edited by William Barret (Garden City, N.Y.: Doubleday & Company, Anchor edition, 1956), contains selections from four of Suzuki's earlier works on Zen. The essays in this volume, by the Japanese Buddhist who gained a reputation as the foremost interpreter of Zen to English-reading peoples, aim at tracing the development of Zen Buddhism and explores the practical meanings of the central concepts of Zen. Comparisons with the West are usually based on deep insight and are extremely illuminating.

H. G. Creel's *Chinese Thought from Confucius to Mao Tse-tung* (New York: New American Library, Mentor edition, n.d.) is an extremely lucid account of the main trends in Chinese philosophy. This is a history of the outlines of the historical development of Chinese thought designed for the non-specialist. *A Short History of Chinese Philosophy* by Fung Yu-lan (New York: Macmillan, Macmillan paperback edition, 1960) is an excellent scholarly account of the development of Chinese philosophy, written by one of China's outstanding contemporary philosophers. The *Short History* is a shorter version of the two-volume work by Fung entitled *A History of Chinese Philosophy* (Princeton: Princeton University Press, second printing, 1959–60) which is generally acknowledged to be the most comprehensive and authoritative survey of Chinese philosophy available. For the reader interested in studying neo-Confucian philosophy there is the excellent two-volume study by Carsun Chang, *The Development of Neo-Confucian Thought* (New Haven: College and University Press, 1963). Wing-tsit Chan's *Religious Trends in Modern China* (New York: Columbia University Press, 1953) focuses on the practical aspects of Chinese thought, providing a basis for reflections about the future of China.

Finally, for the reader interested in comparing concepts of different cultures, East and West, there is the excellent collection of essays on the nature of man in *The Concept of a Man*: A Study in Comparative Philosophy, edited by S. Radhakrishnan and P. T. Raju (London: Allen & Unwin, 1969).

Glossary of Oriental Words

In order to facilitate pronunciation of Oriental terms and names a phonetic spelling has been provided as a guide. No indications have been provided for accenting syllables because according to native grammarians Sanskrit and related languages place equal emphasis on each syllable. However, since in practice pronunciation without accenting a particular syllable is extremely difficult, the rule generally adopted by modern grammarians and linguists is to accent the last syllable containing a long vowel.

The glossary is organized so that the first column gives the term or name as it appears in the text. The next column provides the usual scholarly transliteration wherever this differs from the form given in the first column. In cases where Sanskrit and Pali terms are sometimes used interchangeably the correct transliterations for both languages are given. The letter *P* next to a word indicates that it is the Pali form; the letter *S* next to a word indicates that it is the Sanskrit form. The third column gives a phonetic pronunciation of the name or term. The fourth column provides information about the items in the first column.

WORD AS IT APPEARS IN THE TEXT	SCHOLARLY TRANSLITERATION	PHONETIC PRONUNCIATION	EXPLANATION
Abhidharma		ah bee dar mah	Collections of advanced reflections on *dharma*
Abhidhar- makosha	*Abhidharmakośa*	ah bee dar mah ko shah	A systematic treatment of Abhidharma philosophy from the Sarvāstivādin viewpoint by Vasubandhu
Agni		ugh nee	Vedic fire god
Aham Brahman Asi		ah hum brah mun us ee	"I am Brahman"
Ahamkara	*Ahaṁkāra*	ah hum kah rrah	In Sāṁkhya, the principle of individuation. (Lit. "I-maker.")
Ahimsa	*Ahiṁsā*	ah him sah	Non-hurting
Alaya-Vijnana	*Ālaya-Vitjñāna*	ah lye ah vih gnyah nah	Source of consciousness
Anatta		ah not ah	No permanent self
Anicca		ah nee chah	Impermanence of all existence
Aparashailas	*Aparaśailas*	ah pah rah shy lus	A Mahāyāna school of thought
Aranyaka	*Āraṇyaka*	ah rahn yah kah	A portion of the Veda containing reflections on sacrifice
Arhat		are hot	In Theravāda Buddhism, a person enobled by becoming perfect
Arjuna		are joo nah	Leader of the Pāṇḍavas to whom Kṛṣṇa conveys the teachings of the *Gītā*
Artha		are tah	Means of life
Artha Shastra	*Artha Śāstra*	are tah sha strah	Treatise on politics by Kauṭilya.
Aryadeva	*Āryadeva*	are yah day vah	Mādhyamika philosopher who was a pupil of Nāgārjuna

WORD AS IT APPEARS IN THE TEXT	SCHOLARLY TRANSLITERATION	PHONETIC PRONUNCIATION	EXPLANATION
Asatkaryavada	Asatkāryavāda	ah sot kar yah vah dah	The theory that a cause brings some new being into existence
Ashrama	Āśrama	ahsh rah mah	A stage in life; a place "to do one's thing"
Ashvaghosa	Aśvaghosa	ahsh vah gho shah	Buddhist philosopher who emphasized the "thusness" of all existents
Ashvapti Kaikeya	Aśvapti Kaikeya	ush vup tee kye kay ah	A much respected sage referred to in the *Chāndogya Upaniṣad*
Atharva Veda		ah tarh vah vay dah	The fourth Veda, representing ancient popular Indian religion
Atman	Ātman	aht mun	The innermost self
Aurobindo	Aurobindo Ghose	oro been dough	Twentieth-century Indian philosopher who championed the spiritual nature of man and the world
Ayatana	Āyatana	i ah tah nah	Basis of sensation
Badarayana	Bādarāyaṇa	bah dah rah yah nah	Author of the *Vedānta Sūtra*
Bahushrutiyas	Bahuśrutīyas	bah hoo shroo tee yahs	An early Mahāyāna school
Bhadrayaniyas	Bhadrāyaṇīyas	bha drrah yah nee yahs	One of the Sthaviravādin schools, most likely an offshoot from the Vātīputrīyas
Bhashya	Bhāṣya	bhosh yah	Commentary on a text
Bhaskara	Bhāskara	bhosh kah rah	Ninth-century Vedānta philosopher
Bhava		bah vah	Becoming
Bhavacakra		bah vah chock rah	Wheel of becoming
Bhikku		bhih koo	Buddhist monk
Bhishma	Bhīṣma	beesh mah	One of the heroes of the *Mahābhārata*

WORD AS IT APPEARS IN THE TEXT	SCHOLARLY TRANSLITERATION	PHONETIC PRONUNCIATION	EXPLANATION
Bodhisattva		boh dhee sah twa	An enlightened and compassionate being
Brahmacarya		brrah mah cha rree yah	Student stage of life
Brahman		brrah mun	The ultimate reality
Brahmana	Brāhmaṇa	brrah muh nah	A member of the priestly class; the ritual portion of the Veda
Brihadaranyaka	Bṛhadāraṇayaka Upaniṣad	brrih had dah rahn yah kah oo pah nee shod	One of the oldest Upaniṣads
Buddha		boo dhah	Enlightened; honorific title given Gautama
Budila Ashvatarashvi	Buḍila Aśvatarāśvi	boo dill ah ahsh vah tah rahsh vee	One of the five householders who sought Self-Knowledge from Aśvapti Kaikeya in the Chāndogya
Buddhaghosa		boo dha gho shah	Buddhist philosopher of the Theravāda tradition, fourth century A.D.
Buddhi		boo dhe	Enlightenment
Caittikas		chye tih kahs	One of the early Mahāyāna schools
Candrakirti	Candrakīrti	chan drrah keer tee	A Mādhyamika philosopher, sixth century A.D.
Carvaka	Cārvāka	char vah kah	A materialistic and skeptical Indian philosophy
Ch'an	Ch'an	chaan	The Chinese school of Buddhism which in Japan came to be known as Zen
Chanagankas		cha nah gahnk us	A Theravāda school, most likely a branch of the Vātsīputrīya school
Chandogya Upanishad	Chāndogya Upaniṣad	chun dogh yah	One of the earliest Upaniṣads

WORD AS IT APPEARS IN THE TEXT	SCHOLARLY TRANSLITERATION	PHONETIC PRONUNCIATION	EXPLANATION
Chang tsai		jung tzie	Neo-Confucian philosopher of the eleventh century A.D.
Chang tung-sun		jung doong soon	Twentieth-century Chinese philosopher
Ch'eng		jheng	Sincerity
Ch'eng hao		jheng how	Eleventh-century Neo-Confucian philosopher
Ch'eng I		jheng ee	Eleventh-century Neo-Confucian Philosopher
Chen-yen		jhen yen	Chinese Buddhist school
Ch'i		jhee	Material force; concrete thing
Chih		chee	Moral Wisdom
Chih liang-chih		chee lang chee	Doctrine of the extension of the innate knowledge of good
Ch'in		chin	The Chinese state from which the name "China" derived
Ching-t'u		jing too	Pure Land school of Buddhism
Chou Tun-i		chou toon ee	A pioneer of Neo-Confucianism (1017–1073)
Chuang Tzu		jwung dzuh	Taoist philosopher of the third or fourth century B.C.
Chu Hsi		jhoo she	A major Neo-Confucian philosopher (1130–1200)
Ch'un Ch'iu		choon chew	Spring and Autumn
Ch'ung Yung		jhoong yoong	Doctrine of the Mean
Citta		chih tah	Mind-stuff
Darshana	Darśana	dahr sha nah	Vision
Dharma		dhahr mah	Rightcousness; duty as determined by righteousness

WORD AS IT APPEARS IN THE TEXT	SCHOLARLY TRANSLITERATION	PHONETIC PRONUNCIATION	EXPLANATION
Dharma Shastra	Dharma Śāstra	dhahr mah sha strah	Treatise on dharma
Dharma-guptakas		dharh mah goop tah kahs	A school of Theravāda Buddhism
Dharmakirti	Dharmakīrti	dhar mah keer tee	A Buddhist logician of the sixth century
Dharmottara		dharh moh tah rah	Ninth-century Buddhist logician of the Sautrāntika school
Dharmottariyas		dharh moh tah rree yahs	A school of Theravāda Buddhism
Dhatu	Dhātu	dah too	Element of existence
Dinnaga	Diṅnāga	dingh nah gah	A Buddhist logician, pupil of Vasubandhu
Dukkha		doo kah	Suffering, unwholesomeness
Ekavyava-harikas	Ekavyava-hārikas	eh kah veeah vah ha rree kahs	A Mahāyāna Buddhist school
Fung-yu-lan		foong you lon	Twentieth-century Chinese philosopher
Gaudapada	Gauḍapāda	gwad ah pah dah	Early Vedāntic philosopher
Gautama Siddhartha	Gautama Siddhārtha	go tom ah sid darh tah	The founder of Buddhism
Grihastha	Gṛhastha	grrih hah stah	Householder stage
Gunas	Guṇas	goo nahs	In Sāṁkhya, the material constituents of things
Guru		goo roo	Spiritual teacher
Haimavatas		hye mah vah tahs	Early school of Theravāda Buddhism
Han fei tzu		hun fay dzuh	Early Chinese philosopher identified with the Legalist school
Han yu	Han yü	hun yewh	One of the earliest Neo-Confucianists (768–824)
Harada-roshi		hah rah dah row she	Twentieth-century Japanese Zen master
Hetu		hay too	Reason (for something)
Hsi-shih		she she	Legendary beauty of ancient China

WORD AS IT APPEARS IN THE TEXT	SCHOLARLY TRANSLITERATION	PHONETIC PRONUNCIATION	EXPLANATION
Hsiung shih-li		shoong she lee	Twentieth-century Chinese philosopher (b. 1885)
Hsiao		showe	Familial love
Hsun tzu	Hsün tzu	shoon dzuh	Naturalistic Confucian philsopher (third century B.C.)
Hua-yen		whah yen	School of Chinese Buddhism
Hui Shih		hoo she	Chinese logician, fourth century B.C.
I-ching		ee jhing	Book of Changes
Indra		in drrah	Vedic god of the heavens
Indradyumna Bhallaveya	Indradyumna Bhāllaveya	in drrahd youm nah bhah lah vay ah	In the *Chāndogya*, a householder seeking Self-knowledge
Ishvara Krishna	Īśvara kṛṣṇa	eesh vah rah krish nah	Sāṁkhya philosopher, author of the *Sāṁkhya Kārikā*
Jana sharkarakshya	Jana Śārkarakṣya	john ah sar kah rahks yah	In the *Chāndogya*, a householder seeking Self-knowledge
Jati	Jāti	jah tee	Birth; class determined by birth
jen		wren	Humanness of a person
joshu		jah shoo	Buddhist monk to whom the mu-koan is attributed
Kama	Kāma	comma	Pleasure
Kama shastra	*Kāma Śāstra*	comma shah strah	A treatise on the pleasures of love
Kamashila	Kamaśīla	comma she la	A Yogācāra philosopher, probably eighth century
Kanada	Kaṇāda	kah nah dah	Vaiśeṣika philosopher, author of the *Vaiśeṣika Sutra*, probably third century B.C.
Kapilavastu		kah pih lah vus too	Birth place of the Buddha

WORD AS IT APPEARS IN THE TEXT	SCHOLARLY TRANSLITERATION	PHONETIC PRONUNCIATION	EXPLANATION
Karma		car mah	Action; effect of action
Kashyapitas	Kāśyapītas	kahsh yah pee tahs	School of Theravāda Buddhism
Katha Upanishad	*Kaṭha Upaniṣad*	Kah tah oo pah nih shod	One of the older Upaniṣads
Kena Upanishad	*Kena Upaniṣad*	kay nah oo pah nih shod	One of the older Upaniṣads
Koan		cone	Problem set for a Zen pupil
Krishna	Kṛṣna	krrish nah	An incarnation of the ultimate reality, Arjuna's teacher in the *Bhagavad Gītā*
Kshatriya	Kṣatriya	kshot ree yah	Class of the protectors of society
Kukkulikas		koo koo lih kahs	An early school of Mahāyāna
Kumarajiva	Kumārajīva	koo may hrah jee vah	Mādhyamika philosopher, probably fourth century
K'un		koon	Earth; hexagram representing earth
Kung-sun Lung		koong soon loong	Chinese logician, fourth century, B.C.
Kuo Hsiang		Kwo shang	Third century Neo-Taoist philosopher
Lankavatara	Laṅkāvatāra	lahnk ah vah tah rah	The *Laṅkāvatāra Sūtra* is one of the very early Mahāyāna texts.
Lao Tzu		lao dzuh	Early Taoist philosopher, probably fifth century B.C.
Li		lee	Principle
Li Ao		lee ow	Eighth century philosopher instrumental in reviving Confucianism
Li Chi		lee chee	Book of Rites
Lokottaravadins	Lokottaravādins	loh koh tah rah vah dins	Early Mahāyāna school
Lu		loo	Native state of Confucius

WORD AS IT APPEARS IN THE TEXT	SCHOLARLY TRANSLITERATION	PHONETIC PRONUNCIATION	EXPLANATION
Lu Chiu-yuan	Lu Chiu-yüan	loo choo yoon	Neo-Confucian philosopher (1139–1193)
Lun Yu	*Lun Yü*	loon you	Analects or sayings of Confucius
Madhva		mudh vah	Dualistic Vedānta philosopher
Madhyamika	Mādhyamika	mah dhyah mee kah	Relativistic school of Buddhist philosophy
Madhyamika Karika	*Mādhyamika Kārikā*	mah dhyah mee kah kah ree kah	One of the main critical works of Nāgārjuna
Mahabharata	*Mahābhārata*	mah ha bha rah tah	One of two main long epics of India
Mahasanghika	Mahāsanghika	mah ha sangh hee kah	The large group of Buddhist monks who split off from the rest of the order in the third century B.C.
Mahat		mah hot	"The great one"
Mahayana	Mahāyāna	mah ha yah nah	One of the two main groups of Buddhists
Mahishasakas	Mahīśāsakas	mah hee shah sah kahs	An early school of Theravāda Buddhism
Manu		mun ooh	Indian social philosopher, probably fourth century B.C.
Mao Tse-tung		Mao dzuh doong	Chinese communist leader
Mencius		muhn shoos	Idealistic Confucian philosopher, fourth century B.C.
Mimamsa	Mīmāṁsā	mee mahm sah	Ritualistic school of Vedānta
Ming		ming	Destiny
Mohism		mo izm	Utilitarian school of philosophy named after Mo Tzu
Moksa	Mokṣa	moke shah	Liberation
Mo Tzu		mo dzuh	Utilitarian Chinese philosopher of the late fifth century B.C.
Mu-koan		moo kone	One of Joshu's famous answerless Zen questions

WORD AS IT APPEARS IN THE TEXT	SCHOLARLY TRANSLITERATION	PHONETIC PRONUNCIATION	EXPLANATION
Mundaka Upanishad	*Muṇḍaka Upaniṣad*	moon dah kah ooh pah nih shad	One of the early Upaniṣads
Nagarjuna	Nāgārjuna	nah gar joo nah	Mādhyamika philosopher, second century
Nama-rupa	Nāma-rūpa	nah mah roo pah	Mind-body complex
Nastika	Nāstika	nah stee kah	Unorthodox schools of Indian thought
Nibbana	Nibbāna (S. Nirvāṇa)	nee bah nah	The Buddhist goal of sufferingless existence
Nyaya	Nyāya	nyah yah	Indian school of logic
Paksha	Pakṣa	pahkh shah	Minor term of a syllogism
Panchatantra	*Pañcatantra*	pah cha tahn trah	Collection of Indian fables and stories
Paravidya		pah rah vih dhyah	Higher wisdom
Pataliputta	Pāṭaliputta	pah tah lih puh tah	Place of the third Buddhist council
Patanjali	Patañjali	pah tahn jah lee	Author of the *Yoga Sūtras*
Paticca Samuppada	Paṭicca Samuppāda (S. Pratītya Samutpāda)	pah tee cha sah moo pah dah	Dependent origination
P'eng-tsu		peng dzuh	Legendary Chinese Methusala
Pracinasala Aupamanyava	Prācīnaśāla Aupamanyava	prra chih na shah lah oh pah mah nyah vah	In the *Chāndogya*, one of the Householders seeking Self-knowledge
Prajapati	Prajāpati	prah jah pah tee	Hindu Lord of Creation
Prajnaptivadins	Prajñaptivādins	prah gnyahp tee vah dins	Early school of Mahāyāna
Prakriti	Prakṛti	prah krrih tee	In Sāṁkhya, the source of the material universe
Pudgala	(P. Puggala)	puhd gah lah	Substratum of personality
Purusha	Puruṣa	puh roo shah	In Sāṁkhya, the source of spirituality
Purushartha	Puruṣārtha	puh roo sharh tah	Aim in life

WORD AS IT APPEARS IN THE TEXT	SCHOLARLY TRANSLITERATION	PHONETIC PRONUNCIATION	EXPLANATION
Radhakrishnan		rah dah krrish nun	Twentieth-century Indian scholar, philosopher, statesman
Raja	Rāja	rah jah	King
Rajagaha	Rājagha	rah jah gah hah	Place of the first Buddhist council
Rajas		rah jus	The active element in existence
Rama	Rāma	rah mah	Main hero of the *Rāmayāṇa*
Ramanuja	Rāmānuja	rah mah noo jah	Theistic Vedāntic philosopher of the eleventh century
Ramayana	*Rāmāyana*	rah mah yah nah	One of India's two major epics
Ranee	Rāni	rah nee	Queen
Rigveda	*Ṛgveda*	rrig vay duh	One of the four Vedas making up the ancient Indian vedic literature
Sadhya	Sādhya	sahd yah	Major term of a syllogism
Sama Veda	*Sāma Veda*	sahm vay duh	One of the four Vedas making up the ancient India vedic literature
Samhita	Saṁhīta	sahm hee tah	Portion of the Veda containing hymns of praise and speculation
Samkhya Karika	*Sāṁkhya Kārikā*	sahm khyah kah ree kah	A basic Sāṁkhya text by Īśvara Kṛṣṇa
Sammitiyas	Sāṁmitīyas	sahm ih tee hays	A Theravāda school, probably an off-shoot of the Vātsīputrīyas
Samnyasa	Saṁnyāsa	sahm nyah sah	Stage in life devoted to complete spiritual realization
Samsara	Saṁsāra	sahm sah rah	Round of births and deaths
Sankhara	Saṅkhāra (S. Saṁskāra)	sahn kah rah	Impulses to action
Sanna	Sañña	sah nah	Perception

WORD AS IT APPEARS IN THE TEXT	SCHOLARLY TRANSLITERATION	PHONETIC PRONUNCIATION	EXPLANATION
Sarvastivadins	Sarvāstivādins	sahr vah stee vah dins	Realistic Buddhist philosophers, including Vaibhāṣikas and Sautrāntikas
Satkaryavada	Satkāryavāda	saht car yah vah dah	Theory that effects pre-exist in their causes
Satori		sah tory	Zen enlightenment
Sattva		Saht twa	One of the three guṇas constituting all material things
Satyayajna Paulishi	Satyayajña Pauluṣi	soh yah yah gnyah paw loo she	In the *Chāndogya*, one of the householders seeking Self-knowledge
Sauntrantikas	Sautrāntikas	saw trahn tee kahs	A critical school of Buddhist realists
Shabda	Śabda	shahb dah	Word; testimony
Shamkara	Śaṁkara	shum kah rah	Non-dualistic Vedāntic philosopher, eighth century
Shandilya	Śāṇḍilya	shahn deal yah	Indian sage referred to in the Upaniṣads
Shantarakshita	Śantarakṣita	sah tah rahk she tah	A later Yogācāra philosopher
Shatapatha Brahmana	*Śatapatha Brāhmaṇa*	shah tah pah tah brrah mun ah	Vedic text explaining the significance of various religious practices
Shih Ching	*Shih Ching*	she jhing	Book of Poetry, one of the Five Classics
Shudra	Śūdra	shoo drrah	Laboring class
Shunya	Śūnya	shoon yah	Empty
Shunyata	Śūnyatā	shoon yah tah	Emptiness
Shurya	Śurya	shoo ree yah	Indian sun god
Shvetaketu	Śvetaketu	shveh tah kay too	In the *Chāndogya*, the recipient of the famous "tat tvam asi" teaching
Sthaviravada	Sthaviravāda	shtah vee rah vah dah	"Teachings of the Elders." The early followers of the Buddha

WORD AS IT APPEARS IN THE TEXT	SCHOLARLY TRANSLITERATION	PHONETIC PRONUNCIATION	EXPLANATION
Sung		soong	Chinese dynasty (960–1279)
Sutra	Sūtra	soo trrah	aphorism or collection of aphorisms
Svatantra		Swa tahn trrah	A Buddhist school midway between Sauntrāntika and Yogācāra
Svabhava	Svabhāva	swah bah vah	Independent existence
Ta Hsueh	*Ta Hsüeh*	dah sheeh	Great Learning
Tai-chen		dye jhen	Chinese empirical philosopher of the eighteenth century
Tai-chi		dye jhee	Great ultimate
Taittiriya Upanishad	*Taittīriya Upaniṣad*	tye tee ree yah oo pah nee shod	One of the early Upaniṣads
Tamas		tom us	One of the three guṇas making up all things
Tathagata	Tathāgata	tah taah gah tah	"Thus gone." Honorific title of Gautama Siddhārtha
Tao		dow	The way of ultimate reality
Tao Te Ching		dow day jhing	Basic text of Taoism, attributed to Lao Tzu
Tathata	Tathāta	tah taah tah	The "thusness" of things
Tat Tvam Asi		tut twum us ee	"Thou art That"
Te		day	Virtue; power
Theravada	Theravāda	tehr rah vaah dah	The more conservative branch of Buddhism
T'ien-t'ai		dee en die	School of Chinese Buddhism
Tung Chung-shu		doong choong shoo	Confucian philospher responsible for making Confucianism the state ideology (second century)

WORD AS IT APPEARS IN THE TEXT	SCHOLARLY TRANSLITERATION	PHONETIC PRONUNCIATION	EXPLANATION
Turiya	Turīya	too ree yah	The fourth stage of consciousness wherein the real Self is discovered
Uddalaka Aruni	Uddālaka Āruṇi	oo dah lah kah ah roo nee	The sage in the *Chāndogya* who teaches his son "tat tvam asi"
Upanishads	Upaniṣads	oo pah nee shods	The concluding portion of the Vedas, containing reflections about ultimate reality
Upanishat	Upaniṣat	oo pah nee shot	Secret; the secret about ultimate reality
Uttarashailas	Uttaraśailas	oo tah rah shy lus	An early school of Mahāyāna
Vacchagotta		vah cha go tah	Man who questioned the Buddha about the nature of the self
Vaibhashika	Vaibhāṣika	vy bah she kah	School of Buddhists who are direct realists
Vaisheshika	Vaiśeṣika	vy shesh ee kah	Hindu system of philosophy that is realistic and pluralistic
Vallabha		vah lah bah	Fifteenth-century Vedantic philosopher
Vanaprastha	Vānaprastha	vaah nah prrah stah	Third stage in life according to the āśrama theory
Varna	Varṇa	vahr nah	Class
Vasubandhu		vahs oo bahn dhoo	Sautrāntika and Yogācāra philosopher of the fifth century
Vatsiputriyas	Vātsīputrīyas	vaht see put rree yahs	Early school of Theravāda Buddhism
Vatsyayana	Vātsyayāna	vaaht see ah yaah nah	Author of the *Kāma Sūtra*
Vayu	Vāyu	vaah yoo	Ancient Indian god of the wind
Vedana	Vedanā	vay dah nah	Sensation or feeling

WORD AS IT APPEARS IN THE TEXT	SCHOLARLY TRANSLITERATION	PHONETIC PRONUNCIATION	EXPLANATION
Vedanta	Vedānta	vay daahn tah	The system of philosophy with its basis in the Upaniṣads
Vesali	Vesālī	veh saah lee	Place of the second Buddhist council
Vinnana	Viññāna (S. Vijñāna)	vih naah nah	Consciousness
Virocana		vee row cha nah	A chief demon in Hindu mythology
Wang Yang-ming		wang yang ming	Idealistic Neo-Confucian philosopher (1472–1529)
Wu-wei		woo way	No artificial action
Yajnavalkya	Yājñavalkya	yaah gnyah vul khyah	Famous sage in ancient India
Yajur Veda		yah joor vay dah	One of the four Vedas of sacred texts of Hinduism
Yamuna	Yāmuna	yaah moo nah	Theistic Vedāntic philosopher of the tenth century
Yang		yang	Active principle of the universe
Yang Chu		yang choo	Early Taoist philosopher who emphasized self-preservation
Yashomitra	Yaśomitra	yah show mih trah	A Sautrāntika philosopher of the sixth century
Yi		yee	Righteousness
Yin		yin	Passive principle of the universe
Yin-yang		yin-yang	Theory of the interaction between yin and yang as a cause of all things
Yoga		yoh guh	Discipline
Yogacara	Yogācāra	yoh guh cha rah	Idealist school of Buddhism
Zanzen		za zen	Zen discipline
Zen		zen	Form of Buddhism developed and practiced in China, Korea, and Japan

Index